THE NĀYAKAS OF IKKĒRI

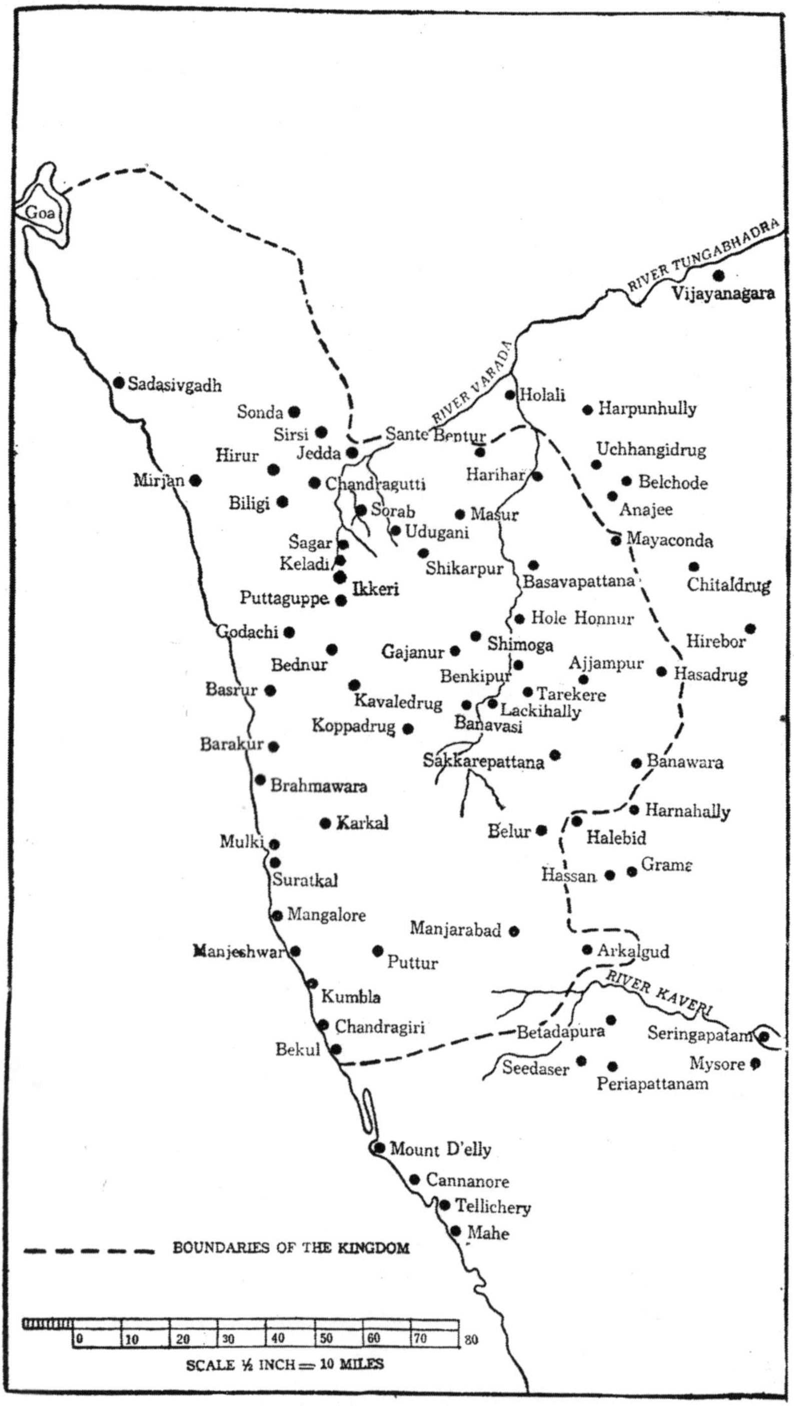

MAP OF THE IKKĒRI KINGDOM

THE NĀYAKAS OF IKKĒRI

K.D. SWAMINATHAN

MANOHAR
2025

First published 1957
Reprinted 2021, 2022, 2023, 2024, 2025

ISBN 978-93-90035-83-0

Published by
Ajay Kumar Jain *for*
Manohar Publishers & Distributors
4753/23 Ansari Road, Daryaganj
New Delhi 110 002

Printed at
Replika Press Pvt. Ltd.

ACKNOWLEDGEMENTS

This book on the Nāyakas of Ikkēri is the ultimate outcome of an opportunity I had for some initial research on the subject during the time I was a Research student in the Department of Indian History and Archaeology at the University of Madras between 1951-53. I pursued the study of the subject after leaving the University and joining the office of the Government Epigraphist for India at Ootacamund. The Government Epigraphist gave me all facilities for consulting inscriptions, published and unpublished, and I am deeply indebted to him for this invaluable help. I have also extensively consulted the *Epigraphia Carnatica* and the *Mysore Archaeological Reports* for writing this book. I am under obligation to the authorities of the Departments of Archaeology, Governments of India and Mysore for giving me permission to reproduce some select photographs, the copyright for which rests with them. I have made use of many Portuguese documents in the Indian Historical Research Institute, St. Xavier's College, Bombay, to which I had access by the kindness of the late Rev. Fr. Heras, S.J.

Dr. T. V. Mahalingam, M.A., D.Litt., now Professor of Archaeology in the University of Madras first set me to research on this subject and guided me when I was in the University. He continued his unstinting help when I pursued the study later; and all along I have received from him much encouragement in writing this work, but for whom I would never have been able to complete my study of the subject. I am very grateful to him for all the immense help I have received from him. My thanks are due to Sri N. Lakshminarayanrao, M.A., formerly Government Epigraphist for India for the valuable suggestions he gave me in the course of preparing this book. I am indebted to Fr. Fernandes of the Orphanage at San Thome, Madras, for kindly translating for my use the Portuguese documents relevant to this study.

I tender my warmest thanks to the G. S. Press for the expeditious and excellent printing and get up of the book.

Ootacamund, K. D. Swaminathan
3-1-1957.

CONTENTS

APPENDIX B

LIST OF ILLUSTRATIONS

ABBREVIATIONS

APO.	Archivo Portuguese Oriental.
ARIE.	Annual Report on Indian Epigraphy.
ARSIE.	Annual Report on South Indian Epigraphy.
ARASI.	Annual Report of the Archaeological Survey of India.
Annals SVOI.	Annals of Śrī Venkaṭēśvara Oriental Institute.
Bull. DCRI.	Bulletin of the Deccan College Research Institute.
Ep. Ind.	Epigraphia Indica.
EC.	Epigraphia Carnatica.
Ind. Ant.	Indian Antiquary.
IHQ.	Indian Historical Quarterly.
JA.	Journal Asiatique.
JBBRAS.	Journal of the Bombay Branch of the Royal Asiatic Society.
JBHS.	Journal of the Bombay Historical Society.
JOIB.	Journal of the Oriental Institute, M. S. University of Baroda.
JOR.	Journal of Oriental Research.
JRAS.	Journal of the Royal Asiatic Society of Great Britain and Ireland.
KHR.	Karnataka Historical Review.
KNV.	Keladinṛpavijayam.
MAR.	Mysore Archaeological Report.
Proc. IHRC.	Proceedings of the Indian Historical Records Commission.
QJMS.	Quarterly Journal of the Mythic Society.
SII.	South Indian Inscriptions.
STR.	Śivatattvaratnākara.
Vij. Sex. Com. Vol.	Vijayanagar Sexcentenary Commemoration Volume.

CHAPTER I

INTRODUCTORY

Studies of small kingdoms and their rulers appear to be appreciated very little obviously because their history affords no scope for a spectacular narrative. There are not many exciting events which we may find in the history of big empires. Also living as we do in the present age with its complex political machineries of Government and the puzzling problems that arise therefrom, its breath taking methods of warfare and their colossal consequences, and their economic enterprises of an international character, these small dynasties and their achievements might well be insipid. But this is no warrant for ignoring them if we really want a true history of our past. It must be conceded that to those rulers and their surroundings the events of their days were as momentous as ours are at the present day. To judge and appraise the importance of a study of these humble rulers from the present or spectacular points of view would go against the very objective of history. "To weigh the stars, or to make ships sail in the air or below the sea, is not a more astonishing and ennobling performance on the part of the human race in these latter days, than to know the course of events that had been long forgotten and the true nature of men and women who were here before us." History is not surely limited to the history of big empires and big empires have had to depend for their very stability sometimes on the effective aid of their feudatories. During the latter half of the Vijayanagar empire, the kingdom was stabilised only by the effective aid of feudatories like the Nāyakas and other minor rulers. To omit a study of these small kingdoms would be like a chain missing many of its links. Little events have sometimes played a great part in shaping the history of big empires and small personages have shown a heroism at critical hours and stood by their masters in goodstead and saved them from terrible disasters. We have for example in the history of the Ikkēri Nāyakas the loyal and noble part played by Śivappa Nāyaka during the dark days of Śrī Raṅga III. The History of South India, would therefore be a maimed picture without an account of these small rulers, their political, social, economic, religious and literary activities.

The Nāyak rulers of South India are bye-products of the provincial administration adopted by the Vijayanagar emperors. It provided for a feudal type of Government in which the chieftains of small principalities were vassals of the sovereign emperor. In return for the privileges of almost autonomous rule in their own territories they were required to fulfil certain obligations to the emperor. They were mainly military aid by the maintenance of local armies and their supply to the emperor in times of adversity. They were also required to contribute specified sums of money annually to the Central treasury. One of the main reasons for the institution of this feudal type by Vijayanagar was the building of the military strength of the empire to enable it to beat off the Muslim attempts to extirpate the Hindu Kingdoms of South India. This feudal administration eventually led to the formation of small dynasties of rulers in tiny principalities and these rulers were known as the Nāyakas. Thus we have the Nāyakas of Madura, Tanjore, Jinji and Ikkēri, each of whom have played their parts in the History of South India. Books have already appeared on the first three[1] Nāyaka rulers but no systematic study has yet been made of the Ikkēri rulers and the gap is sought to be filled up by the present work.

The Ikkēri kingdom comprised at its zenith an area corresponding to the whole coast of Kanara from Goa in the North to Cannanore in the South as also parts of the Shimoga District of Mysore.

From its nebular beginnings from about 1500 A.C. under Keladi Chauḍappa Nāyaka to its end in 1763 A.C. under

1. R. Satyanatha Iyer—The Nāyakas of Madura. (Annamalai University, 1924).
V. Vriddhagirisan—The Nāyaks of Tanjore. (Annamalai University, 1942).
C. S. Srinivasachari—A History of Gingee and Its Rulers. (Annamalai University, 1943).

tragic circumstances there is a period of two centuries and a half. No less than eighteen kings and queens ruled from the Ikkēri throne. Among the kings the three at least were prominent; Sadāśiva (1540-65) who was the real founder of the Ikkēri kingdom, stabilised the infant Nāyakship; Venkaṭappa I (1586-1629) raised the prestige of the dynasty to such an extent that Ikkēri was practically recognised as an independent kingdom by all the chiefs of the coast; and under Śivappa Nāyaka (1645-1660) the dynasty reached the peak of its power and influence so much that Śivappa was able to give shelter to the fugitive Vijayanagar emperor, Śrī Raṅga III. More noteworthy is the fact that there were two queens in the dynasty; one was the heroic ruler Cannammāji between 1671 and 1696. She had the daring to defy no less a muslim emperor than Aurangazeb and even the renown of defeating his army. Less fortunate and the last in the dynasty was Vīrammāji (1756-1763), who was caught up in calamitious circumstances and had to flee from Bednur, the capital of the kingdom, all her resources to save it from Hyder's invasion, having failed. Hindu South India may well be proud of the fact that in this small kingdom two queens occupied the troubulous throne and one atleast ordered the affairs of the State with as much competence as a mighty king. The last words of counsel of Cannammāji to her successor, Basavappa, given in the Śivatattvaratnākara (Kallōla VIII, Taraṅga VIII), are at once a tribute to the glory of a South Indian Queen.

The political history of the Ikkēri kings and queens is in the main a record of several suppressions of many rebellious minor chieftains from time to time, the wars which they waged with the rulers of Mysore, the Maratha Rajas and the ruling houses of Malabar, besides the clashes with the foreign trading companies, the Portuguese, the Dutch, the French and the English, who had a vital interest on the west coast in order to establish themselves in security for purposes of trade in pepper and rice. These political events of this small dynasty of rulers may not be of much interest in themselves but their study cannot be ignored. As Vincent Smith rightly remarks "The more attractive story of Indian thought as expressed in religion and philosophy, literature, art and science cannot be written intelligibly unless it is built on the solid foundations of dynastic history which alone furnishes the indispensable chronological basis." More attractive than the political record are the social, economic, religious, literary and artistic activities of these rulers. "The Social Scene" writes G. M. Trevylyan, "grows out of the economic conditions to much the same extent that political events in their turn grow out of social conditions. Without social history, economic history is barren and political history unintelligible." The main chapter in the economic history of the Ikkēri kingdom may be said to lie in the relations of these rulers with the foreign companies mentioned above, which in themselves constitute an important phase in the growth and decline of their prosperity. We get an authentic picture of the rivalries that obtained among them, their struggles to get into the favour of the Ikkēri rulers who themselves at times courted their help in the wars against their enemies, their rise and fall and the influence which the patronage or otherwise of the Ikkēri rulers had over their fortunes.

The social history of the period consists of the life of the people, their customs and manners, the protection they enjoyed under the rulers. We have graphic accounts of the practices of their people, their festivities, dress, education, music, dancing etc., from foreign travellers who visited the Ikkēri kingdom. The Ikkēri rulers were great patrons of learning. Some of them were themselves poets and scholars. Venkaṭappa Nāyaka and Basavappa Nāyaka were themselves scholars and authors. Men of letters versed in several branches of learning flourished in their court. Some of the celebrities of the period were Bhaṭṭōji Dīkshita, Rāmānujāchārya and Ranganātha Dīkshita. Numerous grants of lands testify to the partiality which these rulers evinced for the literary arts. Their religious bent of mind is borne out in almost every ruler and their activity in this direction is marked by several grants to temples, maṭhas and other religious institutions besides remissions of state taxes. It is noteworthy that they observed toleration in religious matters. Even the muslims and the Christians have had their share in the grants which they have made for religious purposes.

Venkaṭappa Nāyaka made a gift to a Muslim Mosque erected in Bhuvanagiridurga.

Art and Architecture received the prompt attention of the Ikkēri rulers. The Malnad style of architecture is the distinct contribution of the Ikkēri Nāyakas to the history of South Indian Architecture. It is a harmonious blending of the Hoysala and the Dravidian styles of architecture, the best example of which is the Aghōrēśvara temple at Ikkēri. On the whole the picture that we get of the Ikkēri kingdom during these two and a half centuries of their rule would justify the observation that it may be regarded as one of the typical small kingdoms in South India during the 16th and 17th centuries.

Sources

Our sources for the study of the Ikkēri rulers are very copious and they may be divided as primary and secondary.

Primary: Epigraphy supplies us with a large number of inscriptions. In the present thesis nearly 600 inscriptions have been studied and the footnotes to the text amply bear out the substantial aid available from this source in the construction of this history. Inscriptions are by far the most important source for a true and logical narration of facts. The inscriptions throw a flood of light on the life of the sovereigns and the people over whom they ruled. Important incidents are recorded in them. Their evidence in many cases is contemporary and generally precise. Sometimes they supply or strengthen a weak link in literary accounts known to us. They give an idea of the institutions prevalent in the country at the time of their record. They supply us with the names and designations of officers of State to whom different functions were allocated. The prosperity of the country and the privileges of merchant guilds are therein pictured. The religious faith, toleration or bigotry, endowments and charities for temple and other benevolent institutions are recorded. The inscriptions also furnish a good deal of geographical information as also details about weights and measures. But there are however difficulties. Much caution has to be exercised in dealing with the informations they give.

Allowance has to be made for royal and Governmental rodomontade. Spurious and forged grants have to be guarded against. Some times we come across conflicting inscriptions which render the construction of the chronology not very accurate. Used with discrimination this source can be made to furnish us with genealogical details and connected facts. In the main, the inscriptions form an important primary source, as it always is in the history of South India. Some of the Nāyaka inscriptions have been published in publications like Epigraphia Carnatica, Epigraphia Indica, South Indian Inscriptions and the Mysore Archaeological Reports. Most of them are briefly noticed in the Annual Reports on South Indian Epigraphy.

The monuments erected during the Nāyaka period and which still exist in different stages of dilapidation, are found in the Shimoga District of Mysore. The Aghōrēśvara temple at Ikkēri, the Rāmēśvara temple at Kēladi, the Pārvati temple, the Nīlakaṇṭēśvara temple; Āñjanēya temple and Gudde Venkaṭaramaṇa temple at Nagar, the Raṅganāthasvāmin temple at Chitaldrug, the palace of Śivappa Nāyaka and the fort of Śivappa Nāyaka are of great interest to the student of the architecture of the period.

Among the indigenous literary sources two deserve important mention namely the *Śivatattvaratnākara* in Samskrit and the *Keladinṛipavijayam* in Kannaḍa. The *Śivatattvaratnākara,* written by Basavarāja (1698-1715) a ruler of the Ikkēri dynasty is an encyclopediac Samskrit poem consisting of 108 taraṅgās grouped into 9 kallōlas. The subjects dealt with are of varied interest. Chapters 36, 37, 39, 41, 43, 62, 76, 90, 93, 96 and 99 deal with the history of the Ikkēri and Keladi kings, beginning with the founder of the dynasty Chauḍappa to the period of Śōmaśēkhara Nāyaka and Cannamma, the parents of Basavarāja. The general plan of the work is unique and betrays the motive of the author in composing the work namely to immortalise the achievements of his ancestors. The author conceived the idea of issuing a cyclopedia of knowledge in Samskrit, where prominence is usually given to subjects treated of instead of the glorious feats of one's ancestors. Most authors indulge in the glorification of their ancestors at the beginning or end of their works. But Basavarāja, adopting a different mode, compels the reader to hear his tale. The subjects treated of do really come in a certain order determined by antiquity and importance as conceived in his days but are introduced to the reader in relation to the exploits of one or the other of his ancestors, whose knowledge in the subjects was pre-eminent. Thus the adventures of each of his ancestors take a historic order, but after the intrusion of exhaustive treatises on certain subjects. The work *Śivatattvaratnākara* is very interesting from the point of view of Indian Culture. It may be considered a quasi-historical work. The value of the *Śivatattvaratnākara* as a source book for the history of the Ikkēri Nāyakas can hardly be exaggerated. It gives an all round account of the achievements of the kings of the dynasty. The only blemish which the work suffers from is that it does not give a chronological account of the political destinies of the Ikkēri rulers. But it has the merit of being a contemporary work written by a cultured man, who possessed all the necessary information.

The other literary work *Keladinṛpavijayam* describes in fuller detail the history of the Nāyakas of Keladi. This was written by a Brahmin court poet called Lingaṇṇa who lived during the first or last quarter of the seventeenth century. The work has been published under the authority of the University of Mysore by Dr. Shama Sastri. A palm leaf copy of the work is in the India Office Library at London. It contains some slight variations but is substantially the same. The work, however, has not been translated into any other language.

The *Keladinṛpavijayam* is a valuable historical work inasmuch as it gives a lucid and clear account of the Keladi kings from the foundation of the Nāyakship to its final overthrow by Hyder Ali in 1763 A.C. It also contains much useful information about the gradual expansion of Bijāpur into the Karṇāṭaka country. The earlier chapters of the *Keladinṛpavijayam* are not quite reliable as they abound in factual and chronological errors but the later chapters contain valuable information. Being a later work, it is probable that the details of Basavarāja's rule (the author of the

Śivatattvaratnākara) and those of his ancestors contained in the *Keladinṛpavijayam* must have been taken mostly from the *Śivatattvaratnākara*. A co-ordinated and analytical study of the inscriptions and the *Keladinṛpavijayam*, would help us in solving the chronological and factual problems confronting us.

Equally important if not more is the abundance of material in the shape of original documents in Portuguese, Dutch and English. These have not yet been published or studied adequately for exploiting their use for the writing of South Indian History. They are dependable in regard to the accuracy of their statement for we find confirmation from other sources. The Portuguese documents, such as the Moncões do reino, Instrucões, Pazes-E-Tratados etc., are kept at the 'Archivo da Secretaria Geral do Governo', Panjim and Lisbon. Fortunately the photostat copies of some of the documents are available at the Indian Historical Research Institute, St. Xaviers College, Bombay. Most of the documents are in the form of letters written by the Portuguese Governors at Goa to their home authorities, while others contain extracts of treaties concluded by the Portuguese with the native powers of India. These yield valuable information about the commercial and political relations of the Ikkēri Nāyakas with the Portuguese and other foreign powers. They also afford us glimpses of the political struggles in the country during particular times. The historian of political events will gain considerable material if he dives deep into these documents. The history of the later Nāyakas of Ikkēri can hardly be written with sufficient fullness but for these records. A critical, annotated English edition of the Portuguese documents at the Panjim Archives, Goa, by a scholar well acquainted with South Indian History in the 17th and 18th centuries, in all its various aspects, is a desideratum, the importance of which can hardly be exaggerated.

The Dutch documents in the Batavia Dagh Register deal mainly with the relations of the Ikkēri Nāyakas with Dutch power. The English Factory Records and Correspondence from Tellicherry, Karwar and Bombay, which are mostly unpublished supply us with information regarding the trade and commercial relations of the Nāyakas with the English in particular and other foreign powers in general. They also throw much light on the economic and political conditions of South India during the period. By a comparative and careful study of the Portuguese, English, and Dutch documents, it is possible to sketch in vivid detail the relative positions of the three trading powers and their strongholds in the west coast, during the latter half of the 17th century. These documents have not yet been studied or published adequately for exploiting their use for the writing of South Indian History. They are dependable in regard to the accuracy of their statements for we find confirmation from other sources.

The accounts of foreign travellers like Della Valle, Peter Mundy, Dr. Fryer, Pinkerton and Abbe Carei form yet another valuable source. They throw a flood of light on the social, economic, political and religious practices of the period. The records of these travellers who as disinterested spectators, faithfully recorded whatever they saw, have some freshness about them, though at times they are superficial. The necessity of enhancing their own labours, might well have led them, consciously or unconsciously into exaggerations and mis-statements. A foreign colour might have been given to and strange ideas read into transactions and events. Making due allowance for some of these defects a foreigner's account can well serve as supplementary and corroboratory evidence. We have also the Persian work of Ferishta, which gives in detail the campaigns of Bijāpur and Ahamednagar Sultans against Ikkēri. Though the version given is biassed, we can make reasonable inferences from the statements. The Pēshva Daftars or Despatches in Marāṭhi form an important source for the history of the later Nāyakas of Ikkēri. The Daftars contain much information about Marāṭha incursions into the Carnatic and the occasional invasions of Bednur by them.

Besides these, there are other indigenous sources like a number of native chronicles and memoirs, some of which have been collected by Col. Mackenzie and which are preserved in the Government Oriental Manuscripts Library at Madras. The following Manuscripts are useful:

(a) The Rājavamśāvaḷi, containing genealogical accounts of the kings of the Ikkēri dynasty.

(b) Tuḷu Konkaṇa Rājara Śāsanagaḷu, dealing with the wars and conquests of the kings of the Tuḷuva and Konkaṇa and their relations with the muslims.

(c) Biligi Araśara Vaṁśāvali, dealing with the history of Biligi.

(d) Kānthirava Narasarāja Vijaya, Maisūru Araśugaḷa Pūrvābhyudaya Kadattam and Chikkadēvarāyavijayam, dealing with the history of Mysore and an account of the relations of Mysore with Ikkēri kingdom.

(e) Arasugaḷa Parampare, Gersoppa Samsthānada vishaya, containing information about Gersoppa Principality.

(f) Velugōṭivarivaṁśāvali, dealing with Velugōṭi chiefs,

AND

(g) *Kaifiyats.*

  (i) Ustangi Ventike Saluva Sānte Bennūr Kaifiyat,
  (ii) Kaifiyat of Udugaṇi,
  (iii) Kanara Kaifiyat,
  (iv) Kaifiyats of Mardala Mākaṇi, Arikuthāra, Basrūr, Kundāpūr, Kabbunādu, Kadari, Halsanāḍ, Kāpi, Hosaṅgaḍi, and Bidarūr.
  (v) Hyder Kaifiyat.

All these probably written at a later period, do not have the same value as contemporary evidence. But they may be taken to reflect genuine local tradition. They were apparently compiled with the help of the then existing records. They are at best secondary evidence. Col. Mackenzie, whose object was merely to collect them could not have exercised sufficient discriminative judgment in recording the statements and notices he received. Though some of them cannot stand strict internal criticism, their usefulness in investing history with real flesh and blood cannot be overlooked. An impartial and collated study of these native chronicles must serve as a substantial basis for the reconstruction of the history of the Nāyakās of Ikkēri.

Thus the sources for the study of the history of the Nāyakas of Ikkēri are varied and interesting spread over the languages of Samskrit, Kannaḍa, English, Portuguese, Dutch, Persian and Marāṭhi.

History of Previous Research: The earliest attempt in drawing up a genealogy of the Ikkēri Nāyakas was made by Robert Sewell in his "Sketch of the Dynasties of Southern India (1884)." This genealogy of the Rājas of Keladi, Ikkēri or Bednur, drawn up by Sewell was revised by L. D. Barnett in the Journal of the Royal Asiatic Society, 1910. In 1921-22, Dr. Shama Sastry sketched the history of the Mālnāḍ chiefs in the Quarterly Journal of the Mythic Society, (Bangalore). In 1930-31, S. N. Naraharayya contributed a paper on the Keladi dynasty in the same journal. In 1931, Mr. M. S. Puttaṇa wrote a small book in Kannaḍa on the "History of Ikkēri" based purely on literary and legendary sources. The work was published by Śrī M. P. Sōmasēkhara Rao of Bangalore in 1931. In 1936, Mr. N. Lakshminarayan Rao, in his paper on the "The Nāyakas of Keladi" in the Vijayanagar Sexcentenary Commemoration Volume, has fixed the chronology of the chiefs, besides giving a brief account of the dynasty as gathered from inscriptions. Father Heras in his book on the "Aravidu Dynasty" has given a brief account of the Ikkēri Nāyakas. Except for these, there has been no serious attempt to write a comprehensive and connected history of the Nāyakas of Ikkēri.

I have carefully studied the views of the earlier writers on the subject and discussed my differences with them regarding problems of chronology and identifications in my own statements. I am however indebted to these scholars who have worked earlier in the field.

It is hoped that the present study would, for the first time, place before the public an authentic account of the Ikkēri rulers so far as it could be authentic from the source material available at present.

CHAPTER II

ORIGIN AND FOUNDATION OF THE NĀYAKSHIP OF IKKĒRI

The study of the origins and early history of any kingdom bristles with many difficulties on account of their humble and almost unnoticeable beginnings. The materials for such a study are also usually inadequate and often not fully dependable because they combine a large amount of fiction with a few grains of fact. As will be seen from the sequel, the question of the origin and growth of the Nāyakship of Ikkēri is no exception to this.

There are diverse and contradictory accounts about the rise of the Nāyaks of Ikkēri to power. The *Śivatattvaratnākara*, gives the following account of the origin of the Nāyakship. In the town of Keladi there lived a person of moderate means named Basavappa with his wife Basavammā. They had four sons two of whom were respectively named Chauḍa and Bhadra. Basavappa and his two unnamed sons predeceased Basavammā. Hence Chauḍa and Bhadra were left to the care of their mother. One day Chauḍa went to inspect the crops in the family fields. Finding that he had not returned home, though it was late, the mother went to the place anxious to know what could have detained him. To her surprise and bewilderment she found him fast asleep under the shade of a mango tree with a serpent spreading its hood over his head. On her approach the reptile glided away; and Basavammā roused Chauḍa from his sleep and told him of what had happened. Both of them went home reflecting on the truth of the saying

"Raṇe vane jale śaile suptam mattam ca dehinām|

Purākṛtāni puṇyāni rakṣanti na vai mṛṣa"||[1] Some other incidents are said to have followed closely. A cow belonging to them would return home every evening with absolutely no

1. 'On mount, on water, in war, in sleep or under drinks, protecting agents, it is true are Man's actions' links. *Śivatattvaratnākara* (Ed. by B. Ramarao and P. Sundara Sastriar, 1927) *Kallola* v, *Taraṅga* ii, verse 39.

milk in her udder and the cow boy who used to graze her was suspected as the probable thief. Himself anxious to know the real fact, one day the cowherd watched the movements of the cow and discovered that she went to a thicket and shed her milk there. So in order to prove his innocence he reported the incident to his master. Thereupon Chauḍa went there with his relations and servants to see the strange sight; and on digging the ground he found in it a liṅga with an inscription. The name of the liṅga was stated in the epigraph to be Rāmēśvara. He took the liṅga home and worshipped it every day. A few days after Chauḍa had a dream predicting the existence of a treasure trove which he would get. Later on, while ploughing his field, he came across a buried chest containing treasure. Chauḍappa secured it and gradually increased his power and influence and gathered round himself a number of retainers. On account of his influence in the area he became its *grāmādhipa*. The Emperor of Vijayanagar, hearing of the influence of Chauḍa, summoned him to his presence and appointed him Governor of Pulladēśa with the title *Keladi Chauḍappa Nāyaka*.[2]

The *Keladinṛpavijayam* agrees with the *Śivatattvaratnākara* with regard to the account of the buried treasure. It further adds that Kṛṣṇadēva Rāya, the Vijayanagar Emperor, summoned Chauḍa and Bhadra to his court thinking that they would be helpful to him in stemming the tide of Muslim advance and requested them to remain at his court and help him in his military undertakings. At that time the Śabaras and other petty chiefs set up the standard of revolt and harassed the Empire. The Rāya despatched an army under Chauḍa to suppress them. Chauḍa defeated them and took several of them prisoners. Kṛṣṇadēva Rāya being immensely pleased with him, bestowed on him many gifts. After a short time, Kṛṣṇadēva Rāya who feared a Muslim invasion, decided that the defence of his northern frontier should be entrusted to the brothers Chauḍa and Bhadra. So he summoned them to his presence and invested them with the powers of the lords of the Marches to protect the northern

2. *STR*, *Kallola* v, *Taraṅga* iv, vv. 40-42. The work does not, however say who the Vijayanagar Emperor was.

frontier stationing themselves at Candragutti and Keladi. He also granted them the eight *māgaṇis* of Keladi, Ikkēri, Perbayal, Eḷagalaḷe, Mōdūr, Kalise and Lātavādi to be held by them and their descendants as a *jāgir*. Chauḍappa came to be called Chauḍappa Nāyaka of Keladi Mūla Samsthāna. Later he formally installed himself as chief at Ikkēri on Māgha Śu 3 of the year Siddhārti, Śaka 1422 corresponding to 8th January, 1500 A.C.[3]

A few other accounts regarding the origin of the Ikkēri Nāyaks are contained in some of the manuscripts collected by Col. Mackenzie in the first quarter of the last century. The *Ustangi Ventike Salluva Sante Bennūr Kaifiyat* relates that since his servant, Yādava, who was looking after his cows died while unearthing a treasure for his master, Chauḍa built a fort in his name. The Narapati kings of Vijayanagar Acyuta Rāya and Sadāśiva Rāya who heard of this sent for Chauḍa and granted him some territories.[4]

To all these accounts much historical importance cannot be attached for similar stories are current regarding the origin of many a dynasty. The Nāyakship of Jiñji, according to some accounts, had a similar origin. It is said that Ānanda Kōn, a shepherd by caste, accidentally found a treasure in a cavity and made himself the head of a small band of warriors, defeated the petty rulers of the neighbouring villages and laid the foundations of the Nāyakship. In many cases where persons have risen from a humble position to power and distinction stories of their association with serpents auguring their good future and prosperity were often fabricated. For instance, a similar account is known about Kempe Gauḍa of Māgadi, the founder of Bangalore. Such stories were apparently due to the popular belief and to the attempt of the panegyrists to colour their stories by introducing supernatural elements indicating divine sanction in favour of the foundation of the dynasties.

3. *Keladinṛpavijayam* edited by R. Shama Sastry, Mysore, 1921, Canto I, p. 28. If Chauḍappa's installation took place on this date, the Vijayanagar king could not have been Kṛṣṇadeva Rāya as he ascended the throne only in 1509 A.C.

4. Mackenzie Collection, 18-15-7 Sec. 12.

From the available evidence regarding the origin of the Nāyakship of Ikkēri, it is not possible to say anything definite about the circumstances under which it was founded. Instead of being uniform in their details, the accounts contain many contradictory and unbelievable statements.

There is an inscription of Chauḍa dated Śaka 1429, Kshaya, Mārgaśira bahuḷa 10 (9th December 1506 A.C.). It records the gift of some land by Chauḍa to the children of Vīrapaya, a stone carver of the village Ḳalise.[5] He is mentioned therein as *Keladīya Chauḍa Gauḍa;* and it does not refer to the paramount sovereign Immaḍi Narasimha. From this it may be reasonably inferred that Chauḍa had begun his independent career even before 1506 A.C., when Immaḍi Narasimha was the Emperor of Vijayanagar. We do not find any reference to Chauḍappa in the inscriptions of the Vijayanagar Emperor. Lewis Rice and N. Lakshminarayan Rao think that Chauḍa and Bhadra rebelled against the Tuḷuva king Vīra Narasimha in the general confusion of the period. According to Mr. Rao the brothers were seized by the sovereign and imprisoned at the capital. On an opportunity presenting itself, the brothers offered their services to put down a rebellious chief and, when they succeeded in their undertaking, the king appointed Chauḍa as the chief of Keladi.[6] It is not known on what evidence this statement has been made by them. An inscription in the Kalasēśvara temple at Kalse, Mudgere taluk, dated Śaka 1438, Dhātu, Śrāvaṇa Śuddha 15 (1516 A.C.) during the reign of Kṛṣṇadēva Rāya of course mentions an expedition of Bhujabala Mahārāya (Busbal Rao of Nuniz) into the Tuḷu rājya and his camp at Mangalore to quell a rebellion of his feudatories in the area.[7] Curiously enough we do not find any reference to Chauḍa in the epigraph. Probably Chauḍa who was independent from an earlier period did not join the rebels against the paramount power and hence there was no need to mention him in the inscription.

5. *Mysore Archaeological Report,* 1930, No. 65.

6. Rice : *Mysore Gazetteer,* II, p. 458; *Vijayanagar Sexcentenary Commemoration Volume,* p. 256.

7. *Epigraphia Carnatica,* VI, Mg. 41.

An inscription of the time of Chauḍa's successor, Sadāsiva Nāyaka, gives a genealogical list of the members of the family before Chauḍa Gauḍa.[8] It states that Dēva Gauḍa of Keladi had a son named Gōpa Gauḍa whose son was Basava Gauḍa, the father of a Chauḍa Gauḍa Bhadraguṇḍaraśa.[9] It deserves to be noted that the suffix *araśa* meaning king is given only to Chauḍa and not to any one of his ancestors which makes one infer that Chauḍa was the first prominent member of the family. What all could possibly be said about Chauḍa is that he was a loyal subordinate of the Vijayanagar Emperors in the early sixteenth century enjoying a large measure of autonomy in his territory and at the same time doing loyal service for them.

However, we have no means of ascertaining the early history of Ikkēri upto the time of Kṛṣṇadēva Rāya. The political condition of the Vijayanagar Empire was far from satisfactory, when Kṛṣṇadēva Rāya ascended the throne in 1509 A.C. Some of the local chiefs in the Karṇāṭaka country were at large and the authority of the Central Government was not very effective. In 1511 A.C., Kṛṣṇadēva Rāya undertook an expedition against Ummattūr. The *Rāyavācakamu*, a work in colloquial Telugu, purporting to have been written by one Viśvanāthanāyanayya, the governor of a province under Kṛṣṇadēva Rāya and his agent (*Sthānāpati*) at his imperial headquarters, and giving an account of the emperor's campaigns, says that after his Ummattūr campaign, Kṛṣṇadēva Rāya proceeded towards Śrīraṅgapaṭṇam, where he examined his fortifications and worshipped god Ādi Raṅganātha of the place. From there he marched towards Ikkēri Araṅgam, inspected the troops of a certain Śukkula Nāyaka and directed his army towards Bījāpur.[10] The *Kṛṣṇa Rāya*

8. *MAR.*, 1928, No. 65.

9. The astronomical details contained in the inscription say that in Śaka 1431, Vibhava, Kārtika ba. 3 there was a solar eclipse. But there was no such eclipse on that day. From that point of view the reliability of the inscription may be questioned. But on no account one need not disbelieve the genealogy regarding the ancestors of Chauḍa.

10. S. Krishnaswami Aiyangar : *Sources of Vijayanagar History*, p. 111.

Vijayamu, a Telugu poem written by Kumāra Dhūrjaṭi, celebrating the victories of Kṛṣṇadēva Rāya concurs with the account given by the *Rāyavācakamu* and says that Kṛṣṇadēva Rāya, shortly after leaving Śrīraṅgapaṭṇam, effected a junction with the troops of Śankula Nāyaka (probably the same as the Śukkula Nāyaka of the *Rāyavācakamu*) of Ikkēri and marched against the frontier fortress of Bījāpur.[11] It is not known who this Śukkula Nāyaka was. Probably he was a lieutenant of Chauḍa. Other sources, however, are silent about this incident.

In those days, the kings used to create a number of worthy chiefs or vassals, grant them territories within the kingdom or empire, so that they might keep up their dignity and maintain an efficient force for the government. Kṛṣṇadēva Rāya seeing the necessity for having a vassal chief in the region round about Keladi, could have raised Chauḍa to the rank of a Nāyaka or feudal chief granting him some territory known as Malladēśa. And the territory received by Chauḍa from the Emperor besides his hereditary possessions obviously formed the nucleus of the future Keladi kingdom.

The campaigns of Chauḍa may now be briefly reviewed from the available literary evidence. Mention has been made earlier about the subjugation of the Śabaras by Chauḍa. He is also said to have been sent against the Kirātas. According to the *Viṣṇu Purāṇa,* they were a class of hunters in the hilly region and dwelt on the eastern part of Bhārata.[12] But it is not likely that Chauḍa would have gone so far away from his territory. It is more likely that the Vijayanagar king would have sent him against the tribes of the hilly region, near Keladi. According to the *Keladinṛpavijayam* Chauḍa was given large powers to defend the frontiers of the Empire on that side.[13]

At Keladi Chauḍa built a temple of Rāmēśvara and gave large endowments to it. This temple was originally built of

11. *Ibid.,* p. 131.
12. II, 3, 8. Also H. H. Wilson, Viṣṇupurāṇa (London 1840), p. 175.
13. *KNV., op. cit.,* Canto I.

wood.[14] He installed in it the *linga* he is said to have found and became a devotee of Śiva.

Family: Chauḍa had two sons, Sadāśiva and Bhadra. On the birth of Sadāśiva Chauḍa gave much wealth in charity. He taught his sons several *śāstras* and royal acts which they learnt with considerable skill.[15] The *Keladinṛpavijayam* attributes the founding of Ikkēri to Chauḍappa.[16] The new city was enlarged later on by Venkaṭappa Nāyaka.[17]

The reign period of Chauḍappa cannot be fixed with precision. The *Rājavamśāvaḷi* says that Chauḍa became ruler in Śaka 1422 (1500 A.C.) and ruled for a period of 13 years.[18] The relevant prose portion of the *Keladinṛpavijayam* says: "Thus Chauḍappa ruled virtuously for 13 years and six months from his accession to the third of the first fortnight of Śrāvaṇa, Śrīmukha in Śaka 1436" thereby giving him a rule from 1499 A.C. to 1513 A.C. The only epigraph of Chauḍa, as said earlier, is dated Śaka 1429, Kshaya, Mārgaśira bahula 10 corresponding to 9th December 1506 A.C.[19] It is unfortunate that the dates assigned to the Nāyakas of Keladi in the literary works upto the time of Venkaṭappa Nāyaka I, do not tally with those obtained from inscriptions.

We have two other records that throw some light on the reign of Chauḍa. An inscription of Acyuta Rāya dated Śaka 1456, Vijaya, Āṣāḍa Śu 11 (1534 A.C.) mentions a certain Koṇḍappa Voḍeyaru as governing Bārakūr Rājya under the orders of a Śankaṇṇa Nāyaka.[20] Another epigraph of Acyuta Rāya from Uppūru in the South Canara District dated Śaka 1457 (1535 A.C.) states that the Mangaḷūru and Bārakūru rājyas were given to Śankaṇṇa Nāyaka, who in turn gave them over to Koṇḍappa Voḍeya.[21] The earliest known

14. *Ibid.*
15. *STR.*, V, 4, ll. 46 ff.
16. *KNV.*, *op. cit.*, Canto I.
17. *STR.*, VI, 1.
18. *Mac. Coll.* 18-15-15, section v.
19. *MAR.*, 1930, No. 65.
20. *ARSIE.*, No. 422 of 1927-28.
21. *Ibid.*, 487 of 1928-29.

inscription of Sadāśiva Nāyaka, son of Chauḍa, is dated 1544 A.C.[22] The *Śivatattvaratnākara,* says that Sadāsiva had two sons, Doḍḍa Śankaṇṇa and Chikka Śankaṇṇa.[23] The Śankaṇṇa referred to in *ARSIE* 422 of 1927-28 cannot be either of these two. He must be a predecessor of Sadāśiva not mentioned in the *Śivatattvaratnākara* or in the *Keladinṛpavijayam.* It is possible that Śankaṇṇa may have been a surname of Chauḍa, the father of Sadāśiva Nāyaka, especially as the sons of Sadāśiva Nāyaka are given the names of Doḍḍa and Chikka Śankaṇṇa, perhaps the name of their grandfather according to the accepted usage among Hindus and it is reasonable to think that Chauḍa ruled atleast till 1535 A.C. or probably even till 1540 A.C. and his territories included Keladi, Bārakūru and Mangaḷūru in the latter part of his reign. But it is not known how or when he became the overlord of that region.[24]

It is likely that Chauḍa associated his sons Sadāśiva and Bhadra with the administration of his infant principality. In the evening of his life, he appears to have crowned his son, Sadāśiva, retired from active politics and later died.[25] His brother, Bhadra also seems to have died soon after.

22. *EC.,* VII, Shikarpur, 255.
23. *STR.,* V, 5, vv. 2-5.
24. Otherwise we must admit the existence of a large gap between the end of the reign of Chauḍappa and the accession of Sadāśiva Nāyaka.
25. *STR.,* V, 4, Verse 93 ff.

CHAPTER III

SADĀŚIVA NĀYAKA—1540 (?)—1565

Accession: We have no means of fixing the exact date of Sadāśiva Nāyaka's accession. The *Keladinṛpavijayam* makes one think that he ascended the throne in Śaka 1435, Śrīmukha, Śrāvaṇa śu 3 (5th July 1513 A.C.)[1] and that he continued to rule till 1545 A.C. The following reign period has been assigned to him.

Sewell	A.C. 1560-1576[2]
Shama Sastry	A.C. 1545-1561[3]
Rice	A.C. 1513-1545[4]
Rajavamśāvali	A.C. 1513-1545[5]
Aygal	A.C. 1513-1545[6]

It is not clear on what evidence the above dates have been suggested for the commencement and end of Sadāśiva Nāyaka's reign. The earliest reliable inscription of Sadāśiva Nāyaka, which is dated in the cyclic year Krōdhin, (1544-45 A.C.), records a grant for worship of God Mallikārjuna of Togarashe.[7] And among other inscriptions referring to him are two which are dated Śaka 1487 (1565 A.C.).[8] It has been shown that Chauḍappa ruled till atleast 1535 A.C. Since the first known and dependable inscription of his successor, Sadāśiva Nāyaka is dated 1544, it is possible that he succeeded to the throne between A.C. 1535 and 1544, perhaps some-

1. *KNV.*, II.
2. *List of Inscriptions and Dynasties in Southern India*, Vol. II, p. 177.
3. *QJMS.*, XII, p. 47.
4. *EC.*, VII, Intro., p. 42.
5. *Mac. Coll.* 18-15-15.
6. Aygal., *History of South Kanara*, p. 188.
7. *EC.*, VII, Sk. 255. A copper plate grant (MAR. 1928, No. 65 referred to earlier) dated Śaka 1431 (current), Vibhava, kārttika, ba 3, Ravivāra, solar eclipse purports to belong to his reign. The inscription does not seem to be dependable. There was no solar eclipse in the month of kārttika in the cyclic year Vibhava. Further, the date appears to be too early for Sadāśiva, as it would be improbable that he did not issue any record for 35 years after he began to rule.
8. *ARSIE.*, 292 and 301 of 1932.

where about 1540 A.C. Again as two of his inscriptions are dated in 1565 A.C., it may be assumed that he ruled atleast till that year.[9]

With the accession of Sadāśiva Nāyaka, the Nāyakas of Ikkēri, emerge from a period of comparative obscurity to political limelight. Till then they had merely acquired some influence playing some subordinate part in the affairs of the Vijayanagar kings. It was Sadāśiva Nāyaka who laid the foundations of the future greatness of Ikkēri. By taking part in the wars of Vijayanagar and winning its goodwill he was able to secure the stability of the infant Nāyakship, which enabled his successors to build up their power and influence in spite of the rivalries and jealousies of their neighbours.

Sadāśiva Nāyaka was a great warrior, and made a bold bid for fortune and fame. He spent the early part of his career in rendering military service to the Vijayanagar Emperor, Sadāśiva Rāya. The political condition of the Deccan at that time forced Vijayanagar to wage a series of wars; and Sadāśiva as one of the loyal feudatories of the emperor was naturally led to participate in them.

The *Keladinṛpavijayam* and the *Śivatattvaratnākara* contain details of the military exploits of Sadāśiva Nāyaka. The former opens the account of his military career with a description of his march against the Muslim ruler of Ahmednagar, Bhaire Nijama Pātuṣa (Hussain Nijām Pāṣā) for capturing the forts of Kalyāṇī and Kulabarige (Gulburga) under the orders of Rāma Rāja.[10] The Sultān of Ahmednagar sent his regiments commanded by his generals, Feroja Khān, Tālita Khān, Sañjār Khān, Sāthe Khān, Munila Khān, Vajra Khān, Rāvuta Khān and Bokka Śingha to oppose the invader.[11] In the conflict that ensued Sadāśiva Nāyaka

9. N. Lakshminarayan Rao, however, thinks on the basis of Sadāśiva's inscription of 1544 A.C. that he must have ascended the throne in that year. See *Vij. Sex. Com. Vol.*, p. 257.

10. *KNV.*, II, p. 30. The work wrongly places the event in Kṛṣṇadēva Rāya's reign. But the *STR.* places the event correctly in the reign of Rāma Rāja.

11. *KNV.*, II. This is confirmed by the *Burhan-i-Masir.* See *IA.*, Vol. L, 1921, p. 105.

pushed forward, and in an encounter with Bokka Śingha he received a sword thrust on his back. Notwithstanding the injury Sadāśiva by his steadfastness and courage led the Hindus to victory. Bokka Śingha was taken prisoner and led before Rāma Rāja. The victory was followed by the storming of the fort of Kalyāṇi. The work further adds that Rāma Rāja, who was very much pleased with Sadāśiva Nāyaka, bestowed on him great honours and conferred the title Immaḍi Sadāśivēndra. Meanwhile, the garrison of the fort of Kalubarige opposed them. Rāma Rāja halted at the place, and having thrown his *jamuvaḍi* into the fort, commanded the chiefs who accompanied him to fetch it. When all others hesitated, Sadāśiva Nāyaka attacked the fort, captured it and got back the *jamuvaḍi.* In recognition of his valour the Rāya gave him the title, *Kōṭe Kōlāhala* (Destroyer of Forts). The fort of Iṣṭa Kōṭe was also taken by Sadāśiva Nāyaka.

However, according to the *Śivatattvaratnākara* which deals with Sadāśiva's attack on Kalyāṇī and Kalburgi (Gulburga),[12] it was the army of the lord of Vijayāpur (Bījāpur) that opposed Sadāśiva. The Muslim army was, however, defeated and driven away. It also mentions Rāma Rāja's throwing his *yama damṣṭra* into the fort and Sadāśiva's subsequent recovery of it, when all other chiefs remained silent. In recognition of the services rendered by him on this occasion, Rāma Rāja bestowed on him the titles, *Kōṭe Kōlāhala* and *Rāya Nāyaka* and gave him the provinces of Gutti, Bārakūr and Mangaḷūr.[13]

12. *Kallola* V, *Taraṅga* 5, Verse 7.

13. It may be noted that in the earliest reliable inscription of Sadāśiva dated 1544-45 A.C., noticed above, he is not mentioned as governor of any of these districts. But in an inscription dated Śaka 1474 (1550 A.C.) he is for the first time stated to have been ruling the Āraga (18 *kampaṇas*) under the orders of Emperor Sadāśiva Rāya. (*EC.*, VIII, Nagar 77). Evidently he was made the ruler of the region between 1545 and 1550 A.C. Again one of the inscriptions of the reign of Sadāśiva Rāya dated Śaka 1476 (1554 A.C.) (*ARSIE*, 433 of 1927-28) mentions Sadāśiva Rāya Nāyaka as administering Bārakūr rājya, while another record of the reign of Sadāśiva Rāya (*SII.*, VII, No. 366) states

We get a good picture of the details of the campaign by collating together all the available evidence on it. The Muslim troops were led by the Sultan of Ahmednagar and the Vijayanagar forces were led by Sadāśiva Nāyaka of Ikkēri. In the fight that ensued Sadāśiva Nāyaka fully justified the trust reposed in him. Rāma Rāya joined him and they encamped under the walls of fortress of Kalyāṇi. Having decided to besiege it, they effectively cut off the supplies to it. But the Muslims successfully cut the lines of communication of the Hindus. A Council of war seems to have been held to consider the situation that had arisen. Most of the generals were for raising the siege but Sadāśiva Nāyaka encouraged by the success he had already met with was able to prevail upon the rest to consent to attacking the enemy. The next dawn they surprised the Muslim armies with a terrible onslaught. The attack was so unexpected, sudden and forceful that the Muslims fled, leaving their tents, baggage and artillery all of which were taken by the victors. A determined attack was then made on the fort which surrendered with little opposition.[14] The date of this battle is placed by Fr. Heras in about 1549 A.C.[15] and this seems to be acceptable.

Sadāśiva Nāyaka and Bījāpur: The *Keladinṛpavijayam* also contains the following short account of a war between the Sultan of Bījāpur and the Rāya of Vijayanagar: 'The king of Bījāpur without paying due regard to the might of the Rāya, sent an army against him under the command of Sathēya Khāna, one of his ministers, but Sadāśiva Nāyaka defeated him in battle.'[16] The name of the Sultan of Bījāpur and the time of the invasion are not however mentioned therein. But a reference to the accounts contained in the writings of the Muslim historians helps one to trace the events

that it was Mahāmaṇḍalēśvara Venkaṭādri Rāja that had entrusted him (Sadāśiva Nāyaka) with the administration of Bārakūr. This Venkaṭādri was obviously no other than the brother of Aḷiya Rāma Rāya, who was weilding considerable influence.

14. Briggs: *Ferishta*, III, pp. 102-3.
15. *Aravidu Dynasty*, pp. 79 ff.
16. *KNV.*, II.

relating to this war. During Rāma Rāja's period Ibrāhim Ādil Shāh and his son ruled in Bījāpur. Ādil Shāh's son never fought against Rāma Rāja excepting in the wars which terminated in the battle of Rākṣasa Tangaḍi in 1565 A.C. But Ādil Shāh was engaged in a war with Rāma Rāja at first though he sought Rāma Rāja's support later to ward off the invasions of his dominions by Burham Nizam Shāh of Ahmednagar and his allies. The Sultan of Bījāpur who sent an army against Vijayanagar as stated in the *Keladinṛpavijayam* seems to have been Ibrahim Ādil Shāh I. Ferishta confirms this when he states that Ibrahim Ādil Shāh I marched against Vijayanagar and succeeded in adding greatly to his territories by his conquests from that Kingdom.[17] But the invasion does not seem to have produced any substantial results for there was no appreciable territorial loss to Vijayanagar.

Another military exploit of Sadāśiva Nāyaka was his expedition against Barid Shāh of Bidār under instructions from Rāma Rāja to put down his increasing insolence. The *Keladinṛpavijayam* gives a graphic account of it. Barid, hearing of this invasion met it with a large army of elephants, horses and foot soldiers. The battle raged in fury. Barid rallied his followers but it was of little avail. 'Like a tiger falling on a herd of sheep, Sadāśiva shattered to pieces the army of the Yavanas with arrows, spears and swords.' He took Barid Shāh captive with his generals, shield, umbrella, banner, seal-rings and elephants and presented them to Rāma Rāya. The Rāya honoured him with jewels, ornaments and betel leaves and gave him the rights of *meghaḍambara* (sounding of drums) and daylight lamps. He also gave him the title of *Śatrusaptāṅgaharaṇa* (Capturer of the seven *aṅgas* of the enemy).[18]

The *Śivatattvaratnākara* also refers to this battle. It states that Sadāśiva brought the *Pādusha* (Barid Shāh) prisoner with a large amount of plunder. For this achievement he was given the title of *Śatrusaptāṅgaharaṇa* besides

17. Briggs: *Ferishta*, III, p. 387.
18. *KNV.*, II.

valuable marks of honour such as a red flag (*aruṇa dhvaja*), five instruments of band (*vādhyapañcaka*) besides others.[19] The causes of this war are not however known. The Muslim chronicles from which some account may be expected are practically silent about it. The *Narasabhūpālīyamu*, a literary work in Telugu by Bhaṭṭa Mūrti *alias* Rāmarāja Bhūṣaṇa, says that Rāma Rāja's brother Venkaṭādri led the campaign against Barid and that he was assisted by Narasarāja of Torgal besides Sadāśiva Nāyaka and other officers.[20] From this it may be inferred that along with Sadāśiva Rāya Nāyaka there were also some other Vijayanagar feudatories who participated in the campaign. The *Keladinṛpavijayam* places this war after Rāma Rāja's first invasion of the Nizām Shāhi kingdom. This is indirectly supported by some Muslim authorities. According to Ferishta 'Ali Barīd Shāh joined Rāma Rāja and Ali Ādil Shāh in their campagin against Ahmednagar';[21] and his presence in their army during the war with Ibrahim Qutub Shāh of Golkonda is also noticed by the same historian.[22] Hence this war with Barid Shāh seems to have taken place before Rāma Rāja's second invasion of Ahmednagar. It is not, however, possible to fix the date of this war precisely.

Other Campaigns of Sadāśiva Nāyaka: Sadāśiva Nāyaka was then sent to subdue the chiefs of the Tuḷuva country. He led a successful expedition to the south as far as Kāsargode, and planted a pillar of victory there to commemorate his conquest.[23] Subsequently he seems to have been made also the ruler of the newly conquered country to keep control over the chieftains in it; and he ruled over the area till about 1565 A.C.[24] During the days of Rāma Rāja, an expedition was sent under Viṭṭhala against the Tiruvāḍi rājya (Travancore) which was ruled by Bhūtala Vīra Keraḷa Varma.[25]

19. *STR.*, *Kallola* V, Taraṅga 5, Verse 5.
20. S. K. Aiyangar: *Sources of Vijayanagar History*, pp. 224 ff.
21. Briggs: *Ferishta*, III, p. 120.
22. *Ibid.*, (App.), p. 406.
23. *STR.*, V. 5; Verse 83 ff., *KNV.*, II.
24. *ARSIE.*, 433 of 1927-28.
25. Nagam Aiya: *Travancore State Manual*, I, p. 297.

Rāma Rāja Viṭṭhala was helped in the expedition by some feudatories of the Vijayanagar Emperor. Viśvanātha Nāyaka of Madurai offered every help to Viṭṭhala to carry out his enterprise. Likewise Sadāśiva Nāyaka also participated in this expedition.[26] Maddaraśa of Bankāpura was the next victim of Sadāśiva Nāyaka. For some unknown reason he was attacked, taken prisoner and led in chains to the presence of the royal master. A certain Sāḷuva Nāyakendra of Candragutti finding the distracted condition in Vijayanagar made a bold bid for independence. Hence Sadāśiva Nāyaka as a loyal feudatory of Vijayanagar stormed the fortress of the rebel chief and took him prisoner. Probably in recognition of that he seems to have been granted the ownership of the 18 kampaṇas of Āraga.[27]

An inscription of Sadāśiva Rāya of Vijayanagar dated Śaka 1473 (1551 A.C.) mentions Keladi Sadāśiva Rāya Nāyaka as ruling over the Āraga kingdom.[28] Hence this campaign appears to have been completed before the year 1551 A.C. Again an inscription of the reign of the same Emperor ruling from Vidyānagari dated Śaka 1479 (1557 A.C.) says that Honnali Śīme had been given to Sadāśiva Rāya Nāyaka of Keladi as an *amara māgaṇi*.[29]

The *Keladinṛpavijayam* mentions that Eḍava Murāri who was the chief of Jaḷayapayal did not pay allegiance to the Emperor and so Sadāśiva Nāyaka took the responsibility for leading an expedition against him, captured his fort and took him prisoner. The Emperor who was highly pleased with this feat of the Nāyaka, gave him the title of *Eḍava Murāri*.[30] This and the title *Kōṭekōlāhala* were hereditary *birudas* of

26. Heras: *Aravidu Dynasty*, p. 142.
27. *STR.*, V, 5, Verse 98, *KNV.*, II.
28. *EC.*, VIII, Nr. 77.
29. *EC.*, VII, Hn. 9.
30. *KNV.*, II. About the origin of this title there are different versions. In explaining the origin of the Nāyakship it is said that Chauḍa in order to commemorate the names of his two slaves Yādava and Murāri, whom he is supposed to have sacrificed to unearth the treasure, took the title of *Yādava Murāri* (See Rice : *Mysore and Coorg*, p. 156). But the *Keladinṛpavijayam* mentions Yādava Murāri as one person.

the family borne by all rulers from Sadāśiva Nāyaka onwards. For different expeditions undertaken against the Muslims, he was awarded such titles as *Ekāṅgavīra, Balavanta* etc. All these bear testimony to the valuable services of Sadāśiva Nāyaka to Vijayanagar and his striking contribution to its strength and stability.

Other victories are also credited to Sadāśiva Nāyaka. He is said to have put down a number of *Pāḷaiyagars* such as (a) Ikkēri Malla Gauḍa, (b) Nellūr Puṭṭe Gauḍa, (c) Nurguppe Puṭṭe Gauḍa, (d) Malati Puṭṭe Gauḍa, (e) Vṛdhi Muppina Gauḍa, (f) Mañcala Puṭṭe Gauḍa and (g) Yelegaḷḷi Puṭṭe Gauḍa. The identification of these chiefs and their places is however by no means easy in the present state of our knowledge. Likewise he is said to have reduced other minor *pāḷaiyagars* as (a) Vīraṇṇa of Andige, (b) Muppina Gauḍa of Bavuduri, (c) Puṭṭe Gauḍa of Vēlūr, (d) Puṭṭe Gauḍa of Mabasale, (e) Puṭṭe Gauḍa of Kanave and (f) the Jain *Pāḷaiyagars* of Sirvanti.[31] With the available meagre evidence it is equally difficult to identify the above persons and places.

Extent of the Nāyak Kingdom: The territory governed by Sadāśiva Nāyaka is stated in an inscription of 1563 A.C. to have covered Āraga, Bārakūru and Mangaḷūru.[32] He was the ruler of Tuḷurājya also.[33] In order to be prepared for any contingency Sadāśiva seems to have built a number of forts in and around his territory, such as at, Keladi, Ikkēri and Kāvaledurg.[34] The twelfth queen of Gersoppa, a neighbouring kingdom, who was a contemporary of Sadāśiva Nāyaka, finding that she could not rule efficiently gave the overlordship to Sadāśiva Rāya Nāyaka and became his vassal.[35]

Other activities of Sadāśiva Nāyaka: According to the *Keladinṛpavijayam* Sadāśiva Nāyaka is said to have founded

31. *Mac. Coll.* 18-15-7, Section xii.
32. *SII.*, IX, pt. ii, No. 674.
33. *ARSIE.*, 433 of 1927-28.
34. Buchanan: *Journey through Madras*, etc., III, pp. 255 and 283.
35. *Mac. Coll.* 19-1-14.

the Sadāśivapura agrahāra on the banks of the Kuśāvatī river.[36] The *Śivatattvaratnākara* also gives the same details when it says that he built a town called Sadāśivapura and an agrahāra on the river Kuśāvatī.[37] A consideration of the name would suggest that there could have been two reasons for its being called so. Firstly Sadāśiva Nāyaka would have founded the place and named it after the Emperor Sadāśiva Rāya. Secondly, the town might have been named after its founder Sadāśiva Nāyaka himself.[38] Sadāśivapura situated as it was in the midst of places like Ikkēri, Śrāvanti, Yelegalli and Keladi gained much importance. In order to populate it Sadāśiva Nayāka is said to have offered liberal concessions to the merchants and others by way of inducement to them to settle there.[39] The *agrahāra* on the Kuśāvatī granted to the Brahmans consisted of a row of houses to each of which a strip of land adequate to maintain an average family was added. The grantees were scholars of the best type who were provided each with a house to live and propagate *Dharma* by example and precept and guide and keep society in the path of righteousness.[40]

Sadāśiva Nāyaka's Religious Activities: Sadāśiva Nāyaka was well known for his piety and generous disposition to-

36. See *KNV.*, II.

37. *STR.*, *Kallola* v, *Taraṅga* 5.

38. In his account of the Malnad chiefs compiled from local tracts Dr. Shama Sastry says that it was Chauḍa who built a bazaar known as Sadasivasagar. (*QJMS.*, XII, p. 46).

39. Among them were: the rulers of the place were to have no right to punish even such offences as murder of parents or cheating committed by them, or levy fines, or tolls on them or compel them to do free labour, for a period of 30 years. Under these conditions a number of prominent merchants set up their trading houses in the bazaar street. Some other interesting details about the Sadāśivapura bazaar are also available. The streets were square and straight, constructed on a level. To the east of them was built the palace. The town contained 16 divisions: (a) Banajigar with a Talavare katte or Police station, (b) Divisions of Brahmans, (c) potters, (d) copper and bronze smiths, (e) merchants, (f) gardeners, (g) cowherds, (h) weavers, (i) shepherds, (n) washermen, (k) spinners, (1) wrestlers, (m) vegetable dealers, (n) Konkanas, (o) Gavuzas, and (p) prostitutes. *QJMS.*, XII, pp. 45-47.

40. *Ibid.*, XXI, pp. 377-78.

wards religious institutions like temples and maṭhas. In the *agrahāra* which he founded for Brahmans, he constructed three temples consecrated respectively to Rāmēśvara, Amṛtalingēśvara and Mallikārjuna. For conducting worship in the Rāmēśvara temple, Sadāśiva granted a number of fertile villages. In Sadāśivapura there was a Lingāyat maṭha built by Hovina Hampayya, a local merchant. This was called the Mahant Maṭha. Different kinds of merchandise were brought by 1000 bullocks every year for the maṭha. The villages of Nandigrāma, Kambali Koppa, Halaśirakoṭṭadagrāma, Kallukoppa, Hohalagrāma and Sogimane grāma yielding 1000 *varāhas* per annum were endowed to it. This continued till the days of Hyder Āli, who reduced the income of the maṭha to 30 *varāhas*.[41] According to later accounts Sadāśiva Nāyaka built the Īśvara temple at Ikkēri.[42] Under his orders a *Nandimaṇḍapa* was erected in the Rāmēśvara temple at Keladi.[43]

Sadāśiva Nāyaka's inscriptions reveal a good deal of his religious bent of mind. He made a gift of *sarvamānya* lands yielding produce worth 4 *varāhas* for the service of *dīpārādhana* to Mallinātha, the tutelary deity of the village Ālahaḷḷi in the Holalūru hobaḷi.[44] To the Subrahmaṇya temple at Kukke, he granted the village of Balpa in the Mangaḷūru Śime.[45] Apart from such royal grants, there were a good number of donations by private individuals during his rule to temples and for the maintenance of *satras* and *maṭhas*.[46]

Sadāśiva Nāyaka had also close association with the gurus of Sṛṅgeri maṭha.[47] Though an orthodox Hindu with a predilection for Śiva, Sadāśiva was tolerant of other religions also. His catholicity is amply borne out by a copper plate inscription of his reign dated Śaka 1479 (1557 A.C.), which registers a grant of land by him to Dharmanātha, the fifteenth

41. *Mac. Coll.*, 18-15-7, Sec. xii, *Account of Honnali.*
42. Buchanan: *Journey through Madras*, etc., III, p. 257.
43. *KNV.*, II.
44. *MAR.*, 1923, No. 120.
45. *ARSIE.*, 348 of 1930-31.
46. *EC.*, VII, Sk. 55; *ARSIE.* 392 of 1927 and *EC.*, VIII, Tl. 103.
47. *KNV.* II. There is a long description of Sṛngeri Maṭh and its Gurus in *MAR.*, 1928, pp. 15 ff.

Jīna Tīrthankara. The gift was made at the instance of the Jaina teacher Dēvacandradēva for the spiritual welfare of his Guru Municandradēva, the disciple of Abhinavakīrtidēva.[48]

Coins of Sadāśiva Nāyaka: It is interesting to note that Sadāśiva Nāyaka issued some gold coins which bear on the obverse the figure of Śiva holding the trident in the right hand and the antelope in the left with Pārvatī seated on his left thigh, while on the reverse there is the legend *'Śrī Sadāśiva'* in two or three horizontal lines in Nāgari characters.[49]

Domestic life of Sadāśiva Nāyaka: Sadāśiva Nāyaka married, during the life time of his father, two wives Vīramāmbe and Bhadramāmbe.[50] Through the former he had a son named Doḍḍa Śankaṇṇa and through the latter Chikka Śankaṇṇa. He had them properly educated in the arts and *śāstras* and also got them married.[51] The *Śivatattvaratnākara* says that Sadāśiva Nāyaka installed his brother Bhadrappa on the throne and retired to the forest.

Estimate of Sadāśiva Nāyaka: Sadāśiva Nāyaka was one of the less known able rulers in South India in the sixteenth century like Viśvanātha Nāyaka of Madurai and Acyutappa Nāyaka of Tanjore, all of whom evolved order out of the existing political confusion and built up strong principalities in their respective areas and strengthened the hands of the imperial house. Though Chauḍappa has been credited with the foundation of the Nāyakship Sadāśiva Nāyaka was its real founder. The stability he gave to the infant Nāyakship enabled his successors to build up a powerful and influential kingdom, which, more than once, was able to give shelter to the Emperor of Vijayanagar. His strength and character were so much in high esteem that he was considered as "Bhīma in battle, Suradruma in enjoyments, Sōma in tranquillity and Rāma in truthfulness."

48. *Ep. Ind.*, XX, pp. 89-90.

49. A specimen of this type is preserved in the office of the Government Epigraphist for India, Ootacamund.

50. *KNV.*, II.

51. *STR.*, V. 5, Verse 104.

CHAPTER IV

IMMAḌI SADĀŚIVA NĀYAKA AND DOḌḌA ŚANKAṆṆA NĀYAKA

(1566-1571 A.C.)

The question as to who the successor of Sadāśiva Nāyaka was is a matter for conjecture. According to some of the available sources it was Sadāśiva Nāyaka's son, Doḍḍa Śankaṇṇa Nāyaka that succeeded to the throne after Sadāśiva, while according to a few others it was Sadāśiva's brother Bhadrappa. The *Śivatattvaratnākara* says that after Bhadrappa's return from his pilgrimage from Banares, Sadāśiva Nāyaka bestowed on him the title of Immaḍi Sadāśiva Nāyaka, performed his coronation and retired to the forest. After ruling for some time, Bhadrappa nominated the elder of his nephews Doḍḍa Śankaṇṇa as his successor and the younger Chikka Śankaṇṇa as heir-apparent.[1] According to the *Keladinṛpavijayam,* however, after the death of Sadāśiva Nāyaka, his eldest son Doḍḍa Śankaṇṇa succeeded to the rulership of Ikkēri.[2] Some literary sources in the Mackenzie collection do not mention Bhadrappa Nāyaka at all. There are a few interesting inscriptions, all of them dated Śaka 1488 (1566 A.C.) referring to the reign of an Immaḍi Sadāśiva Rāya Nāyaka[3] and mentioning him as the ruler of the Āraga Rājya. But they do not help us to understand whether this was his name or surname, or the relationship that he bore to his predecessor. But the title Immaḍi Sadāśivēndra according to the *Keladinṛpavijayam* was the one bestowed on Sadāśiva Nāyaka by the Vijayanagar Emperor.[4] As said above the few inscriptions of Immaḍi Sadāśiva Nāyaka are all dated 1566 A.C., thereby indicating that his reign was short. It may be surmised that this Immaḍi Sadāśiva Nāyaka was the title or name of none else than Bhadrappa

1. *STR., Kallola* V, *Taraṅga* 9, Verse 9.
2. *KNV.,* III, p. 43.
3. *EC.,* VIII, Nagar 1 to 4; *MAR.,* 1923, No. 73.
4. *KNV.,* II.

Nāyaka, the brother of Sadāśiva Nāyaka.[5] Probably the title Immaḍi Sadāśiva Rāya Nāyaka, originally conferred on Sadāśiva Nāyaka by the Vijayanagar Emperor Sadāśiva, was given to his brother Bhadrappa Nāyaka also and he was appointed ruler. The younger Immaḍi Sadāśiva ruled for one year 1566 A.C. On his death probably in that year itself or early in 1567 A.C., he was succeeded by Doḍḍa Śankaṇṇa Nāyaka who ruled upto 1571 A.C., as the earliest known inscription of his successor Chikka Śankaṇṇa Nāyaka is dated 1571 A.C.[6]

The following dates have been assigned to him:

Sewell	A.C. 1585-1596[7]
Rice	A.C. 1545-1558[8]
Naraharayya	A.C. 1545-1558[9]
Buchanan	A.C. 1584-1595[10]
Rājavamśāvali	A.C. 1546-1559[11]

It is not known on what grounds the above dates have been suggested for the commencement and end of Doḍḍa Śankaṇṇa's rule. Doḍḍa Śankaṇṇa began his rule with the approval of the Vijayanagar Emperor as regards his title and territories. He kept up to the traditions of his family when it came to the use of the sword. The jealousies of his neighbours and their anxiety to check the progress of the Nāyakas of Ikkēri drew Śankaṇṇa Nāyaka into a series of wars with them. Political rivalries had existed in earlier times between Virūpaṇṇa Oḍeyār of the Jambūr dēśa and Sadāśiva Nāyaka.[12] But Sadāśiva Nāyaka was too strong for him and

5. Shri N. Lakshminarayan Rao identifies Immaḍi Sadāśiva Nāyaka with Doḍḍa Śankaṇṇa on the basis of a copper plate grant of Venkaṭappa Nāyaka dated 1592 A.C. (*Vij. Sex. Com. Vol.*, p. 259). But the evidence regarding the identification of Immaḍi Sadāśiva Nāyaka is conflicting indeed and difficult to determine.
6. *EC.*, VIII, Sb. 55.
7. Sewell: *List of Inscriptions in Southern India*, Vol. II, p. 177.
8. *EC.*, VII, Intro. p. 42.
9. *QJMS.*, XXI, p. 379.
10. Buchanan: *Journey through Madras, etc.*, III, p. 126.
11. *Mac. Coll.* 18-15-15.
12.. *KNV.*, III.

so Virūpaṇṇa had to wait for more favourable times. An opportunity presented itself to him when the young Doḍḍa Śankaṇṇa succeeded to the throne. Details about the hostility between them are contained both in the *Śivatattvaratnākara* and the *Keladinṛpavijayam*. It is said in the *Śivatattvaratnākara* that Virupaṇṇa of Jambūr showed signs of hostility to the Vijayanagar Emperor who therefore deputed Śankaṇṇa Nāyaka of Ikkēri against him. So Śankaṇṇa led an army against Virūpaṇṇa and took him prisoner. The Emperor highly pleased with Śankaṇṇa Nāyaka's services, invited him to come to the capital and stay there. Śankaṇṇa spent some years there and during this period of his absence, Ikkēri was administered by his brother Chikka Śankaṇṇa Nāyaka.[13]

The *Keladinṛpavijayam* gives more but slightly different details about these events. The Jambūra country was conquered by Śankaṇṇa and the fort of Udugaṇi taken, probably without the permission or knowledge of the Vijayanagar Emperor. As both Śankaṇṇa and Virūpaṇṇa were feudatories of Vijayanagar, the dethroned governor Virūpaṇṇa sought shelter at Vijayanagar finding no other refuge. The Emperor summoned the Ikkēri chief to his presence and ordered him to return the captured territories to the applicant.[14]

The *Keladinṛpavijayam* credits Śankaṇṇa Nāyaka with an expedition against Goa in the company of Viṭṭhala Rāja. Having captured Goa, Śankaṇṇa is said to have gone to Vijayanagar where he was granted the Malena *Hōbaḷi* free from all obligations besides valuable jewels and the title of *Bhīyakīrti*.[15] But as Viṭṭhala's expedition against Goa is not known otherwise, it is not possible to ascertain the authenticity of the account. It is known that Rāma Rāja sent his cousin Viṭṭhalarāja on a number of expeditions against the Portuguese only on the Coromandel coast. The last date when we hear

13. *STR.*, *Kallola* V, *Taraṅga* 7, Verse 56 ff.

14. *KNV.*, III.

15. *Ibid.*, The *STR.* says that under the command of Viṭṭhala Rāja, Śankaṇṇa defeated the Portuguese at Goa, and took its governor as prisoner. For these achievements, the Emperor presented him with the town of Mahādēvapura. (See *STR.*, V., 7, Verse 55).

of the general is 1558 A.C., when his career as the viceroy over the southern part of the Vijayanagar Empire came to an end. After that date no mention is made of him and it may be presumed that he died soon after. Hence it is not possible that Viṭṭhala could have undertaken the expedition.

The *Keladinṛpavijayam* further credits Śankaṇṇa Nāyaka with the conquest of the kingdom of Bhairādēvī of Gersoppa, who had much influence along the coast, her chief port being Bhatkal. But the queen was defeated later by Venkaṭappa Nāyaka, son of Doḍḍa Śankaṇṇa. It has been said earlier[16] that she herself accepted the overlordship of Sadāśiva Nāyaka. Hence the occasion for this invasion is not clearly known. It is possible that a small skirmish took place between the two powers during Doḍḍa Śankaṇṇa's rule.

Śankaṇṇa Nāyaka's next target of attack seems to have been Bhairasa Voḍeya of Karkala. He is said to have collected annual tribute from Bhairasa, after defeating him.[17] Doḍḍa Śankaṇṇa had two sons Rāmarāja and Venkaṭappa.[18] The Vijayanagar Emperor appears to have given the districts of Māsūr, Mallūru and Ponnūru for their upbringing and education.[19]

Having a religious bent of mind, Doḍḍa Śankaṇṇa spent a good part of his life in spiritual matters. Towards the closing years of his life he is said to have gone on a pilgrimage to all the holy places of India. The *Śivatattvaratnākara* and the *Keladinṛpavijayam* describe at great length Doḍḍa Śankaṇṇa's pilgrimage to important religious centres in the different parts of the country.

Doḍḍa Śankaṇṇa was aided in the administration of his Nāyakship by his brother Chikka Śankaṇṇa particularly during his absence from his kingdom. He was also helped by his minister Kalasappayya of Āraga. Naravappayya

16. See *ante*, p. 27.
17. *JRAS.*, 1911, p. 190.
18. *STR.*, V. 7, vv. 49-50. *KNV*, III; Buchanan: *Journey through Madras*, etc., III, p. 126.
19. *KNV.*, III.

and Kēlappa were two generals under him who contributed much to his military successes. Others of note connected with the administration were Añjanayya, Bagara Tammarasayya and Yellappayya.[20]

Fr. Heras, on the strength of the *Keladi Araśuvamśāvaḷi* is of the view that Doḍḍa Śankaṇṇa was deposed by Rāma Rāja for putting a Jangama priest to death.[21] But Śankaṇṇa Nāyaka could not have been deposed by Rāma Rāja as the latter was killed in the battle of Rākṣasa Tangaḍi in 1565 A.C., itself. There could not have been any other deposition. After crowning his brother Chikka Śankaṇṇa at Ikkēri, he died.

20. *KNV.*, III.

21. *Aravidu Dynasty*, p. 180; Wilson: *Mackenzie Collection*, p. 333. Shri Lakshminarayan Rao follows Fr. Heras in holding the view that Doḍḍa Śankaṇṇa was deposed (*Vij. Sex. Com. Vol.*, p. 258).

CHAPTER V

CHIKKA ŚANKAṆṆA NĀYAKA AND RĀMARAJA NĀYAKA

(1570-1586 A.C.)

All authorities are agreed that Chikka Śankaṇṇa Nāyaka succeeded Doḍḍa Śankaṇṇa. The following dates have been suggested for the beginning and end of Chikka Śankaṇṇa's reign:

Rice	A.C. 1558-1570[1]
Sewell	A.C. 1596-1603[2]
Rājavamśāvali	A.C. 1559-1571[3]
Naraharayya	A.C. 1558-1570[4]

But there are some inscriptions which refer to the reign of Śankaṇṇa Nāyaka without the prefix Doḍḍa or Chikka. The earliest of them is dated Śaka 1492 (1570 A.C.)[5] and the latest Śaka 1503 (1580 A.C.).[6] They have probably to be assigned to Chikka Śankaṇṇa Nāyaka. Epigraphs of Rāmarāja Nāyaka, son of Doḍḍa Śankaṇṇa Nāyaka ranging in dates from Śaka 1493 (1570 A.C.)[7] to Śaka 1508 (1586 A.C.)[8] are also found. The overlapping of dates may be explained with the help of a lithic record from South Kanara dated Śaka 1500 (1577 A.C.), which states clearly that Śankaṇṇa Nāyaka and Rāmarāja Nāyaka were together ruling over Gutti, Āraga, Bārakūru and Mangaḷūru.[9] It may therefore be surmised that at least till 1580 A.C., these two princes ruled over their territory jointly. Their loyalty to the imperial authority even after the staggering disaster of Rākṣasa Tangaḍi

1. *EC.*, VII, p. 42.
2. *List of Inscriptions in Southern India,* II, p. 177.
3. *Mac. Coll.* 18-15-15.
4. *QJMS.*, XXII, p. 72. Naraharayya follows Rice in assigning the dates.
5. *SII.*, VII, No. 389.
6. *Ibid.*, No. 375.
7. *ARSIE.*, 574 of 1929-30.
8. *SII.*, VII, No. 321.
9. *ARSIE.*, 267 of 1931-32.

is noteworthy. Most of the records of the two chiefs mention the ruling Vijayanagar sovereigns, Sadāśiva, Tirumala and Śrī Ranga.[10] Though the latest available date for Chikka Śankaṇṇa is only 1580 A.C., one finds inscriptions of his co-regent Rāma Rāja Nāyaka dated Śaka 1503[11] (1582 A.C.) and Śaka 1508 (1586 A.C.)[12] There is however no means of ascertaining definitely whether both the uncle and nephew ruled conjointly even after 1580 or Rāma Rāja Nāyaka ruled independently thereafter.

Campaigns of Chikka Śankaṇṇa Nāyaka: Chikka Śankaṇṇa had already gone through a course of apprenticeship in administration before he succeeded to the Nāyakship. He is said to have defeated Salabhat Khān of Bījāpur, who wanted to enlarge the sphere of his influence, and driven the Muslim forces.[13] According to the *Śivatattvaratnākara*, the Bījāpur general, Mumjula Khān, attacked Śankaṇṇa Nāyaka with a number of horses and elephants.[14] It is however difficult to determine whether it was Chikka Śankaṇṇa Nāyaka who was attacked by the Muslim general. Chikka Śankaṇṇa who wanted to increase his power, undertook an aggressive policy and defeated and brought under him the neighbouring chiefs. He clashed with Bhairādēvī, queen of Gersoppa, whom he defeated. This was obviously the continuation of the animosity that existed even during the time of his brother; it was, however, left to his successors to completely destroy the kingdom of the Queen. The ambitious designs of Chikka Śankaṇṇa are well borne out by a letter of King Philip II of Portugal which reads:

> "You say that the queen of Boticala has not paid the tribute due for many years and that she is now in a great distress on account of one Naique (Chikka) formerly a subject of King Narasinga of Vijayanagar but now risen to power and who gives clear proofs of his

10. *Ibid.*, 487 of 1928-29, *EC.*, VIII, Sb. 35, Tl. 5 etc.
11. *EC.*, VIII, Sb. 232.
12. *SII.*, VII, No. 231.
13. *KNV.*, IV, p. 66 ff.
14. V, 15, Verse 9.

ambition to become the paramount Lord over all those neighbouring kings."[15]

Śankaṇṇa Nāyaka seems to have defeated also Araśappa Nāyaka of Soḍe who tried to extend his influence. An inscription at Siddahaḷḷi in Sorab taluk dated Śaka 1502 Pramāthin, Puṣya Śuddha Dvādaśi (29th December 1579 A.C.), mentions a quarrel between Śankaṇṇa Nāyaka and Araśappa Nāyaka and that the *parapategāra* of Soraba, Virūpākṣaiya and Mandi Kudūr Hēmāji laid siege to Engaḷa and plundered it.[16] Hence this battle must have taken place before 1579 A.C. The fort of Udugaṇi also seems to have been captured by Śankaṇṇa Nāyaka.[17] He is also credited with having built a magnificent palace at Ikkēri. He is said to have constructed a big tank in the village Sangaḷa and laid out a garden containing different kinds of trees and creepers.[18]

Śankaṇṇa Nāyaka had more than one wife, probably at least three, for he had a son named Siddappa through his 'youngest' wife.[19] Siddappa was taught all the *vidyas* by his father.[20] He had two wives. By the first, he had a son, the famous Śivappa Nāyaka and three daughters. By the second wife he had a son called Venkaṭappa Nāyaka, who later succeeded Śivappa Nāyaka.[21]

Śankaṇṇa Nāyaka did not appoint his son Siddappa as his successor. Sewell's statement that he ruled for one year[22] is not borne out by any evidence. The *Śivatattvaratnākara* says that Chikka Śankaṇṇa anointed Venkaṭappa Nāyaka, his elder brother's son, as his successor and his younger brother Rāmarāja as *Yuvarāja.*

Rāmarāja Nāyaka: The *Keladinṛpavijayam* mentions Rāmarāja as the successor of Chikka Śankaṇṇa.[23] It is

15. Letter from King Philip II to Viceroy Conde de Vidigueira, cited in *Archivo Portuguese Oriental,* III, pt. ii, p. 916.
16. *EC.,* VIII, Sb. 301.
17. *Mac. Coll.* 18-15-39.
18. *STR.,* VI, 1.
19. *KNV.,* IV.
20. *STR.,* VI, 1.
21. *JRAS.,* 1911, p. 191.
22. *List of Antiquities,* II, pp. 177, *Buchanan,* III, p. 126.
23. *KNV.,* IV.

obvious that Rāmarāja Nāyaka continued the rule of Chikka Śankaṇṇa Nāyaka after his death in 1580 A.C. as is borne out by the indisputable evidence of inscriptions. No outstanding exploit is known about him. He, however, continued to keep in tact the hereditary territories to which he had succeeded. According to an inscription dated Śaka 1495 (1573 A.C.) he was ruling under the orders Śrīraṅga Rāya, the districts of Āraga, Gutti, Bārakūru and Mangaḷūru and other territories.[24] Yet another epigraph of the same date records that Kalise in the Keladi Śīme was conferred on Rāmarāja Nāyaka of Keladi as *kaṇatci* by the Emperor.[25]

Rāmarāja Nāyaka had two sons, Vīra Oḍeyār and Basavalinga Nāyaka.[26] According to the *Keladinṛpavijayam* his officers were Kalaśappayya of Āraga (Prime Minister), and Chikka Kōlappa (Commander-in-Chief).

Rāmarāja Nāyaka is said to have died at Gersoppa, probably about 1586 A.C.[27] It is not known however what had taken him there; probably he went there to wage a war since the relations between Ikkēri and Gersoppa had not been friendly for some years.

24. *EC.*, VIII, Tl. 5.
25. *MAR.*, 1930, No. 60.
26. *JRAS.*, 1911, p. 190.
27. *KNV.*, IV.

CHAPTER VI

VENKAṬAPPA NĀYAKA I
(1586-1629)

Venkaṭappa Nāyaka, as said earlier, was the son of Doḍḍa Śankaṇṇa Nāyaka and the brother of Rāmarāja Nāyaka.[1] He succeeded to the Ikkēri throne after Rāmarāja Nāyaka. There are no means of ascertaining the exact date of his coronation. The following dates have been assigned by the following for the commencement and end of his reign.

Sewell	A.C. 1604-1626[2]
Rice	A.C. 1582-1629[3]
Naraharayya	A.C. 1582-1629[4]
Rājavamśāvali	A.C. 1583-1629[5]

The *Keladinṛpavijayam* places the initial year of Venkaṭappa's reign in Śaka 1505, Chitrabhānu, Mārgaśira Śuddha 5—Tuesday, 4th December 1582 A.C.[6] But the earliest known date for him from inscriptions is Śaka 1514 Nandana, Āśvija Śuddha 5 corresponding to Saturday, 30th September 1592 A.C.[7] The last date available for him from inscriptions is Śaka 1551 (A.C. 1629),[8] which was also the last year of his reign according to the *Keladinṛpavijayam*.[9] Venkaṭappa Nāyaka seems to have been associated with the administration by Rāmarāja Nāyaka since 1582. He became an independent ruler in 1586 A.C., the last known date for Rāmarāja Nāyaka, and continued to rule till 1629 A.C.

1. It is necessary to draw attention to a serious error in the *STR.*, which, besides mentioning that Chikka Śankaṇṇa was succeeded by Venkaṭappa, makes Rāmarāja, the latter's younger brother, *Yuvarāja* (See V, 15, vv. 11-12).
2. *List of Inscriptions in Southern India,* Vol. II, p. 177.
3. *EC.,* VII, Intro. p. 43.
4. *QJMS.,* XII, p. 73.
5. *Mac., Coll.,* 18-15-15.
6. *KNV.,* V, p. 70.
7. *MAR.,* 1923, No. 108.
8. *EC.,* VIII, Sb., 266.
9. *KNV.,* V.

Venkaṭappa Nāyaka may be taken to have acknowledged the suzerainty of Vijayanagar till atleast 1613 in which year he is stated to have been ruling the Tuḷu and Male Rājyas, as a subordinate of Venkaṭapatidēva Mahārāja.[10] Venkaṭappa Nāyaka raised the prestige of his dynasty to such an extent that Ikkēri was practically recognised as an independent kingdom by all the chiefs of the coast. He began the conquest of neighbouring chieftancies with the definite idea of creating a powerful kingdom for himself, a kingdom that could withstand the shocks of the growing Muslim menace from Bījāpur and the attempts of minor chiefs, who feared, that on account of the increasing power of Venkaṭappa they would be under a new master, the king of Kanara. By a series of successful wars he carried his arms into distant territories. The Italian traveller Pietro Della Valle, who visited Ikkēri in 1623 A.C. says that "this prince Venkaṭappa Naieka was sometimes vassal of one of the ministers of the great king of Vidia Nagar .... but after the downfall of the king ...... Venkaṭappa Naieka remained absolute prince of the state of which he was governor, which also being a good soldier, he hath much enlarged."[11] In an inscription of his grandson and successor Vīrabhadra, Venkaṭappa is described as "a diamond elephant-goad to the rutting elephants, the bounding Tauḷava kings, a sun to the darkness of the Kirātas, a boundary mountain to stop the great ocean of Mlecchas ever seeking to overflow the south in victorious expedition."[12] Finding the states to the north and east of Ikkēri too strong for him, Venkaṭappa Nāyaka concentrated his attention on enlarging and strengthening his kingdom all along the West Coast from Gersoppa in the north to the extreme corner of Tuḷuva in the south. He attained signal success in this object.

Venkaṭappa Nāyaka and the Portuguese: The Portuguese had by that time established themselves at important places along the west coast. They had built forts at Mangalore,

10. *SII.*, VII, No. 297.
11. *Travels of Pietro Della Valle* Ed. by Edward Grey for the Hakluyt Society, Vol. I, p. 191.
12. *EC.*, VII, Sh. 2.

Onore (Honāvar) and Barcelor to protect their trade. They had to war with neighbouring chiefs to better their prospects in trade. Now that Venkaṭappa Nāyaka launched an active policy of conquest, their interests were adversely affected resulting in the dislocations of their trade and loss of prestige.

Venkaṭappa Nāyaka's wars: Venkaṭappa's initial expedition seems to have been against one Hanuma, who made a bid for independence in the area of Hoḷe Honnūru. Hanuma was helped by the Bījāpur forces under Mumjula Khān, but the combined armies were no match for that of Venkaṭappa. He routed them completely and to celebrate his success he erected a pillar of victory at Hangal.[13] Probably Hanuma was killed in battle. His elder son seeing the futility of war against Venkaṭappa, concluded a treaty with him. According to the terms of the treaty Venkaṭappa Nāyaka got the territories of Shimoga, Gājanūr and Lakkuhaḷḷi. Hanuma's younger son, enraged at this humiliating treaty attacked Venkaṭappa's territory. He was, however, overpowered and had to flee and hide himself at Bāṇavara.[14]

Venkaṭappa was soon called to repel the attacks of his enemies at Danivara, Kumbēsi, Yalavandūr, Hebbe Mandagadde, Karabura, Mōrabadi and Sālanāḍu.[15] Then he built strong and impregnable fortresses, at Hebbe, Sāgara, Koṇḍūru, Malakād, Hole Bailūru, Bārakūru, Mallikārjuna, Nagari and Pariyāḷa, apparently to protect his kingdom from foreign attacks.

Venkaṭappa's next expedition seems to have been against Bhairadēvī, the queen of Gersoppa; Gersoppa continued to be one of the richest portions of North Kanara. The large quantity of pepper grown in that kingdom attracted the Portuguese, who at a very early date established commercial relations with its ruler and derived great benefit from the pepper trade.[16] The Italian traveller Pietro Della Valle writing of Gersoppa says: "For this is the country wherein greatest plenty of pepper grows, for which reason the queen

13. *STR.*, VI, 13, v. 140.
14. *KNV.*, V., *Mac. Coll.*, 17 18-15-39 Section v; *QJMS.*, XXII, p. 75.
15. *KNV.*, V.
16. Gracia de orta: *Tratado-delas-drogas*, p. 24.

of Gersoppa was wont to be called by the Portugals *Reyna da Pimenta,* that is queen of pepper."[17] The account of the same traveller contains some information regarding the circumstances under which the kingdom of Gersoppa was annexed by Venkaṭappa Nāyaka. The queen of Gersoppa fell in love with a mean person and a stranger and resigned herself with her whole kingdom to him. Her choice of a lover of base blood was abhorred by her subjects. And the man, so favoured by the queen having thoughts as ignoble as his blood, instead of being grateful to the queen designed to prove false to her and take the kingdom for himself. He met with success in the initial stages by getting around himself the queen's leading vassals. The queen, finding herself oppressed by the traitor, appealed to the Portuguese for help, who willingly helped her. But the traitor appealed to Venkaṭappa Nāyaka for assistance against the queen and the Portuguese. Venkaṭappa, taking advantage of the occasion, entered suddenly into the kingdom of Gersoppa with great diligence and force, drove away the Portuguese and took the queen prisoner. But he did not allow the traitor to go free and punished his intrigue by causing him to be slain. He also burnt Gersoppa and the royal palace in it.[18] This expedition seems to have taken place in 1606 for a letter of the Portuguese viceroy to the king dated 16th January 1607 refers to this event.[19] The effects of this conquest were far reaching. The ports of Onore (Honāvar), Barcelore and Bhatkal came under the control of the Nāyaka. Apart from the prestige Venkaṭappa earned by defeating the Portuguese, he was now master of the entire pepper trade and he held the granary of the West coast under his control. He thus became a power, whose favour was courted by all European trading companies on the coast.

There are two interesting Portuguese letters which contain accounts of the neighbouring kings and things that occurred in Kanara, written in 1629 A.C. and 1630 A.C. to the Portuguese Viceroy. These letters give detailed information

17. *Travels of Pietro Della Valle, op. cit.,* Vol. II, p. 221.
18. *Ibid.,* p. 219.
19. Bulhao-Pato: *Documentos,* i, p. 74.

about the expansion wars of Venkaṭappa Nāyaka of Ikkēri.[20] According to them Venkaṭappa seems to have defeated a number of rulers and chieftains such as Amapa Nāyaka, the king of Basavapaṭṇa, Venkaṭādri Nāyaka the king of Bēlūr, the kings of Sunda and Biligi, the Chauta king, the king Hona of Cambolin, the king of Serra, king Idalcao, the kings of Bamguel, Palpare, Mysore, Gunbira, Nereguy, Agilara, Umzur, Calhator, Battekala, the queens of Ankōla, Gersoppa, Carnate and Ullal, the *balalas* of Manipary, Doltady, Color, Guedumardady, Herar, Penabur, Pedanar, Bedrete, Ermala, Capy, Catapary, Nelebor, Citipary, Belor, Condegere, Mudrady, Hebery, Hiretor, Tombosa, Anagy, Tagrette, Gololer, Agoube, Mutur, Mallor, Modicar, Adolly, Mudoly and Viṭṭala. He also subjugated the people of Baguaner, Quelanar and Canduly and conquered the fortresses of Arguy, Barcelor and Serguo. Since all our knowledge of the wars of Venkaṭappa Nāyaka for the expansion of his kingdom are mainly based on the two letters mentioned above, it is not possible to give a chronological account of them.[21]

Besides his wars with the above rulers and chieftains, Venkaṭappa Nāyaka seems to have subdued other minor chiefs also like Honne Kambali ruling over Hosangadi, Kadari, Baggavāḍi and Kallūru[22] and captured a number of forts like Koṇḍūru Kōṭṭa and Kalidurga. But Venkaṭappa was not able to make much headway against Bījāpur. Ibrāhim Ādil Shāh, its Sultan, hearing about the extended power of Venkaṭappa, ordered all his Havildars commanding the Konkan to march against Ikkēri. Under the command of Sherful Mulk, the Muslim invaders reached as far as Candeśvara, where Venkaṭappa met them. According to the *Keladinṛpavijayam* and the Local Tracts[22a] the Bījāpur forces suffered a reverse for a time and so they had to go beyond

20. Moncões do Reino, No. 12, Ano de 1629, Fol. 448-49. *Ibid.*, Fols. 481-482. Texts and translations published in *Proceedings of the Indian Historical Records Commission,* Vol. XI, pp. 107 ff

21. The Chieftains and places conquered by Venkaṭappa are discussed in alphabetical order with their probable identifications in a note at the end of this chapter.

22. *KNV., op. cit.,* V.

22a. *Mac. Coll.,* 18-19-5.

the river Mirju, which ever after, remained as the northern boundary of the Ikkēri kingdom. But the Portuguese sources record that Venkaṭappa Nāyaka paid 1000 *pagodas* annually to the Ādil Shāh as tribute. We have unfortunately no other means of verifying the details.

Venkaṭappa and the English: Early in the seventeenth century, the English East India Company had but a few factories in India. They were at Agra, Surat, Ahmedabad, Barhampur, and Broach. At that time the power and influence of the Portuguese were still considerably high. The pepper trade of the coast was entirely under the Nāyakas of Ikkēri. Rice was also another important article of trade and it was the rice of Kanara that attracted the English merchants. Soon there was competition between them and the Portuguese. Some details regarding the commercial policy of the Ikkēri rulers are available in the letters of the servants of the English East India Company. A few of these letters were written by Thomas Kerridge and Thomas Ratsell from Surat. Two of them are dated respectively 9th and 15th February 1619 A.C. While describing the voyage of a ship named "The Expedition" they refer to a factory at Calicut. The letters say: "They (the company's authorities) advise the commander to call there to receive if possible the moneys due to the Company. Overtures received from 'a certayne Mallabars who inhabit a country on the sea coast some 20 leagues to the southwards of Goa called Ekaree, the prince, an Indian Raja that hath been long in league with Portingall".[23] William Hoare, in a letter to the Company written in May 1620 says: "It hath been, I presume, long since related unto your worship, how that during your fleetes abode at Swallee, two Mallabar frigotts putt themselves under command of your shippes, affirming themselves subjects to a Ragia of Echaree, neare Goa, and pretending to be sent by the king, their master to capitulate with the English about establishing a trade with him for pepper, his countrey by their report, yielding yearlie sufficient to lade two good shippes, the tryall whereof being by consultation assented to,

23. Foster: *English Factories in India,* 1618-21, p. 56.

they both attended the fleets to this place. And here one of them desired leave to depart before to the king to advize of our cominge, that his pepper might be in readiness against our arrivall, and that an English merchant might accompany him to view the commodity and cutt price with the kinge; for whom sufficient hostage should be left abrood the Dragoon which was likewise agreed upon".[24] The above letters help us to affirm that (a) Venkaṭappa Nāyaka was desirous to secure advantages of trade in pepper with the English (b) he sent two ships to put themselves under the command of the English captain (c) the ships were to effect a bargain with the English to trade in pepper and (d) the final word concerning the price of the commodity lay with Venkaṭappa Nāyaka. It may also be noted that all this was done before he received an embassy from the Portuguese Viceroy at Goa.

Portuguese Embassy to the Court of Venkaṭappa Nāyaka in 1623: Even before the Portuguese ambassador Sig. Fernandez departed from Goa, Venkaṭappa had written to his ambassador Vithula Sinay, that if they sent this embassy to urge the restitution of the Bangher Raja, it was in vain that they undertook the journey; for he was fully resolved not to restore him. Venkaṭappa also felt that the ships from Portugal "which every year take pepper from his dominions and bring him a great sum of money" had not arrived and that the Portuguese were in arrears of payment. Hence he did not care to arrange for the transport, and other facilities for the embassy. However, after prolonged negotiations, mainly due to the efforts of Vithula Sinay, the Portuguese were allowed to go to Ikkēri with the embassy. They arrived at the place on November 6th, 1623. One gets a detailed description of the transactions of this embassy from the accounts of Pietro Della Valle.[25] The embassy was lodged in one of the best houses in Ikkēri and was suitably looked after. On 8th November 1623 A.C., Vithula Sinay, accompanied by Muse Bai, an Ikkēri general and other personages conducted the Portuguese ambassador and his party to the court of

24. *Ibid.*, pp. 69 ff.
25. Pietro Della Valle: *op. cit.*, II, p. 244 ff.

Venkaṭappa Nāyaka. After preliminary exchange of honours and formalities, the Portuguese ambassador Sig. Fernandez, explained the reason for his embassy *i.e.*, to continue the friendship and peaceful relations with Venkaṭappa Nāyaka and handed over some presents (some pieces of cloth) from the Portuguese Viceroy. Venkaṭappa Nāyaka, in turn, enquired him about the health of the king of Spain and the Viceroy at Goa. His discourse with them covered different subjects, chief among them being the question of the arrears of payment and the slowness of the ships that year, which used to come to take pepper. He also discussed matters relating to the war with the Rāja of Banghel as also the peace which concluded the war. He further made other personal enquiries regarding all the members of the embassy. After the negotiations, the embassy was reconducted home, with grand solemnity and company.[26] Inspite of the anxiety of the Portuguese to be on friendly terms with Venkaṭappa Nāyaka, they were however not able to get further concessions.

Venkaṭappa as a builder and patron of religion and learning: In the midst of his very active military career and commercial activity, Venkaṭappa also found sufficient time to devote to activities calculated to improve the good of his subjects and promote the cause of arts, religion and letters. He was a builder of many temples and forts. Within the citadel of Ikkēri he constructed temples for gods Śikharēśvara, Viśvēśvara, Lakṣmīnārāyaṇa and Mailāra. He also built the shrines of Tāṇḍavēśvara and Ranganātha at Antarāśipura.[27] He further built a temple for Gaṇapati at Bāṇavara.[28] Venkaṭappa also renovated the temple of Rāmēśvara at Keladi.[29] He also renovated the temple of Kōṭiśvara through the agency of Mṛityuñjaya Voḍer who was administering the province of Bārakur.[30] He endowed these institutions with munificient gifts of gold and land for their proper maintenance. He gave official sanction and financial help for the renovation of the *Caityālaya* called Tribhuvanatilaka dedicat-

26. Pietro Della Valle, *op. cit.*, II, p. 257.
27. *Mac. Coll.* 19-14-32 *Kaifiyat of Holy Places.*
28. *KNV., op. cit.*, V.
29. *MAR.*, 1938, No. 86.
30. *ARIE.*, C.P. No. 4 and 5 of 1954-55.

ed to Candranāthasvāmi at Bidure.[31] There is an interesting manuscript *sannad* (in paper) in the possession of Śrī Rāma Bhat of Ikkēri, in the Sagar taluk of Shimoga District of Mysore, issued by Veṅkaṭappa Nāyaka. It records on order of Veṅkaṭappa Nāyaka pertaining to the professional (priestly) rights such as *Dēvasthāpana, Saṁprōkshaṇa, Rathōtsava,* and *Ashṭabandha* etc., in the various temples at Ikkēri, Sagar, Keladi, Banavasi, Gutti, Ānantapura and Bidarūru, of a certain Linga Bhaṭṭa of Ikkēri. The rights of this bhaṭṭa seem to have been disturbed by Chennakēśavayya and others of Ānantapura. The order clearly states that the Parepatēgara and Sēnabōvas of the respective areas should put down the mischievous elements and set things right.[32]

At Śṛngeri, Venkaṭappa built a *maṭha* for the accommodation of the venerated *svāmi* (then Abhinava Narasimha Bhārati), presented an agrahara to the Brahmans and earned the title "Re-establisher of Śṛngeri."[33] To the Mahattina maṭha at Ānandapura he granted the village of Khayira, in the Masarūr śīme in Ārgada Veṇṭhe, yielding a revenue income of 196½ *varāhas.* He also remitted taxes on bullocks carrying commodities to the maṭha.[34] To the *maṭha* built by Hiriya Hampayya of Śrīrangapaṭṭaṇa, in Sadāśivasāgara, Venkaṭappa granted the Kadēnahaḷḷi village in the Udunguḍi śīme rated at 477 *varāhas,* 8 *haṇa* and 3 *haga.*[35] The Mahattu maṭha at Bārakūr was also the recipient of a donation from Venkaṭappa of the village of Masige, in the Bārakūr śīme rated at 38 *varāhas.*[36]

Venkaṭappa Nāyaka's religious catholicity is amply borne out by some epigraphs, which record grants to institutions, propagating religions other than the Vīraśaiva faith. For

31. *ARSIE.,* C.P. No. 4A of 1940-41.
32. A photograph of the *Sannad* is in the office of the Government Epigraphist for India, Ootacamund. (Neg. No. 2960). The Sannad is being reviewed in the Annual Report on Indian Epigraphy for the year 1952-53.
33. *EC.,* VI, Sr. 5.
34. *MAR.,* 1923, No. 108, Also *EC.,* VII, Sa. 123.
35. *EC.,* VIII, Tl. 56.
36. *Ibid.,* Tl. 83.

instance, he made a grant of the Tivali village in Haralatu śīme to a *maṭha* of the Rāmānuja sect (Vaiṣṇava) and the god Veṅkaṭeśa.[37] It is interesting to note Venkaṭappa making a gift also to a Muslim mosque erected in the Bhuvanagiri-durga.[38]

Venkaṭappa seems to have beautified Ikkēri by raising parks and building a gorgeous palace at the place. He also built a city called Sadāśivasāgara with a palace and a swimming resort in it and another called Viśvanāthapura on the river Varadā. He is also said to have performed *Vājapeya* and other sacrifices.[39] One of the many *agrahāras* he founded, was called Vīrammā agrahāra in memory of his mother and another of the same name in honour of his wife who was also named Vīrammā. Venkaṭappa also built a horse-stable at Bhuvanagiri and a beautiful lake at Saṅgamēśvara.[40] He was interested in irrigation works too as is testified to by an inscription of his, which records the excavation of a tank.[41]

Venkaṭappa's patronage of learning and literature is borne out by the encouragement he gave to works on *Kāvyas, Nāṭakas, dharma śāstras* and the like. He also patronised the twin arts of music and dance (*nāṭyaśāstra*) and built a *nāṭyaśāla* (theatre) to encourage them. He caused a number of works to be written by his court paṇḍits. Among them were: (i) a metrical translation in Kannaḍa of the *Śiva Gītā* consisting of 18 *adhyāyas* in the *Uttarakhaṇḍa* of the *Padma Purāṇa* by the poet Tirumala Bhaṭṭa. This *Śiva Gītā* is said to have been taught to Rāmacandra by Paramēśvara (ii) The *Śiva aṣṭapadī* was another work in Saṁskrit by the same poet, (iii) A commentary on the Āgama work *Tantrasāra* was written by Ranganātha Dīkṣita, (iv) A large work called *Manapriya* relating to horses, was written by Aśva Paṇḍita[42] and (v) the *Tattva Kaustubha* was written by Bhaṭṭōji Dīkṣita. The opening verses of the last mentioned work, re-

37. *EC.*, VIII, Ng. 79.
38. *Ibid.*, Tl. 38.
39. *KNV.*, *op. cit.*, V.
40. *Ibid.*
41. *EC.*, VIII, Sagar 54.
42. *JRAS.*, 1911, p. 190.

veal that Bhaṭṭōji Dīkṣita wrote it at the instance of a Keladi Venkaṭēndra who may be identified with the king Venkaṭappa. Bhaṭṭōji Dīkṣita calls himself in the *Tattva Kaustubha* as the son of Śrīmad Vidvān makuṭa-māṇikya Lakṣmīdhara-Bhaṭṭa. He may be assigned to the first quarter of the seventeenth century.[43]

It is said that one staunch *Viśiṣṭādvaitin* named Rāmānujācārya (not the founder of the faith, but another scholar of the same name) lived in Venkaṭappa's court. He was famous far and wide as an exponent of *Viśiṣṭādvaita* and won many titles and marks of honour. Bhaṭṭōji Dīkṣita had two grievances against the Śrī Vaiṣṇavas. First, a Śrī Vaiṣṇava author (Ranganātha) had written a criticism of his work, *Manōramā*, giving it the indecent name of *Manōramā Kucamardana,* and secondly the same person had heaped insults on the great Appayya Dīkṣita whom he would refer to by nicknames as *lambakarṇa*, etc. He seems to have challenged Rāmānujācārya and succeeded in the controversy that followed and Rāmānujācārya had to relinquish all his honours in favour of his adversary. Venkaṭappa bestowed on Bhaṭṭōji Dīkṣita the title of *Viśiṣṭha Vaidīka advaita Siddhānta sthāpanācārya* besides extending to him other usual marks of honour and court presents.[44]

Domestic life of Venkaṭappa Nāyaka: Venkaṭappa Nāyaka had two wives named Abhinava Vīramāmba (Vīrammā), daughter of Virūpaṇṇa Nāyaka,[45] and Bhadrammā.[46] Vīramāmbā seems to have erected a maṭha in the Bhaṭṭa-pethe of Ikkēri to which Venkaṭappa Nāyaka granted the Kollakoppa village in the Mantasala śīmē, rated at 49 *varāhas* and also freedom from toll on bullocks carrying articles to the *maṭha*.[47] She also granted for the service of goddess Mūkāmbikā at Kollūr two solid metallic figures of *dvārapālakas* weighing 17 maunds, 13 seers and 16 maunds, $5\frac{3}{8}$ seers respectively at the time of the Śivarātri.[48]

43. *Karnataka Historical Review,* Vol. IV, p. 98.
44. *QJMS.,* XXII, p. 78.
45. *MAR.,* 1944, No. 52; *EC.,* VIII, Tl. 97.
46. *KNV., op. cit.,* V.
47. *EC.,* VIII, Tl. 97.
48. *MAR.,* 1944, No. 52.

The queen Bhadrammā seems to have died on 29th October 1623.[49] From what he had heard, Pietro Della Valle narrates the following story regarding her :

> "They say that twelve or thirteen years since, when she was about five and thirty years old, it came to her ears that Venkaṭappa Naieka, her husband, having becoming fond of a Moorish woman, kept her secretly in a Fort not far from the Court, where he frequently solac'd himself with her for two or three days together; whereupon Badra Ama, first complaining to him not only of the wrong which he did thereby to her, but also more of that which he did to himself, defiling himself with a strange woman of impure race and of a Nation which drank wine and ate flesh and all sort of uncleannesses, told him that, if he had a mind for other women of their own clean race without contaminating himself with this Moor, and she would have suffered it with patience; but, since he had thus defiled himself with her, she for the future would have no more to do with him; and thereupon she took an oath that she would be to him as his Daughter and he should be to her as her Father; after which she shew'd no further resentment, but liv'd with him as formerly keeping him company in the Palace, tending upon him in his sickness and doing other things with the same love as at first, helping and advising him in matters of government, wherein she had always great authority with him; and in short, excepting the Matrimonial Act, perfectly fulfilling all other offices of a good wife. Venkaṭappa Naieka, who had much affection for her notwithstanding the wrong he did her with his Moor, endeavoured by all means possible to divert her from this her purpose and to persuade her to live a Matrimonial Life still with him, offering many times to compound for that oath by the alms of above 20,000 pagodas but all in vain, and she preserv'd constant in this resolution till death; which, being undoubtedly an act of much constancy and virtue was the cause that Venkaṭappa Naieka loved her always so much the more."[50]

49. Pietro Della Valle: *op. cit.*, II, p. 207.
50. Pietro Della Valle: *op. cit.*, II, pp. 208-9.

Venkaṭappa had a daughter named Hiriyammā, who was married to Vīrūpaṇṇa Oḍeyār of Jambūr. Bhadrappa, the only son of Venkaṭappa had two wives. One was Bhangārammā, daughter of Venkaṭādri Nāyaka of Bēlūr. He had two sons Rāmalinga and Vīrabhadra and a daughter who married Sadāśivayya, the only son of Hīriyammā and Virūpaṇṇa Voḍeyār. Rāmalinga seems to have died young. Bhadrappa, the son of Venkaṭappa was of an ascetic temperament, and became a recluse and predeceased his father.[51]

Siddappa Nāyaka, son of Chikka Śankaṇṇa Nāyaka, and first cousin of Venkaṭappa Nāyaka, had a son called Śivappa Nāyaka and three daughters by his first wife and a son Venkaṭappa Nāyaka II, by his second wife.

Last years of Venkaṭappa Nāyaka: About the year 1623, there seems to have been some uneasiness in the Ikkēri court regarding the successor of Venkaṭappa Nāyaka. There were two sons of Rāmarāja Nāyaka, Vīra Voḍeyār and Basavalinga, who had a claim to the throne of their father. It was quite likely that Vīra Voḍeyār would make a bid for the throne; the scene was further tangled by the presence of Sadāśivayya (grandson of Venkaṭappa Nāyaka), and Śivappa Nāyaka. Obviously Venkaṭappa was anxious that the Nāyakship should continue in his own line and hence according to Pietro Della Valle he had already imprisoned two of his nephews, apparently to avoid any trouble after his death.[52] That Venkaṭappa was not wrong in his fears is shown by the attempt of Vīra Voḍeyār to seize the throne during the time of Vīrabhadra Nāyaka. The death of Siddappa, son of Chikka Śankaṇṇa was another event which added to the gloom of the closing years of the glorious reign. Age crept on him and as death seemed nearer, he prepared his grandson Vīrabhadra in handling state matters by teaching him everything to be learnt by kings. He seems to have died in 1629 A.C.[53]

51. *JRAS.*, 1911, p. 191.

52. Pietro Della Valle, *op. cit.*, II, p. 284.

53. *KNV.*, *op. cit.*, V., *Notions of the Reign*, No. 14, 1630 Fol. 212-13, No. 84.

Note on Venkaṭappa Nāyaka's Expansion Wars

The following is the alphabetical list of countries with their probable identifications with which Venkaṭappa Nāyaka waged wars as revealed by the documents.

Adolly: Not identifiable.

Agilara: Agilara may be identified with Ajilara (near Mulki). The chief of Agilara ruled from Venur, in South Kanara. Being a Lingāyat, Venkaṭappa Nāyaka dispossessed the ruling family of Agilara as its members were Jainas.[1]

Agoube: It may be identified with Agumbe, a place on the ghats, north of the Udipi taluka and within the limits of South Kanara.

Anagy: Not identifiable. It could be Konaje under the Balalas[2] of Mavalli[3] or Amunje within the jurisdiction of the Balala of Manel.[4]

Ancola: The place is still called Ankola in North Kanara. The ruins of its fort remind one of the ancient grandeur of the place. It was in fact one of the largest kingdoms siezed by Venkaṭappa as it yielded 3,00,000 pagodas. According to the second letter its queen was Bhairadēvi. Apparently there had never been independent rulers or chiefs in Ankola.[5] Probably this Bhairadēvi was the same Bhairadēvi, queen of Gersoppa, defeated and dispossessed by Venkaṭappa Nāyaka, and the so called kingdom of Ankola after all formed part of the kingdom of Gersoppa. This is confirmed by Ceaser Frederick who when passing

1. Aygal: *History of South Canara,* p. 313 ff.
2. A *balāla* is a Canarese denomination given to chieftains inferior to the petty kings in power. The word is still in use; in fact there are still several balālas in South Kanara.
3. Aygal: *op. cit.,* p. 393.
4. *Ibid.,* p. 390.
5. *Gazetteer of the Bombay Presidency* (*Kanara*), Vol. XV, pt. II, p. 258 (1883).

through Ankola in the second half of the 16th century expressly states that Ankola belonged to the queen of Gersoppa.[6]

Arguy: (Fortress) not identifiable

Baguanor: (Fortress) not identifiable.

Bamguel: May be identified with Bangher, north of Mangalore, now included within the city of Mangalore between Kodailbail and Urwa. The chiefs of Bangher rose to power after the second half of the 11th century.[7] The king of the place was called Lakshmaṇa Bangharasa; he was married for mere political reasons to the Queen of Uḷḷal, Abagadēvi, but their strained relations finally caused the downfall of both. Lakshmaṇa Bangharasa was helped by the Portuguese and the Queen of Uḷḷal appealed to Venkaṭappa Nāyaka against both. "Venkaṭappa Naieka" says Pietro Della Valle, "sent a powerful army in support of the queen, took all the territories of the king of Banghels and made them his own, destroying the fort which was there."[8] The Portuguese had thus unsuccessfully helped the Bangher chief against Venkaṭappa.[9] This war may have taken place towards the end of 1615, for the king of Portugal wrote on the subject to his viceroy on 14th March 1616.[10] Venkaṭappa Nāyaka subjected the queen of Uḷḷal to his overlordship and forced her to resign to him Berdrette which was the best and richest city she had, together with a large territory, which formed a good part of her dominions.[11]

Barcelor: It may be identified with Basrur on the river Gangoli. The Portuguese had built near this city a fortress called Barcelor, within the modern town of Kundāpur. It is not known as to who governed Kundāpur then. During the time of the wars of Venkaṭappa the city apparently was not ruled by a king for the letters mention only the chief merchants of the place. The son of Alfonso d' Albuquerque speaks of

6. Purchas: *His Pilgrims,* X, p. 99.
7. Aygal: *op. cit.*, p. 276.
8. Pietro Della Valle: *op. cit.*, II, p. 314.
9. Faria-Y-Souza: *Asia Portuguesa,* III, p. 325 ff.
10. Bulhao Pato: *Documentos,* III, p. 478.
11. Pietro Della Valle: *op. cit.*, II, p. 315.

one Retelim Cherim (Rādāliṅgam Chetty) the chief noble at the court of Kṛṣṇadēva Rāya, who was "the governor of Barcelor" in 1514.[12] But other authorities speak of a monarchical ruler of the city. Faria-y-Souza says that the city belonged to the chief of Polar in 1569,[13] while Ferishta speaks of the Rāṇi of Barcelor in 1575.[14] After considering these one is inclined to think that Basrur was a semi-independent town, a free city within the empire of Vijayanagar ruled by a Governor or a Council in the manner of a republic.

Barcellor de Sima: This is upper Barcelor, the real Hindu town of Basrur called by the Portuguese Upper Basrur to distinguish it from their fort Barcelor or Basrur, situated in Kundāpur. Some walls of this fort are seen still.

Batecella: May be identified with Bhatkal in the North Kanara District. It was a famous port in ancient times. The second letter referred to above speaks of "The recently crowned king of Bathecala, elected by the people a few days ago." Yet one hears of a king of Bhatkal only once. In 1502, when Vasco da Gama landed at Bhatkal he found there a king.[15] But a queen was the sovereign of Bhatkal in 1540,[16] 1543,[17] and 1548.[18] Ceaser Frederick when passing through Bhatkal in 1567, also found there a queen.[19] King Philip II writing to his Viceroy in 1596 again speaks of the queen of Bhatkal.[20] Bhatkal was a principality subordinate to Vijayanagar, as the Italian traveller Corsali had noted so early as 1517.[21] Peter Mundy records the fact that Venkaṭappa took possession of Hadivalli, the residence of the queen of Bhatkal.[22]

12. Commentaries do Grande Alfonso de Albuquerque, IV, p. 139.
13. *Asia Portuguesa,* II, pp. 469-70.
14. Briggs: *History of the Rise of the Mohomedan Power in India till the year* 1612 *A.C.*, (1829), III, p. 140-141.
15. Danvers: *The Portuguese in India,* I., p. 81-82.
16. Correa: *Lendas da India,* IV, p. 252.
17. *Ibid.*, pp. 257-262; Faria-Y-Sousa, *op. cit.*, II, pp. 117-120.
18. Limafelner: *Subsidos,* pp. 242-243.
19. Purchas: *op. cit.*, X, p. 101.
20. Heras: *Aravidu Dynasty,* I, p. 569, No. V.
21. Gubernatis: *Storia dei Viaggiatori,* p. 117.
22. Mundy: *Travels,* III, p. 76.

Battapatao: It may be identified with Basavapaṭṭaṇa situated in the Shimoga district of Mysore. In the first letter the place is also mentioned as Basavapatao and its king as Amapa Naique. Fr. Heras wrongly cites the *Śivatattvaratnākara* in stating that the king of Basavapaṭṭaṇa came to terms with Venkaṭappa and offered him the cities of Lakkuhalli, Gājanur and Shimoga.[23] These cities were ceded to Venkaṭappa by the elder son of Hanuma of Hole Honnuru as said earlier.

Bedrete: It may be identified with Mudubidri in the Karkala taluk of South Kanara district. The town is still called Bidri (Bamboo), Mudu, meaning east, Mudubidri may be interpreted to mean 'Eastern Bamboo'. The place belonged to the queen of Uḷḷal, and was siezed by Venkaṭappa Nāyaka. The city called Vēṇupura, in ancient days seems to have been attacked by Venkaṭappa. The governor who defended it was a Brahman named Śankaranārāyaṇa Bhaṭṭa. After defeating him Venkaṭappa spared his life since he was a Brahman.[24] This governor may be identified with one Sao Carno Botto mentioned in several Portuguese documents.[25]

Belar: It may be identified with Bellare, a village in the Uppinangadi taluk in the South Kanara district.[26] Venkaṭādri Nāyak was the chief of the place, who was also related to Venkaṭappa Nāyaka of Ikkēri by marriage.

Bellur: There are several places bearing the same name and hence it is rather difficult to identify it. The following suggestions may however be offered. (i) Belur, chief town of Belur taluk, Hassan district in Mysore also called Belapura or Velāpura in early inscriptions. The Nāyaks of Belur became prominent during the period of the third and fourth dynasties of Vijayanagar. (ii) Another Bellur is to be found in the Karkala taluk. It was under the Ajilara family ruling from Venur in the South Kanara district.[27]

23. Proceedings, *IHRC.*, XI, p. 117; see also *STR.*, VI, 13.
24. *STR.*, *op. cit.*, VI, 13.
25. Heras: *Aravidu Dynasty*, I, pp. 416, 417, 427.
26. *South Kanara Manual*, Vol. II, p. 271.
27. Aygal: *op. cit.*, p. 316.

(iii) Beluru, in the Nalvatanāḍ Magane, in the Udipi taluk, 17 miles north of Udipi. In the Śiva temple in this village there is an inscription dated 1561 recording a grant made by one Mahādēva Uḍaiyar to the said temple.[28]

Nevertheless the place meant by the Portuguese document does not seem to be any of these towns. The second document says that the king of Bellur was allied to the king of Battapatao (Basavapaṭṭaṇa). This town, as has been seen, is in the Shimoga district in Mysore. It seems but natural that Bellur should be in its neighbourhood. So it may be taken that the city of Bennur or Sante Bennur seems to be the one referred to by the document.

Belor: It may be identified with Bolur or Bolor in the neighbourhood of Mangalore.[29]

Biliguy or Bilgim: The place may be identified with Bilgi in the Siddapura taluk of North Kanara. It was formerely called 'Śvētapur' or 'White city'.[30] It seems to have been founded in 1593.[31] So it was not very old when Venkaṭappa captured it.

Cambolin: This may be identified with Gangoli in the Kundāpur taluk in the South Kanara district. The village is on the small peninsula-like strip of land between the sea and the River Kundāpur on the North Bank. The Portuguese had built a fort half a mile north of the village and dug a canal from the sea to the river in order to separate their fort from the main land, thus making it (as they supposed) impregnable. Some traces of this canal are still seen half a mile south of Kirimuneshwar. The fort was finally taken by Śivappa Nāyaka of Ikkēri (1645-1660). Remains of this fort are still found half a mile north of Gangoli. Faria-Y-Souza says that the king of Cambolin was subject to Vijayanagar.[32] He also says that the king of Cambolin was in

28. Sewell: *List of Antiquities,* I, p. 231.
29. *South Kanara Manual,* Vol. II, p. 258.
30. Burgess-Cousens: *Revised list of Antiquarian Remains in the Bombay Presidency,* p. 191.
31. Faria-Y-Souza: *Asia Portuguesa,* II, pp. 469 and 474.
32. *Asia Portuguesa:* II, pp. 476-79.

league with the king of Tolar. Cambolin was however the seat of a Jain principality and hence Venkaṭappa who was a Śivabhakta could have destroyed it. This defeat of Hōna shows the anxiety of Venkaṭappa to bring this port under his control.

Calhator: It may be identified with Kāsargode, 27 miles south of Mangalore. Pyard de Laval, who visited Malabar and Kanara in 1607, a few years before Venkaṭappa's conquest of the place, says the following about Kāsargode:

> "Congelotte, another harbour of the Corsairs, who rule a great extent of countries and peoples.... They have certain lofty buildings erected upon piles on the sea shore, there they keep sentinels to scan the horizon. They know within a little when the Portuguese fleet may be expected and keep intrechments ready on land to obstruct their landing."[33]

Capy: It may be identified with Kapy, in ancient days Kap. The traditional name of the balalas of the place seems to be 'Kap Marda Hegde'. They ruled over Padu, Mallaru, Muluru, Paduva, Heruru, Mujuru, and Innange in the Udipi taluk.[34]

Carnate: This place was formerly called Carcara and Carnati.[35] Now it is called Karnad, a small hamlet nearly 5 miles south of Mulki. The queen of the place is spoken of by Pietro Della Valle. He says that she "was also confederate with the Portugals and no friend to her of Olala (Uḷḷal)."[36] "I prepared myself to go to Carnate" continues this traveller, "to see the queen whose territory and city is, as I have said elsewhere, two or three leagues distant from Mangalore upon the sea coast, towards the North. The city stands upon a river which compasses it and overflows the country round about. It was to be very strong both by Art and situation; but during the war of Mangalore, Venkaṭappa Naieka, coming with a great army to subdue and pillage all

33. Pyard de Laval: *Travels,* I, pp. 344-45 (Haklyut Society Edn.).
34. Aygal: *op. cit.,* p. 417.
35. Yule: *Cathay,* III, p. 45.
36. Pietro Della Valle: *op. cit.,* II; p. 314.

these countries, sent for this queen to come and yield obedience to him. The queen, who as I have heard, is a lady of much virtue and prudence being unwilling to render herself to Venkaṭappa summoned her captains together, told them that she was ready to spend and give them all the money and jewels she had, and not be wanting on her part to exert her utmost power, if they would prepare themselves to defend the state. But the Ministers, through cowardice or treachery would not attempt a defence. Whereupon the poor queen who as a woman could do little by herself (her son also being very young) seeing her people disheartened, resolved by their advice to surrender herself to Venkaṭappa Naieka, and accordingly prepar'd to go to him with a good guard of soldiers. Hearing which, he sent to her to come alone without other company than her attendants, which she did, not voluntarily but constrained thereto by her hard fortune and the treachery of others. Venkaṭappa received her honourably and took her into his friendship and protection but with all he caus'd the city to be dismantled of the strong walls it had, to prevent her rebelling against him afterwards, and left her as before, the Government of the state, tying her only to obedience, the payment of a tribute, and the profession of an honourable vassalage to him. When they dismantled the city the queen (they say) unable to endure the sight retir'd into a solitary place a little distant, cursing, in her solitude the pussilanimity and infidelity of her own people, no less than the bad fortune and weakness of the Portugals, her defenders to whom she had been a faithful friend. At this time she lived with her young son either in Carnate or some other place thereabouts."[37]

Catapary: May be identified with Katupad or Katpadi. The balalas of this place were called *'Kattupadi Dore Balalas'* and they ruled over the Kattupadi Savira *śime*, including Mudubettu, Kote, Mattu, Uliyargot, Pangala, Belle, Enugudde, Kurkala, Manipura and Alevuru, all in the Udipi taluk.[38]

37. Pietro Della Valle: *op. cit.*, II, pp. 352-53.
38. Aygal: *op. cit.*, p. 316.

Chater: The Chater family was the family of Uḷḷal. In the first document the queen of Uḷḷal is not mentioned. She is undoubtedly meant by this reference, though only the king is referred to. The king could be her son, Sāluva Rairu, who though not actually reigning, received the title of king.[39]

There is a reference to a negotiation by a Chauta king with Venkaṭappa Nāyaka against a Bhairasa Woḍeyar in the Kanara Kaifiyats collected by Col. Mackenzie.[40] Chikka Rāya Chauta, according to the Kaifiyat wanted to take revenge on the Bhairasa Woḍeyar of Karkala and applied for help to Venkaṭappa Nāyaka to which he readily agreed. Karkala was invaded on both sides and Bhairasa Woḍeyar was killed. The whole of Karkala was annexed by Venkaṭappa, who gave only Sannur Grāma as an *umbaḷi* to Chikka Rāya Chauta. The *Keladinṛpavijayam* also confirms the above account of Bhairasa Woḍeyar's death at the hands of Venkaṭappa Nāyaka.[41] With the assistance of the Chautas, Venkaṭappa proceeded to Bārakur passing through the country by Moolike, the *sāvanta* of which also concluded a treaty with him. The Patte Grāmas of this Moolike country were given as *umbaḷi* to the Chautas. Venkaṭappa also gave Mandkur *magani* and Hejamadi *magani* as an *umbaḷi* to Chikka Rāya Chauta and returned to his capital.[42]

Citipary: It may be identified with Chittupadi in the Udipi taluk. The balalas of the place were originally Jainas and ruled over Heraga, Badagabettu, and Marane.[43]

Color: It may be identified with Kulur, nearly two and a half miles north of Mangalore along the coast. The chiefs of the place were called 'Kulur Karnantaya Balalas'. Their territory comprised of Pangimogara, Padukodi, Kāvūru, Kungatabailu, Marakaḍa and Kuḷūr.[44] The Kuḷūr chief who

39. Pietro Della Valle: *op. cit.*, II, p. 316.
40. *Mac. Coll.* 18-15-6 Kanara Kaifiyats, Kaifiyat of the Chauta kings.
41. *KNV.*, *op. cit.*, V.
42. *Mac. Coll.*, 18-15-6; Kanara Kaifiyats: Kaifiyat of the Chauta kings.
43. Aygal: *op. cit.*, p. 419.
44. *Ibid.*, p. 389.

was a contemporary of Vīrabhadra Nāyaka seems to have rebelled against him, with the help of the Portuguese as is evident from Portuguese sources.[45]

Condegere: This name seems to be much changed from its original form, and may stand for Konnara. The chiefs of the place were called 'Pani pila Konnara kings'. They ruled over portions of the Karkala taluk. They seem to have been independent for some time but were later subdued by the Bhaira kings of Karkala,[46] who as said above, were overpowered by Venkaṭappa.

Doltady: This may be identified with Dolpadi, one of the divisions in the territories of the Edambur Balalas of the Uppinangady taluk.[47]

Ermala: It may be identified with Yermala, 18 miles from Mangalore.

Gololer: The place is not identifiable.

Guedumardady: This name sounds very much like Kidumardady, but cannot be identified.

Gunbia: This may be identified with Kumbla, 20 miles off Mangalore. The ruins of the old fort are still seen. The king of this place according to Della Valle was called Ramo Nato Ari (Rāmanātha Ādi) and he married a daughter of the queen of Uḷḷal.[48]

Hebery: This may be identified with Hebri. These balalas ruled over Hebri, Balinge, Kacapura, Jara, Kerebettu, in the Karkala taluk. They were related to the Balalas of Kap by marriage.[49]

Herar: Herar seems to be the same as Herur. There are two places with this name which might possibly be meant (a) Herur ruled over by Kap Marda Heggade, in the Udipi

45. Panjim Archives: Moncões do Reino, from the Viceroy to the king, Goa, February 20, 1630.
46. Aygal: *op. cit.*, p. 360.
47. Aygal: *op. cit.*, p. 403.
48. Pietro Della Valle: *op. cit.*, II, p. 318.
49. Aygal: *op. cit.*, p. 318.

taluk,[50] and (b) Hirur in the Hangal taluk of Dharwar district.[51]

Hiretor: It is difficult to identify this place.

Idālcão: It is the Portuguese corruption of the word Ādil Shāh and means therefore the Sultan of Bījāpur. It is not possible to verify the historicity of the statement that Venkaṭappa Nāyaka defeated Bījāpur.

Mallor: This name stands for Mullur. But there are three places having the same name. (a) Mullur in the Karkala taluk, (b) Mullur in the Kappa magane, ten and a half miles south of Udipi,[52] and (c) Mullur in the Kaval magane near Udipi. These balalas belonged to the Bangher royal family and ruled over Kaval magane, Sishula magane, Pagiradka magane, and Beltangady magane, at the foot of the ghats.

Manipary: The place may be identified with Manipura in the Udipi taluk one of the centres of the Kattupadi Dore Balalas.[53]

Mayzur: Obviously it is a reference to Mysore. During Venkaṭappa's time, Mysore was ruled by Cāmarāja Woḍeyar V (1617-1637). Venkaṭappa seems to have encroached upon the Mysore territories, through his General Singala Rāya, who helped Bommarasaiya, the minister of Nanjuṇḍa Arasu of Periyapaṭṇa, when the Mysore forces under Basavaliṅgaṇṇa laid siege to Periyapaṭṇa in 1626.[54] Singala Rāya was however, chastised by the Mysore army and this seems to have formed the starting point of hostility between Mysore and Ikkēri.

50. *Ibid.*, p. 417.

51. *Karnata desa inscriptions*, I, p. 144; *Bombay Gazetteer*, I, pt. II, p. 436.

52. Sewell: *List of Antiquities*, II, p. 232.

53. Aygal: *op. cit.*, p. 418.

54. See Chikkadēvarājā Vaṁśāvaḷi, 33; [Karṇātaka Kāvya Mañjari, Vol. 3] Chikkadēvarāya Vijayam, II, 68, [Karṇātaka Kāvya Mañjari Series, No. 17] and Mysore Dhorēgala Vaṁśāvali, Ms. No. 62 P. L. and No. B. 336, p. 26 ff [Mysore Oriental Library].

Modicar: This sounds like Mudicaru or Mudikeru. The latter place is now called Mudgere or Mudagere, the capital of Mudagere taluk in Mysore.

Mudoly: Two places may be equated with this name (a) Muduri balalas of the place were chieftains under the Bangher Rajas,[55] (b) Muduly—This was one of the little known principalities under the Bangher Rajas of Mandavar.[56]

Mudrady: May be identified with Mudradi. The balalas of the place ruled over Shivapura, Mudradi, Kabbinale, Varanga, and Padukuduru in the Karkala taluk. They were Jainas,[57] and hence Venkaṭappa could have conquered them.

Mutur: The identification of the place is difficult. It may be (a) Mudur in the Hangal taluk of Dharwar[58] or (b) Muttur, in the Mangalore taluk, the balalas of which place had other centres as Amunge, Ulipadi, Kattemara, Kirale, Niddodi and Mangage.[59]

Nelebor: It may be identified with Nilambur. The Balalas of the place ruled over Shivalli, Kadekeru, Kidiyuru, Ambalpady, Mudunidambur, Putturu, Kodavuru, Badaganinidiyuru, Tenkandiyuru, Kelar Kabettu and Tonase all in the Udipi taluk. They were originally Jainas though later they became followers of Mādhva.[60]

Nereguy: It may be identified with Nerenki, now called Halenenki, or old Nerenki. The balalas here were called 'Nerenki Chavadi Hegde' and ruled over Hale Nerenki, Alangaru, Rāmakuṅga, Alanpaya, Honalu, Golitattu and Basatura in the Uppinaṅgadi taluk of South Kanara. They were Jainas.[61]

55. Hedge: *History of South Kanara*, p. 211.
56. *Ibid.*, p. 199.
57. Aygal: *op. cit.*, p. 414.
58. *Bombay Gazetteer*, I, pt. II, p. 562.
59. Aygal: *op. cit.*, p. 390.
60. *Ibid.*, p. 419.
61. *Ibid.*, p. 411.

Olala: The place seems to be the same as Uḷḷal, three miles south of Mangalore. The name of this queen was Abaga Dēvi according to Della Valle.[62] There were three powers contesting for the supremacy over Mangalore, the Queen of Uḷḷal, Rāja of Bangher and the Portuguese.[63] Uḷḷal is situated to the south of Mangalore with only a river to separate the two. The king of Bangher had a palace and fort at Mangalore. The Portuguese had a fort at Mangalore and they carried on trade in rice. Kanara was a rice exporting centre during the period. The Portuguese joined hands with the Rāja of Bangher whenever the local chiefs were on inimical terms.

On her accession Abaga Dēvi (or Bukka Devi) was married to the Rāja of Bangher but the marriage was a failure. Some other unfortunate incidents followed and the queen made preparations for war with the Rāja of Bangher.

Venkaṭappa Nāyaka, by this time, had carried out his policy of aggrandisement and was anxious to bring Mangalore under his control. From the letter of the Portuguese Viceroy dated 29th December, 1616 to the king of Portugal, it appears that the Portuguese had been on friendly terms with Venkaṭappa till then, because of the good profits the pepper trade brought them from his country. But this friendship was not to last long. Venkaṭappa is represented in the letter as being at the gates of Mangalore, threatening to drive out the king of Bangher.[64]

In 1617 the Portuguese concluded an alliance with the king of Bangher, who made over the fortress of Bangher, to them for defence. The fort was reinforced by soldiers and by the arrival of a fleet of eight ships under Francisco Miranda Henriques. In the engagements that followed the Portuguese were successful and it is recorded that 4,000 Canarese were slain.[65]

62. Pietro Della Valle, *op. cit.*, II, p. 311.

63. Moraes: *Mangalore*, p. 15.

64. Panjim Government Archives: Moncões do Reino: Anno de 1614, fol. 302.

65. Faria-Y-Souza: *op. cit.*, III, pp. 325-26.

An unfortunate turn came to the Portuguese. They captured a ship belonging to the queen of Uḷḷal who sent an invitation to Venkaṭappa Nāyaka, for attacking her husband and the Portuguese. Venkaṭappa Nāyaka who was waiting to humiliate the Portuguese invaded the Bangher Rāja's territories aided by the Queen's armies. The territories of the Rāja were conquered and the fort set fire to, though the Portuguese were in charge of it. Venkaṭappa also captured the ensign of the Portuguese. Their captain Henriques revenged himself by attacking Uḷḷal but he was soon forced to raise the siege.[66] In 1618, the Portuguese made another attempt, by bringing fresh reinforcements from Malabar but they were once again defeated by Venkaṭappa Nāyaka, who had at his command more than 12,000 Canarese. A treaty was however signed with the Portuguese according to the terms of which Venkaṭappa restored to them the ensign he had captured and in return he got the fort of Bangher. Though the Queen of Uḷḷal gained freedom from the Portuguese, she had only to fall under the suzerainty of Venkaṭappa Nāyaka. Venkaṭappa Nāyaka was now the undisputed master of Kanara.[67] The Rāja of Bangher was in exile, being deprived of his kingdom worth 1,25,000 pagodas.[68] It was this expedition which forced the Portuguese to send an embassy to Ikkēri to regain their lost favours and to reinstate the Rāja of Bangher. The details of this embassy have been furnished earlier.

Palpare: This may be identified with Palpare in Southern Coorg.

Pedanar: This place is difficult the identify. It may be Pegavar in the Mangalore taluk, the seat of some Balalas.[69]

Penabur: This may be identified with Penabur in the Mangalore taluk. The Balalas of the place ruled over Penabur, Hosabettu, Baikampali and Kulai.[70]

66. Moncões do Reino, 12; Anno de 1629 Fols. 448-449.

67. Varkey: *History of Uḷḷal*, Mangalore College Magazine, VI, No. 2.

68. Moncões do Reino, No. 12, Anno de, 1629, Fols. 448-449.

69. Aygal: *op. cit.*, p. 387.

70. *Ibid.*, p. 388.

Quelanar: It is difficult to identify the place.

Saura: It is difficult to identify the place. Can it be Soratur, 12 miles south of Gadag?

Serguo: It is not identifiable.

Serra: The Portuguese phrase 'O Rey sa Serra' may be rendered as 'the king of the Mountain'. There were many petty chieftains in the Ghats. The kingdom of Serra was probably in South Kanara bordering on Malabar.

Sunda: It may be identified with Sunda in the Sirisi taluk of North Kanara. It was in ancient times called Sindhapura. The chiefs of Sunda continued in their capital even after their defeat by Venkaṭappa.

Tagrette: The place is not identifiable.

Tomboso: It may be identified with Tombattu in South Kanara.

Umzur: It may be identified with Umunjur or Vamaṇjur in the Mangalore taluk. The principality consisted of Tiruvailu, Bodantila, Ulaya, Bettu, Mulu, Mudu-Perar and Padu Perar. The chiefs of the place were Jainas and seem to have been connected with the Chauta rulers. Della Valle speaks of this chief as one of the feudatories of Venkaṭappa Nāyaka to whom he paid an yearly tribute of 800 pagodas. The total yearly revenue of his state was 2,000 *varāhas*. Della Valle further says that he was styled Omgiu Arasa, his name being Ramo Rau (Rāmarao).[71]

Vitala: The place may be identified with Vithala, twenty miles north-east of Kāsargode. It seems that its chiefs were called Heggades of Vithala. Their territory was called the 'two thousand śime of Vithala.' They were originally feudatories of the Bangher rulers, and their principality consisted of Vithala, Kolanadu, Mani, and Saletore in the Uppinangadi taluk.[72]

71. Pietro Della Valle, *op. cit.*, II, p. 305-6.
72. Aygal: *op. cit.*, p. 365.

CHAPTER VII

VĪRABHADRA NĀYAKA (1629-1645 A.C.)

Vīrabhadra Nāyaka succeeded to the throne after the death of his grandfather Venkaṭappa Nāyaka.[1] As said earlier, Bhadrappa Nāyaka had, according to the *Śivatattva-ratnākara,* died even during the life time of his father.[2] The *Keladinṛpavijayam* corroborates this when it says that Vīrabhadra Nāyaka succeeded to the throne after Venkaṭappa. Vīrabhadra Nāyaka's earliest date, as gathered from inscriptions, is Śaka 1552, Śukla, 10th lunar day of the bright half of Puṣya (15th December 1629 A.C.)[3] which was also the first year of his reign as given in the *Keladinṛpavijayam.*[4] From this reign onwards the dates assigned in this work to the Nāyakas of Ikkēri may be regarded as fairly correct. The last known date for Vīrabhadra according to epigraphs and the *Keladinṛpavijayam* is Śaka 1567, Pārthiva, Chaitra Śudha 10, Wednesday, (26th March, 1645 A.C.).[5]

Vīrabhadra Nāyaka was only twenty when Venkaṭappa died. Hence the administration of the kingdom was entrusted to his uncle Śivappa Nāyaka. The defeated chiefs were so jealous of his accession that they took the earliest opportunity to make an organised attempt to dethrone the young ruler. When the strong arm of Venkaṭappa was removed, the whole kingdom was in the throes of a civil war. Armies

1. Buchanan's statement, "This Vencatuppa's son Bhadruppa Nayaka governed for 23 years nominally as servant of the Rayaru and 12 years as sovereign prince" is not however borne out by the available evidence.—*A Journey from Madras through Mysore, Canara and Malabar,* III, p. 127. Sewell also does not mention the rule of Vīrabhadra. See *List of Inscriptions in Southern India,* II, p. 177.
2. *VI.,* 13, Verse 135.
3. *MAR.,* 1916, p. 65, also 1933, No. 28.
4. *KNV.,* VI.
5. *EC.,* VIII, Tl. 40; *KNV.,* VI. The following are the dates assigned to him by other scholars: Rice 1629-45 (*EC.,* VII, p. 43); Naraharayya 1629-45 (*QJMS,* XXII, p. 79); Mackenzie 1630-36, (18-15-15, *Rajāvaṁśāvali*).

marched from different sides; and but for the military genius of Śivappa Nāyaka, the Ikkēri dynasty would have sunk into oblivion after an existence of only about a century.

Vīrabhadra Nāyaka and Bījāpur: As soon as news of the death of Venkaṭappa reached Bījāpur, the Ādil Shāh sent his ambassador Mīra to Ikkēri to demand nine million gold pieces, five elephants, 200 Arab horses, besides 80,000 *pagodas* which Venkaṭappa Nāyaka owed to him. Vīrabhadra Nāyaka was extremely annoyed at this demand, and in order to avoid war with a powerful neighbour he offered him 30,000 *pagodas* on condition that the Ādil Shāh would help him to suppress the revolts of the minor chiefs under him.[6] But this was not acceptable to the Sultan. He was anxiously waiting for an opportunity to wage war.

Vīrabhadra Nāyaka and local rebellions: All the balalas and minor chiefs of the Karṇāṭaka area who were conquered by Venkaṭappa Nāyaka[7] revolted against the authority of Vīrabhadra Nāyaka. The rising was a general and wide-spread one and all the territory from Bhatkal to Kāsargode was a seething mass of rebellious chiefs. Vīrabhadra's power seemed to be crippled for a time. It took him nearly six protracted years to suppress all the rebellions and re-establish his authority firmly over them. This is indicated by a letter of the Portuguese Viceroy to the king dated 6th February, 1635, which mentions Vīrabhadra Nāyaka's taking possession of all the kingdoms that rebelled.[8] The two Portuguese letters which give details about the expansion wars of Venkaṭappa Nāyaka also refer to the rebellion during the time of Vīrabhadra Nāyaka. These rebellions seem to have taken place during the years 1629-1635.[9]

Vīrabhadra Nāyaka and Vīrappa Nāyaka: Vīrabhadra Nāyaka had troubles nearer home also. Taking advantage

6. Moncōes do Reino, No. 12, Ano de 1629, Fols. 481-82.
7. See *infra,* Chapter VI.
8. Moncoes do Reino, No. 19 Anno de 1633, Fol. 563.
9. For details and identification of all the places and *balalas* who rebelled against Vīrabhadra Nāyaka see *infra* note to Ch. VI

of these events, the cousins and uncles of the Nāyaka schemed and plotted against him; Vīra Voḍeyār or Vīrappa Nāyaka, son of Rāmarāja Nāyaka made a bold bid for the throne. A few Portuguese documents throw much valuable light on the attempted usurpation by Vīrappa Nāyaka. If succession to the Ikkēri throne was by primogeniture, Vīrappa Nāyaka had a better right than Vīrabhadra. But succession by primogeniture was not an inviolable rule. Venkaṭappa Nāyaka fearing that Vīrappa Nāyaka would contest for the throne, had imprisoned him. However, on the death of Venkaṭappa, Vīrappa Nāyaka managed to escape. Once out of prison, he found a fertile field to sow seeds of dissension among the minor chiefs. The vassals sympathised with the claims of Vīrappa and thought that by supporting him they would be able to work up for their own freedom. Vīrappa Nāyaka seems to have proclaimed himself independent in 1630 A.C. as is evidenced by a copper-plate grant of his dated Śaka 1553, Pramōdūta, Mārgaśira, Śu. 5 (Sunday, 28th November, 1630 A.C.).[10] N. Lakshminarayan Rao surmises on the basis of this grant that Vīrappa Nāyaka ruled for some time conjointly with Vīrabhadra.[11] But other pieces of evidence, such as the Portuguese documents, show that Vīrappa Nāyaka was only an usurper. Further, we find only this inscription of Vīrappa Nāyaka and no other, throughout the reign period of Vīrabhadra Nāyaka. A letter from Conde de Linhares, Portuguese Viceroy at Goa, dated 4th November, 1630, runs as follows:

> "I shall give an account of what happened to Vīrabhadra Naik, and how an uncle of his, who was for more than 30 years in prison and proclaimed king, he came out of the prison with great cunning, not knowing how, not being able to say what the new king will assent to and I shall succeed in what I am already dealing and intend doing by way of industry and intelligence and that I am so careful as I dream of it in my sleep because it is from this land of this king comes the rice, with which this city and the adjacent islands and the places like

10. *EC.*, VIII, Tl. 51.
11. *Vij. Sex. Com. Vol.*, p. 263.

> Bardez, Salsette, Muscat and Mozambique are maintained, which the vessels bring from the kingdom. It is not possible to be at war with this king and I am working with various prevarications to bring him round and force him to come to what is to the credit and reputation of this state, and the service of your Majesty, whose catholic and royal person God may keep."[12]

Vīrappa Nāyaka was able to bring the coastal town of Barcelor under his control and he offered it to the Portuguese in return for help.[13] The Portuguese were not able to decide in favour of any particular claimant. Meanwhile they were anxious to establish a factory at Cambolim.[14]

Instead of direct action against Vīrappa Nāyaka, Vīrabhadra Nāyaka and Śivappa Nāyaka left the usurper in his false security and directed their actions against others. Vīrappa Nāyaka thinking that he had firmly established himself sent an ambassador to the Portuguese Viceroy to scrap up a peace. The Viceroy, Count of Linhares was not in a hurry to conclude peace with Vīrappa Nāyaka as he had intentions of sending a representative to Vīrabhadra Nāyaka.[15]

Realising that the whole kingdom was up against him, Vīrabhadra was anxious to maintain friendly relations with the Portuguese, for though they would not be very useful to him as allies, yet as enemies they would prove troublesome by aiding the rebels. He therefore sent an ambassador to Goa. A letter from the Portuguese Viceroy to the king describes the reception given to Vīrabhadra Nāyaka's ambassador as also the desire of the Portuguese to be on friendly terms with him, so as to have a plentiful supply of rice and chilleys.[16]

12. *Notions of the Reign,* No. 146, Year 1630, Fols. 171-172; No. 25.
13. *Notions of the Reign;* No. 16; Year 1632, No. 6.
14. *Notions of the Reign;* No. 13, Year 1629, Fols. 264-65; *Ibid.,* No. 146, Year 1630, Fols. 171-172; *Ibid.,* No. 14, Fol. 21; *Ibid.,* No. 14, Year 1630, Fol. 218, No. 95.
15. *Ibid.,* No. 14, Year 1630, Fols. 212-13, No. 84.
16. *Ibid.,* No. 13, 1629, Fols. 264-65.

Finding that nearly two years had passed and that Vīrappa Nāyaka had not been dethroned, the Portuguese being anxious to benefit from the trade in commercial crops of Kanara, arranged for a treaty of peace with the usurper. The treaty was concluded on the 7th March 1631 A.C. The terms of the treaty were:

(1) Vīrappa Nāyaka was to grant the possession of the island of Cambolim to the Portuguese with permission to build a fortress therein;
(2) the Portuguese were to be allowed to cut and take timber from his dominions without any tax;
(3) Vīrappa Nāyaka was not to allow the Malavars or others trade in his harbour;
(4) every year he was to pay punctually 500 sackfuls of rice;
(5) dues or levies on Portuguese merchandise were to be abolished;
(6) all the pepper in his dominions was to be freely sold without any difficulty to the buyers;
(7) the Portuguese Viceroy was to act as Judge in differences between Vīrappa Nāyaka and the other kings who were allies of Portuguese;
(8) Vīrappa Nāyaka was allowed to take iron and ten horses without paying tax from Goa;
(9) he was also to have two ships

and

(10) those who violated any clause of the treaty was to pay a sum of 10,000 *pagodas*.[17]

N. Lakshminarayan Rao thinks that Cambolim was ceded to the Portuguese by Vīrabhadra Nāyaka in 1631.[18] But the treaty of peace mentioned above establishes the fact that Cambolim was ceded by Vīrappa Nayaka, the usurper and not by Vīrabhadra. After this, Vīrappa Nāyaka seems to have been powerful till 1633 in which year the Portuguese were thinking of concluding an alliance with Vīrabhadra

17. *Pazes-E-Tratados,* No. 2, Ano de 1715/1716, Fol. 69. See for the text of the treaty Appendix A, No. 1.

18. *Vij. Sex. Com.* Vol., p. 262.

Nāyaka. The letter of the king of Spain to Count of Castro, the Viceroy of India, dated 22nd February 1633, speaks of it as follows:

> "And as regards the peace you contracted with Vīrapa Naique and that you want to renew with Vīrabhadra Naique, it seems to signify to you by this letter that they were made with all good considerations of my service and the reputation of this State and preceeded teneciously not to alter any of the conditions as Vīrabhadra Naique wished to, about which I shall write."[19]

As we hear little or nothing about Vīrappa Nāyaka from Portuguese or other sources after 1633 we may presume that he died soon after.

Other troubles: There were other futile attempts to dethrone Vīrabhadra. Sadāśivayya, cousin and brother-in-law of Vīrabhadra, encouraged by the seeming success of his uncle (Vīrappa Nāyaka), made an attempt to secure the throne. But he had to flee and take refuge at the court of Sōḍe. The ruler of Sōḍe refused to surrender Sadāśivayya and this resulted in a war. The Ikkēri army marched against Sōḍe and defeated the combined armies of Sōḍe and Biligi, the ruler of the latter then being one Ghante Voḍeyār. Meanwhile Sadāśivayya died. The Lords of Sōḍe and Biligi, who, however, wanted to continue the war approached the Sultan of Bījāpur for help. Vīrabhadra hearing of the motives of the enemies, sent his envoy Śankaranārāyaṇa to the Bījāpur court. His appeals were successful and the Sultan declined to help the chiefs of Sōḍe and Biligi. The *Keladinṛpavijayam* says that Śankaranārāyaṇa was granted the title of Sarajarāja by the Sultan of Bījāpur. Further Ghanteyamma, daughter of Ghante Voḍeyār, lord of Biligi, was married to Bhadrayya, son of Sadāśivayya.[20]

Vīrabhadra Nāyaka had to withstand the attack of the Bhairava chiefs of Kalaśa. They took possession of some parts of Ikkēri kingdom measuring six *yōnas* including Śṛngeri.

19. *Notions of the Reign:* No. 17, 1632-33, Fol. 60, No. 30.
20. *KNV.*, VI.

Bhairava attacked the Śṛngeri maṭha and wanted to humiliate its guru Saccidānanda Bhāratī. Being a traditional patron of the Śṛngeri maṭha, Vīrabhadra Nāyaka rose up to the occasion and defeated Bhairava but he was let off to return to his capital. Bhairava made thereafter two more attempts on Śṛngeri, but both of them were repelled by Vīrabhadra's army. From this time onwards the Ikkēri Nāyakas became strong guardians of this famous maṭha.

Vīrabhadra Nāyaka and Bījāpur again: The next onslaught which Vīrabhadra had to suffer from was one from the Bījāpur General Ranadaula Khān (Rustam-i-zaman). Ikkēri was the first kingdom to be invaded by him in his general conquest of the Karṇāṭaka country. The causes for the invasion are not easy to find. According to the accounts of Gōvinda Vaidya and Tirumala Nāyaka, Kenge Hanuma of Basavapaṭṭaṇa who was on inimical terms with Vīrabhadra Nāyaka requested the Sultan of Bījāpur to invade Ikkēri with a view to annihilate it, and promised him large presents in return. According to the *Keladinṛpavijayam*, Venkaṭappa, the chief of Tarikere, apparently another recalcitrant feudatory of the ruler of Ikkēri also appears to have induced the Sultan of Bījāpur to invade the kingdom. In the present state of our knowledge it cannot, however, be made out in what political relationship the chief of Tarikere stood to the Sultan of Bījāpur. Taking advantage of the confused political condition in Ikkēri, the Sultan of Bījāpur sent Ranadaula Khān for the conquest of the kingdom. When the city of Ikkēri was attacked, Vīrabhadra Nāyaka offered resistance for some time, but finding that his position was becoming weak, he retired to the fortress of Bhuvanagiri along with his family. Ranadaula Khān took Ikkēri, and assisted by Kenge Hanuma, attacked Bhuvanagiri with a large army of 40,000 horses, 1,00,000 foot and 40 elephants. Finding further resistance impossible, Vīrabhadra Nāyaka sued for peace; and according to the treaty that was concluded then, he gave up his claims to the conquered forts; and he was allowed to rule over the remaining portions of his kingdom on terms of subordination to the

Sultan of Bījāpur.[21] According to the *Keladinṛpavijayam* the invasion of Ikkēri took place in Śaka 1560, Īśvara, Puṣya, Bahula daśami, corresponding to 30th December 1637 A.C.[22]

Vīrabhadra, however, wanted to punish his erstwhile feudatories, the chiefs of Tarikere and Basavapaṭṭaṇa. In December 1638, he sent an ambassador named Rāmakṛṣṇappa, who was a *niyogi* in his service, with many presents to the Sultan and sought his aid in crushing the power of the two chiefs. According to the *Keladinṛpavijayam* the Sultan sent for a second time a large army under Ranadaula Khān; and Vīrabhadra joined his forces with the Bījāpur army near Harihara on the river Tungabhadrā. The Ikkēri forces were led by Śivappa Nāyaka. The *Muhammadnāmāh,* however, gives a slightly different account. According to it Kenge Hanuma, with whose help Ranadaula Khān conquered the Malnad country, rose in rebellion against the Sultan of Bījāpur. Hence the Sultan sent his general Ranadaula Khān to suppress the rebellion. When he was encamped at Harihara on the river Tungabhadrā he is said to have solicited the help of Vīrabhadra of Ikkēri promising restoration of the territory conquered from him recently. Vīrabhadra took advantage of the situation and joined the Bījāpur General.[23] The combined Ikkēri-Bījāpur armies besieged Tarikere and destroyed it. Next they attacked Basavapaṭṭaṇa and captured it. In the battle fought at the place, the brothers of Kenge Hanuma, who had sided with Ranadaula Khān in the latter's campaign against Ikkēri were captured and sent to Bījāpur.[24] The relationship between Ikkēri and Bījāpur became so cordial that when Ranadaula Khān advanced against Bangalore in 1640 he seems to have been accompanied by the Ikkēri army. It appears possible that Ikkēri, after

21. *Proceedings of the IHRC.,* XVI, pp. 50-51, *Mac. Coll.* 18-15-7 section xii.

22. Canto VI. The *Muhammadnāmāh* assigns the attack of Ikkēri by Ranadaula Khān to 1030 A.H. (1630 A.C.). The date is however too early for the expedition. (See K. A. Nilakanta Sastri and N. Venkataramanayya, *Further Sources of Vijayanagar History,* I, pp. 342-3 n).

23. K. A. N. Sastri and N. Venkataramanayya, *op. cit.,* I, p. 344 ff.

24. *Proceedings of the IHRC.,* XVI, pp. 50-51; see also *Muhammadnāmāh,* translated in *The Modern Review,* July, 1929.

the subjugation and death of Hanuma of Basavapaṭṭaṇa attempted to press the Bījāpur demands upon Mysore.

Though Ikkēri was then in the midst of great difficulties, Vīrabhadra Nāyaka was able to overcome them, regain the lost territories and maintain his kingdom in tact. A letter of the Viceroy at Goa to the king of Portugal dated the 6th February 1635 A.C., speaks of the entire triumph of Vīrabhadra Nāyaka over the kingdoms that had rebelled against him on the death of Venkaṭappa.[25] This is further supported by the fact that Capt. Weddel, who came to Bhatkal in 1637 A.C. makes no mention of any political confusion in the kingdom, although the *Keladinṛpavijayam* states that there was an invasion of Ikkēri in December 1637 by Bījāpur.

Vīrabhadra Nāyaka and the Portuguese: The commencement of the seventeenth century witnessed a set back in the Portuguese power and influence. The Dutch had launched on a vigorous policy of obstruction against the Portuguese and in many engagements they came out in flying colours. Added to this, the English joined the race, for the Portuguese allowed the English free access to the different ports on the west coast.

When Kanara was torn asunder by civil wars, the Portuguese tried to acquire Cambolim taking advantage of the fact that many of the rebellious chiefs applied to them for help. The fortress was garrisoned with 70 marines, and a large quantity of gunpowder. The contingent was reinforced with two hundred infantry and six armed vessels. But upto 4th November 1630 A.C., the strengthening of the fort was not completed. The Government at Goa continued to send *chunam* and stone for the work.[26] Pedro de Silva, the Portuguese Viceroy at Goa, commissioned Martin Teixera, the Portuguese Governor of the coast of Kanara, to meet the king Vīrabhadra Nāyaka, who had delayed the sale of pepper and who was coerced by the English to break his commercial relations with the Portuguese. Vīrabhadra Nāyaka sent

25. Moncōes do Reino, No. 19, Ano de 1633, Fol. 563, No. 8.
26. *Notions of the Reign*, No. 146, Year 1630, Fols. 171-72, *Ibid.*, No. 14, Fol. 21, No. 103.

his ambassador Rāma Pai to Goa, but he seems to have come to no agreement and left Goa on a Portuguese vessel with instructions that he should be left at Barcelor and given asylum.[27] After the death of Vīrappa Nāyaka, the arms of Ikkēri were again triumphant. But its success was not complete as is shown by the hasty and compromising peace signed by Vīrabhadra Nāyaka with the Portuguese in 1633. The Portuguese welcomed Vithula Sinay, the agent of Vīrabhadra; and after preliminary discussions, a treaty was signed. The terms of the treaty were of a very compromising nature. The chief among them were:

(a) The island of Cambolim was to be with the Portuguese;
(b) Vīrabhadra Nāyaka was to give all the rice and victual in his country and a regular tribute of 500 sackfuls of rice per year;
(c) The Portuguese were bound to take 350 *candies* of pepper for each ship at the rate of 22 *pagodas* per *candi*;
(d) The Portuguese were to give Vīrabhadra Nāyaka 12 horses every year and in return he was to give shelter to the ships of the Portuguese plying on the coast;
(e) Vīrabhadra Nāyaka was to be given by the Portuguese three charters of Navigation for his ships to go to Mecca, and Muscat (obviously to bring horses);
(f) The Portuguese were to be allowed to cut all the wood they required for building ships;
(g) The boatmen of Vīrabhadra Nāyaka were to take only the allowed number of boats and not more;
(h) The two ships near the island of Cambolim were to be given to Vīrabhadra Nāyaka.[28]

A perusal of the treaty will show that it was almost on the model of the one concluded earlier between the Portuguese and Vīrappa Nāyaka.

27. Justricoes—1630/1640, Fol. 66.

28. *Pazes-e-Tratados*, No. 1, Ano de 1671, Fols. 17-19. See Appendix A, No. 2 for the text of the treaty.

Meanwhile the gulf between the Portuguese and the English in commercial matters widened. The English offered to buy pepper from Vīrabhadra Nāyaka at a much higher price. In 1637 A.C., the Portuguese were anxious to continue the friendship with Vīrabhadra Nāyaka. The Nāyak at this time was expecting trouble from the Ādil Shah of Bījāpur. Finding that the Portuguese had some influence at Bījāpur court, Vīrabhadra thought of availing himself of their help to check the impending invasion. He sent Rāmappa to Goa with instructions to request the Viceroy to write to the Portuguese ambassador at Bījāpur to settle his affairs with its Sultan. In a written reply to Vīrabhadra the Viceroy at Goa promised to do the needful.[29]

29. Secredo, 1633, Fol. 27. The reply runs as follows: "For king Virabhadra Naique two letters together were given to me by Ramapa, Ambassador of your excellency and both demonstrative of love and friendship which your Excellency has and your ancestors bore to the king of Portugal, and for all the Portuguese who are in this State, the obligations for which will be remembered by me, that I may know how to thank for them with good will.

Together with your ambassador came Antonio Borges, resident of Barcelor and each one for himself said that your Excellency kept a secret within your heart. I listened to everything with much pleasure and replied, which your Excellency will see together with the letters what they spoke about and promised in the name of your Excellency and everything remains a great secret and as your Excellency will swear and promise to keep thus everything. I, also, on my part shall swear and give my word on behalf of myself and other succeeding viceroys of this State just as your Excellency will do on behalf of all the kings who will succeed in this kingdom; your sons, and descendants, so that all the peoples of Canara and all the Portuguese may remain certain that we have peace and friendship for ever, the sun to moon lasts. As soon as these things will have been done and sworn as I say, I shall arrange that the Queen of Banghel may have friendship with you and I have written to my ambassador to be present in the Court of Idalcao and I will write to him again to be in friendship with your-ambassador and to work to help in the business for which he was sent by you to the same Idal Sha; above all I shall ever do the office of a good friend for your Excellency desires much to be with so much truth and for many years.

All other things which are not written in this letter will be told by your Ramapa and Antonio Borges. Now I am certain that this friendship will be for ever between us."

Goa 10th December 1638. (Sd.) Pedro da Silva"

The political atmosphere in Kanara was getting clearer and Vīrabhadra Nāyaka realised that the power of the Portuguese had increased by their erection of a new fort at Cambolim. Vīrabhadra constructed a fort opposite to it and at the same time negotiated with the Portuguese Viceroy to dismantle the fort at Cambolim or Barcelor held by them. The Viceroy in his instructions to Antonio Borges strongly recommended the further fortification of Cambolim and the dismantling of the fort of Barcelor to please Vīrabhadra Nāyaka.[30]

The queen of Banghel seems to have applied to the Portuguese for help against Vīrabhadra Nāyaka, so that she might recover her lost territories. But the Portuguese were anxious to be friendly with both and to keep them in good spirits so that they might benefit in trade from both their countries. In instructing the chief captain of Kanara, Luiz de Cane de Souza, the Portuguese Viceroy wrote:

> "The Queen of Banghel condescended to write to me a letter in which she asks me a favour to help her against Virabhadra Naique in order that she may be able to recover what he had taken from her. I have to say in reply that you have my orders to help her in anything that takes place, if king Virabhadra Naique does not object. I order you that if the said queen asks you to treat this matter, give her to understand that you have my orders to help her wherever you think fit, with many words of favour. However, if she asked a favour against Virabhadra Naique or any other king, you should excuse yourselves with good reasons saying it is impossible and that as you are sent to fill up and keep guard on, you are not able to divert yourself to other things but so that she should not be discomfeited, nor take from her the hope of your help and always with vague words that do not compromise you giving to understand and that this practice and other intimations should not be in

30. *Jus Frucares,* 1631-1640, Fol. 177.

writing, but only by word of mouth, through persons who are experts in those things."[31]

In 1643, Count de Averras, the Viceroy at Goa instructed Antonio Borges to see Vīrabhadra Nāyaka and try to win him over to their side as the English were making rapid progress. The chief instruction was:

> "You shall now show to the king Virabhadra Naique the baby elephant which I send him as a present and as the aim of your journey is that neither the Dutch nor the English should be admitted into Canara, and you shall represent to him about this as is convenient."[32]

Antonio Borges carried out the instructions so carefully and tactfully that Vīrabhadra Nāyaka pulled down the English factory at Bhatkal. Finding that the English were still making inroads, the king of Portugal sent an order in 1644 to the effect that the English should not be allowed to trade in Kanara. To this the Viceroy replied that the best way to drive out the English was to supply him with the necessary money to buy up all the pepper in Kanara. But the finances of Portugual being very slender, the idea was not practicable. Slowly but surely the English were able to dislodge the Portuguese from the Ikkēri territories and get mastery over the entire trade.

Vīrabhadra Nāyaka and the English: During the reign of Venkaṭappa Nāyaka, the English Company had made little progress as the Portuguese influence at the Ikkēri Court was considerable. Even when they were offered Bhatkal, they declined it because of the proximity of the place to Goa. But during Vīrabhadra's reign, being better equipped, they made an attempt to capture the pepper trade of Canara. This attempt is known as the famous voyage of Captain Weddel. In this fleet was Peter Mundy, to whom we owe much of the information regarding the English attempt. Two of Weddel's party, Robinson and Mundy, started on a mission to Ikkēri and reached the place on 25th

31. *Instrucōes*, Fol. 98.
32. *Ibid.*, 1641-1647, Fol. 61.

January 1637. The Rājā received them cordially, granted them a piece of ground to erect a fort, and promised them exclusive rights of exporting pepper from his territory. A factory was established at Bhatkal under the charge of Anthony Vereworthy.[33] Peter Mundy gives detailed information about the embassy.[34]

33. Foster: *English Factories in India,* 1637-41, Intro. p. vi.

34. Peter Mundy: Travels, III, pp. 74-75. "The Sabandar (Shahbandar-Harbour Superintendent) or Customer of the Towne accompanied by the king's merchants came aboard the Dragon and gave us friendlie welcome with full assurance of all good entertainment, putting us in hope of a present quantitie of pepper for the despatch of one of our small ships, and this although they urged somewhat beyond truth to the end we might not goe solemlie from their post, we have since (with some delay) found to be real, and what the issue will be, time will produce to the undoubted profit of successors. A few days after our arrivall, Advice came from the king, who was certified of our being here and a contracte was Made betweene our Principall and his officers to have a shippes loading of pepper, deliver 4 waights of lead for three of pepper. This arrangement included 'customes and all charge and a letter and present were immediately sent to the king, who liveth 3 daes journey upp in the countrie, who by his answere, was pleased to allow what was done and to promise a grant of what we should in reason demand; and so with a present of goats, henns, rice etc., welcomed us to his ports butt shortly they began to cavill protracting Delwere, Demanding part in Ryalls of 8 as allsoe 10 to 12 per cents more in lead than was agreed for. Whereuppon, For redresse hereof as alsoe to procure and confirme a future trade here and an abiding in this country, Mr. Thomas Robinson, was enordered to proceed to the Court to treat with the king about the particulars aforementioned.

Having concluded upon the Shipt Planter to be dispeeded for Europe, we beganne to land of our lead and to waie some small quantities of pepper, which coming down out of the countries very slowly, reason the king and the Portugalls have latelie beene at some differences and thereupon that commoditie was transported overland to Cambia or elsewhere, nor is not at anie time brought tither, but when the merchants are ready to shipp it awaie, the town being of no defence to resist the Malabars or anie other invasive enemies. The king's officers there, fearing our discontent upon their supposed slackness, which might turn to their prejudice if we should depart unsatisfied they pretended diverse soothing excuses and delaied untill at last it was resolved that to understand the certainiety of matters, Thomas Robinson should passe up to the Court and meat with the king about our trade and residence there. In the meantime his Majesty's officer at Batacala

In February 1637, Vīrabhadra Nāyaka hearing about the arrival of Captain Weddel's fleet at Bhatkal wrote to them inviting them to the port and informing them that he had ordered Mange Nāyaka to weigh them out pepper procurable at the moment. He also assured them that he would most willingly embrace the friendship of the English.[35] On the last day of the month, Vīrabhadra Nāyaka entertained the embassy to supper; and after it was over he gave them a *firman* to build a fort at Bhatkal and permission to trade in his country. The members of the embassy were received with usual honours and they were looked after and well treated. All their requests were favourably considered and decided according to their wishes. Peter Mundy gives plenty of details about this embassy.[36]

came aboard the Dragon and requested in his master's behalf to be furnished with a piece of ordnance which was granted and referred to his owne election, and a Demiculverin out of the Dragon was for that purpose with all its apurtences put ashore, the portraiture whereof was drawne out with its proportion and length and sent to the king with a present of Rich Scarlet (broad cloth) and some other things by Thomas Robinson who being accompanied with Peter Mundare and the two English youths to attend them departed Baticala this present evening and the next night with some difficultie attained the height of the mountiynes of Ballaguate arriving the second daie after at the cittie of Itary, the seat of the King."

35. *Extract from Courteen Papers in Ms. Rawl. A.* 299 *Fol.* 188, *at the Bodlean Library.* The extract runs as follows:

"By a letter received from you I am informed of your safe arrivall and that you are invited to this port of Battacalla and that you came in the waie of trafique, I have therefore enordered Mange Naique to take notice of all your merchandise and to weigh you out all the pepper that is to be procured at present and have likewise received the presents which you sent me at your first arrival in the port. Mange Naique writes unto me that you desire much in the behalfe of your kinge to hold amitie with this countrie, which I am heartilie glad to understand as your selfe hereafter shall perceive for I shall most willingle embrace your king's friendship and shall cause to be putt into your hands as well all the pepper as other merchandise of this countrie, desiring likewise that you would bring me whatsoever rarite and goodthings of your countrie. I received your present according to your letter and have likewise returned you such things as by a roll therewith sent will apeare. 'Icarry', 14th February 1637."

36. Extracts from voyages of Weddel's Fleet—State papers, Dom Chas I cccli, No. 3 quoted in Peter Mundy, Travels III, pp. 88 ff. For extract see Appendix A, No. 3.

In March 1637, Vīrabhadra Nāyaka wrote to the English merchants regarding the transactions in pepper. Therein it is stated that he had ordered Mange Nāyak to weigh out 300 *candies* of pepper and another 200 *candies* later to the agent at Bhatkal. The price of pepper was to be 30 *pagodas* per *candi*. This pepper was to be taken in exchange for lead. Further he requested the English to bring good horses from Persia or Arabia for which he would pay in pepper and money.[37] In the second letter, Vīrabhadra wrote to the English thus:

> "The Portugalls tell me they would faine see anie merchandise or good thing come from the English but doe not you esteem their patronage."[38]

Thus in spite of the Portuguese jealousy the English were able to gain considerable footing in the Kanara trade during the reign of Vīrabhadra Nāyaka.

Change of capital to Bednūr: In 1639 A.C. Vīrabhadra Nāyaka, transferred the seat of his government from Ikkēri[39] to Bednūr situated about 20 miles south of it. It was here that the dynasty ruled till the end of its hegemony. Ikkēri though a great place full of fortifications was not quite strong. So finding that this city was subject to great danger when attacked, the city of Bednūr was chosen, possibly under the guidance of Śivappa Nāyaka, who was a rare military genius. Bednūr was originally called Biduruhaḷḷi meaning Bamboo village. In due course it grew up into a great city. Its situation was favourable for trade as many important trade routes, connecting the city of Mangalore and the ghats converged there. The greatest advantage of this city was

37. *Extract from Courteen Papers* (Ms. Rawl.) A. 299, Fols. 188-189 in Peter Mundy, *Travels*, III, p. 92. For details see Appendix A, No. 4.

38. Peter Mundy, *Travels*, III, p. 93.

39. Mac. Coll., *Ikkēri Araśugala Vamśāvali*, 18-15-15. Peter Mundy describes the place as follows: "The town or citty of Icaree is very greatt, with many spatious streetes, bazares, etts places. The houses generally are of tempered morter, low, with one floore, commonly striped on the outside. White and red as hanguings are painted with as in Drincking houses. There are several great tanckes."

its strategic and natural fortification. It was surrounded by a number of wood hills and fortified defiles.[40]

In spite of his active martial policy, Vīrabhadra paid a good deal of attention to administration. He was ably assisted in it by his cousin Śivappa Nāyaka. Vīrabhadra was also helped by an able minister Rāmakṛṣṇa. This *mantri* must have been in high favour with his master, for he figures in several inscriptions of the Nāyaka.[41] In an inscription of Vīrabhadra he is described a "good minister, bearer of the burden of his master's affairs, versed in the Vēdas, Śastras and fine arts, skilled in royal policy, a treasury of six qualities, adorned with the three powers of increase, of the Vāsiṣṭha *gōtra,* Āśvalāyana *sūtra* and Bahuvṛica *pravara,* learned, a brother to the wives of others, great grandson of Nārāyaṇa Prabhu, grandson of the Mantri Rāmakṛṣṇa and son of Mantri Purushōttama." King Vīrabhadra being pleased with the virtuous qualities of his *mantri* like Bṛhaspati with those of Śukra, made to him a grant in the Āraga maṇḍala.[42] Vīrabhadra Nāyaka paid good attention to the welfare of his subjects. He protected the civic rights and privileges enjoyed by the merchants, śeṭṭis, and traders as also the merchant guilds of Bidure, from encroachment by royal officers or by outsiders.[43] In recognition of the services rendered to the palace, Vīrabhadra granted some wet land in the village Malave in the Keladi śīme as *umbali* to a Nilaya's son, Malla of the fisherman caste.[44]

Vīrabhadra Nāyaka's patronage to religion, learning and arts: Vīrabhadra Nāyaka's liberal grants and donations to religious institutions are testified to by many of his inscriptions. An inscription describes him as "skilled in minute researches into the essence of religion, desirous of establishing the Advaita philosophy of the pure Vēdas, possessor of the title Yādava followed by the word Murāri, servant of gods, cows and Brahmins, a head jewel of the faith in Śiva.

40. Buchanan—*Journey Thro' Madras* etc., III, p. 261.
41. *E.C.*, VIII, Tl. 3, 4; *EC.*, VII, Sh. 2.
42. *EC.*, VII, Sh. 2.
43. *ARSIE.*, C.P. No. 8 of 1940-41.
44. *MAR.*, No. 62 of 1928.

The lotus hand of the king Vīrabhadra glitters with water from the tree of the merit nourished by the libations of his gifts. The lotus eyes of the wives of his proud enemies water the tree, his arm of valour and cause it doubly glitter. Seeing the streams poured out with his gifts to Brahmans by the king Vīrabhadra Nāyaka, saying 'I shall be exhausted', the pure water ocean established itself at the farthest point."[45]

To the temple of god Madhuliṅga at Bankāsana, Vīrabhadra granted the village of Bankāsana in Telugade śīme belonging to the Gutti Venthe, on the occasion of his visit to the shrine for worship.[46] The temple at Ratnapurapēṭhe of god Veṅkaṭēśvara was the recipient of a gift of land assessed at 2 *varāha* 5 *haṇa* in order that the authorities of the temple might plant cocoanut and arecanut and thereby increase the income and apply the funds to the service of the god.[47] The village Hotlasaruhina, in Brāhmaṇavāda of Mantalasāle śīme rated at 51 *varāhas* 8 *haṇa* 1 *aḍḍa* was given to Basavalingadēva of the upper cave of Śivagange.[48] Vīrabhadra seems to have founded an *agrahāra* on the banks of the confluence of the Carmavatī and Haridrāvatī rivers. It was called Vīrabhadrapura, probably after his own name. He granted lands in the Mayikoṇḍanakoppa in Pattuguppe for the maintenance of the Brahmans residing there as also for the worship of gods Vīrabhadrēśvara, Hanumān and Vināyaka, setting out the details of expenses to be incurred in the temples.[49] For the service of the god Bhairavadēva on the embankment of the Ikkēri tank, he granted specified wet fields in a number of villages around Keladi.[50] To the Mailhara temple at Ikkēri, Vīrabhadra granted land rated at 12 *varāhas* in the Yelegale village.[51] For the temple expenses of gods Lakṣmīnarasimha and Saccidānandēśvara at Tīrthahaḷḷi, an estate yielding 80 *vārāhas* in Madhuvankanāḍ was granted

45. *EC.*, VII, Sh. 2.
46. *EC.*, VIII, Sb. 451.
47. *Ibid.*, Sagar 157.
48. *Ibid.*, Tl. 58.
49. *MAR.*, 1923, No. 110.
50. *Ibid.*, No. 73.
51. *EC.*, VII, Honnali 83.

with all rights.[52] To the Acyutēśvara temple at Kovade in Mālūr śīme were granted 2½ *vṛttis* of land.[53] Finally for the maintenance of daily offering and worship in the temple of the family deity Mūkāmbikā of Kollūru, Vīrabhadra Nāyaka set apart annual incomes from specified sources in a few villages amounting to 1002 *varāhas* and the income from 9 villages.[54] He further seems to have erected the temples of Tryambakēśa, Vīrabhadra and Gōpālakṛṣṇa in the Trayambakapura agrahāra.[55]

Vīrabhadra was equally liberal in his patronage of other religious institutions like *maṭhas.* He continued the traditional reverence for the Śṛṅgēri maṭha. Saccidānanda Bhāratī was the *guru* of the Śṛṅgēri maṭha during his time. Vīrabhadra granted lands in the village of Candiśetti Koppa in Pattuguppe śime and remitted the local customs duties (*sthala śunka*) on arecanut and pepper grown in the village on the occasion of his visit to the *maṭha.*[56] A complaint seems to have been made to Vīrabhadra Nāyaka by the Śṛṅgēri authorities about one Tirthahaḷḷi Oḍeyār using unauthorised insignia. He readily enquired into the complaint and redressed their grievances.[57]

Vīrabhadra was also munificient to institutions propagating faiths other than Viraśaivism which shows his tolerance of other faiths. To the *maṭha* of the Yeradu daṇḍa Siddhalingadēva's disciple, the Mahantadēva of Ikkēri Hosapetha, he granted the Malare village in the Śūdravāḍa of the Hosaguṇḍa śīme, rated at 200 *varāhas.*[58] To the Mahattu maṭha at Akkipeṭhe of the Keladi śīme, the Haragopa village rated at 61 *varāhas* 4 *huṇa* and 1 *haga* was granted.[59] The Hadarikoppa village was gifted by Vīrabhadra to Cenna Vīradēva and Cennabasavarājadēva, heads of the Mahattina maṭha in

52. *EC.*, VIII, Tl. 3.
53. *MAR.*, 1944, No. 47.
54. *ARSIE.*, C.P. Nos. 3, 4, 6 and 6 A of 1927-28.
55. *EC.*, VII, Sh. 2.
56. *MAR.*, No. 28 of 1933.
57. *MAR.*, 1916, p. 65.
58. *EC.*, VII, Tl. 94.
59. *Ibid.*, Tl. 181.

Sāgar.[60] His sense of religious tolerance is amply borne out by his gift of land as *ubhayam* for 12 *varāhas* in the Yedehaḷḷi village for the religious service in the Muslim mosque built at Tavaregere pond of Malalagopa in the Ānandapura śīme.[61] Vīrabhadra Nāyaka seems to have been a patron of arts and letters. Music received good encouragement at his hands. In 1641 A.C. he granted land from Raghodu village rated at 50 *varāha* to a musician named Śūraṇṇa hailing from Kollūru.[62]

Domestic life: Vīrabhadra was married to Kollūrammāji, daughter of one Revaṇṇa Oḍeyār.[63] But unfortunately he had no issue.

Thus after an eventful rule of sixteen years, Vīrabhadra Nāyaka finding that he had no issue and getting disgusted with the pleasures of the kingdom, abdicated in favour of his uncles Śivappa Nāyaka and his brother Venkaṭappa. He realised the vanity of human happiness and entrusted the kingdom in 1645 A.C. to Śivappa Nāyaka and had his coronation performed. On the death of Vīrabhadra Nāyaka his consort Kollūrammāji committed *sati*.[64]

60. *MAR.*, 1923, No. 93. Various other *maṭhas* were recipients of gifts from Vīrabhadra:
 (a) Mahattu maṭha in Kerekoppa, (*EC.*, VIII, Tl. 84).
 (b) Viraktha maṭha in Cainkaṭṭe (*EC.*, VII, Hn. 82).
 (c) *maṭha* in Danivāse śīme (*EC.*, VIII, Tl. 165).
 (d) *maṭha* in Chakkod (*EC.*, VIII, Tl. 43).
 (e) *maṭha* in Basrūr (*EC.*, VIII, Tl. 88).
 (f) Malali maṭha (*EC.*, VIII, Tl., 101).
 (g) Bhuvanagiri *maṭha* (*EC.*, VIII, Tl. 42 and 49).
 (h) Mandalli *maṭha* (*MAR.*, No. 37 of 1943).
 (i) *maṭha* in the name of Siddammaji (*EC.*, VIII, Tl. 63)
 (j) Ālūr Puraṇa Śetti's *maṭha* (*EC.*, VIII, Tl. 41).
 (k) Siddalinganna's *maṭha* (*EC.*, VIII, Tl. 54).
 and
 (l) Cannamalla Śetti's maṭha (*EC.*, VIII, Tl. 40), etc.

61. *EC.*, VIII, Sagar 108.

62. *EC.*, VIII, Tl. 182.

63. *Ibid.*, Tl. 62.

64. *KNV.*, VI.

CHAPTER VIII

ŚIVAPPA NĀYAKA (1645—1660)

The inscriptions of Śivappa Nāyaka range in dates from 1652 A.C.[1] to 1660 A.C.[2] According to the *Keladinṛpavijayam* he ruled from 1645 A.C. to 1660 A.C.[3] As the latest known date of his predecessor, Vīrabhadra Nāyaka is 1645 A.C., there does not seem to be any difficulty in accepting the period given to him by the Kannaḍa work.

The *Cikkadēva Rāya Vamśāvali* states that Śivappa Nāyaka ascended the throne after murdering Vīrabhadra Nāyaka.[4] This is the only source which stigmatises him with this dastardly act. But one is at a loss to understand how Lingaṇṇa Kavi, the author of the *Keladinṛpavijayam*, who records that Rāmarāja Nāyaka was the murderer of his uncle Cikka Śankaṇṇa Nāyaka, is silent about this if Śivappa had been guilty of such a ghastly crime. As has been seen earlier, he and his nephew Vīrabhadra Nāyaka were closely related and Śivappa Nāyaka had actually helped Vīrabhadra to maintain himself on the Ikkēri throne. In fact he was the chief power behind Vīrabhadra, and as such, he could not have been an usurper. The *Śīvatattvaratnākara* clearly mentions that Śivappa Nāyaka was crowned.[5] Hence one cannot readily rely on the *Cikkadēva Rāya Vaṁśāvali,* in the absence of further reliable evidence.

1. *EC.*, VI, Sr. 11; *MAR.*, 1925, No. 35.
2. *EC.*, VIII, Tl. 81.
3. *KNV.*, VII; the following are the other dates assigned to Śivappa Nāyaka.

Sewell—1649-1671. (*List of Inscriptions in Southern India*, Vol. II, p. 177).

Rice—1645-1660 (*EC.*, VII, p. 43).

Naraharayya—1645-1660 (*QJMS.*, XXII, p. 79).

Mackenzie—1646-1661 (Rājāvamśavali, 18-15-15).

4. Cikkadēvarājavamśāvali; 190, [Karṇāṭaka-Kāvyamañjari Series, No. 13, Mysore, 1896].
5. *STR.*, VI, 17.

Śivappa Nāyaka was the most distinguished among the Nāyak rulers of Ikkēri, and during his reign the glories of his dynasty reached their climax. He had to his advantage the good experience gained by his strenuous and long administration when he aided and guided his nephew Vīrabhadra Nāyaka on the Ikkēri throne; and when he himself succeeded to it, he ruled over the kingdom with great energy and ease keeping under control all the minor chiefs in it. His power and influence were so great that he was able to give shelter even to the fugitive Vijayanagar emperor Śrī Raṅga III.

Śivappa Nāyaka and the Vijayanagar Emperor: The political condition in South India since the accession of Śrī Raṅga III to the Vijayanagar throne was rather confused. The dominions of Śrī Raṅga were hemmed in by the invading armies of Bījāpur and Golkonda in the west and east. By 1644 A.C., he was able to beat an invasion from Golkonda[6] and he ruled from Penukoṇḍa, his recognised capital till about 1649 A.C. In the far south Tirumala Nāyaka of Madurai had been showing signs of severance from the empire and asserting his independence and the Nāyaks of Jiñji and Tañjore were displaying the same tendency. The Bījāpur forces, also directed their attention to invading the western portions of Śrī Raṅga's kingdom as they could not extend their influence beyond the Bangalore and Tumkur districts in Mysore. After the battle of Turuvekere in 1646-47 A.C., Mustafa Khān, the Bījāpur general marched through Śivaganga against Śrī Raṅga's kingdom. Pressed from all sides, Śrī Raṅga negotiated with the Muslim invader in order to dissuade him from invading his territories. But almost simultaneously the Nāyakas of Madurai, Jiñji and Tanjore had sent their envoys to Mustafa Khān tendering their submission to Bījāpur. Śrī Raṅga is said to have set out with his army consisting of 12,000 cavalry and 3 lakhs of infantry against these feudatories who continued to be rebellious. After a protracted and treacherous diplomacy in which Śrī Raṅga's envoy Venkayya Sōmayāji is said to have at first

6. Macleod: *De Oost Indische Compagnie*, II, pp. 180-82. Foster: *English Factories in India*, (1641-45) pp. 115-116.

undertaken to induce Śrī Raṅga to withdraw from the field but subsequently asked him to prepare for war, Mustafa Khān took Kṛṣṇagiri, Vīrabhadrana-durga and Dēva Durga all belonging to Śrī Raṅga. In February 1647 A.C. he finally reached Vellore.

Meanwhile the Golkonda forces under Mir Jumla also proceeded towards Vellore. The Bījāpur and Golkonda generals agreed that Śrī Raṅga's territories and treasures were to be taken and divided between them. In February 1647 A.C. Vellore was besieged and taken from Śrī Raṅga, after a protracted battle by the combined forces of Bījāpur and Golkonda. To raise money for fighting this battle Śrī Raṅga seems to have taken the jewels of the women of Vellore and money from the temple of Tirupati.[7]

In March 1647, Mustafa Khān took possession of Āmbūr, Tirupattūr, Kāvēripaṭṭanam, Hassan, Rāyadurga, Kankagiri, Ratnagiri, Mēlagiri, Arjunkōṭe and Dhulikōṭe all of which belonged to Śrī Raṅga. In November 1648 A.C., Mustafa Khān died and was succeeded by Khān Muhammad (Khani-i-Khanan). Khān Muhammad captured the impregnable fort of Jiñji from Śrī Raṅga. The capture of Jiñji was followed by the submission of the Nāyaks of Madurai and Tanjore to the Muslims. During those organised invasions and conquests by Bījāpur and Golkonda, Śrī Raṅga depended on the shifting and dangerous alliances of his southern feudatories (the Nāyakas of Madurai, Jiñji and Tanjore) and had taken refuge with them and spent some time in the midst of festivities, feasts and pleasures.[8] Neglected again by the Nāyakas and abandoned by his courtiers, Śrī Raṅga now became a king without a kingdom. However he resolved to go to Mysore, and see what little fortune was still in store for him.[9]

Śrī Raṅga received warm treatment at the hands of the Mysore ruler Kaṇṭhirava Narasarāja Woḍeyār. Between

7. Macleod: *De Oost Indische Compagnie,* II, pp. 396, 398.

8. Macleod: *De Oost Indische Compagnie,* II, p. 403.

9. *Ibid.,* p. 405. For general references for details of Śrī Ranga's viscissitudes see *Muhammadnāmāh,* in Modern Review, July 1929, pp. 10-12; *La Mission Du Madura*—Proenza to Nickel cited in R. Sathyanatha Ayyar: *The Nayaks of Madura,* pp. 264-66.

1650-1652 A.C. encouraged by the good reception he had from the ruler of Mysore, he tried to recover his kingdom.[10] He reconquered a part of his lost territories. In 1652 A.C., Bījāpur and Golkonda continued the war in the Karṇātak strenuously. Khān Muhammad laid siege to Penukoṇḍa and took it in March 1653 A.C.[11] Mīr Jumla, the Golkonda general, alarmed at the striking success of the Bījāpur troops made overtures to Śrī Raṅga. Towards the close of 1653 Khān Muhammad marched against Vellore. Śrī Raṅga relying on Mīr Jumla's false promises of aid, left Mysore for Vellore, hoping to drive out the Bījāpuris. Khān Muhammad after a protracted siege captured Vellore in 1654 A.C. and concluded a treaty with Śrī Raṅga, according to the terms of which Candragiri was given to Śrī Raṅga with revenues of certain districts.[12]

The wars of Bījāpur and Golkonda in the Karṇātak were over by 1654 and they even accomplished the division of their new gains in 1656.[13] In the very year of the division of these conquests Muhammad Ādil Shāh of Bījāpur died. Simultaneously Abdulla Qutb Shah of Golkonda had to return to his capital due to a Mughul invasion. Bījāpur and Golkonda were much engrossed in their death struggle against Aurangzeb (the Mughal viceroy of the Deccan). So unable to look after their conquered territories in the South, they had to depend on the local governors. This no doubt proved to be an advantage to the powers in the Karṇātak. In particular Śivappa Nāyaka of Ikkēri succeeded in acquiring Vasudhare, Śakkarepaṭṇa and other places from Bījāpur.

About 1656 A.C., Śrī Raṅga was again betrayed by his vassals (the Nāyaks of Madurai, Tanjore and Jiñji) and was obliged to seek refuge on the confines of his kingdom in the forests where he led a miserable life. But there was one loyal feudatory of his, Śivappa Nāyaka of Ikkēri who boldly

10. Proenza's Letter, in *The Nayaks of Madura*, p. 267.

11. Hague transcripts cited in Foster, *English Factories in India*, (1651-54), Intro. pp. XXV-XXXIII.

12. Foster: *English Factories in India,* 1651-54, Introduction, p. XXIII; *Muhammadnāmāh*, in Modern Review, November 1929, p. 502.

13. Orme: *Historical Fragments*, p. 62.

stood up and offered protection and asylum to the refugee monarch. Between 1656 A.C. and 1659 Śrī Raṅga appears to have stayed at Bednūr[14] after his sojourn at Mysore. Śivappa Nāyaka also seems to have given Śrī Raṅga the governments of Śakkarepaṭṇa, and Vasudhare.[15]

The *Śivatattvaratnākara* gives some details of the expeditions of Śivappa Nāyaka on behalf of Śrī Raṅga. Hearing that the Emperor had been driven out of Vēlāpura, Śivappa Nāyaka, marched to Vēlāpura and encamped near the fort, constructed defences around and blockaded it. He soon reduced it to submission slaying large numbers of the enemy.[16] Śrī Raṅga honoured Śivappa with titles like *Rāmabāṇa Paravāraṇavāraṇa* and presents including a costly ear ornament, the emblems of the conch and the discus, an umbrella called *Jagajhampa* (literally World leap)[17] all of which Śivappa gratefully received at the hands of his overlord, though reduced by his misfortunes to a mere nominal overlordship. The incident narrated above refers to obviously the siege of Bēlūr in the Hassan district as Vēlāpura of the text in the *Śivatattvaratnākara* is only the Sanskritised form of Bēlūr and not 'Vellore' in the North Arcot District of the Madras State as has been identified by scholars like S. K. Aiyangar,[18] R. Sathyanatha Ayyar,[19] N. Lakshminarayan Rao,[20] V. Vriddhagirisan[21] and C. S. Srinivasachari.[22] The old

14. *Cikkadēvarāyavamśāvali*, p. 191; *KNV.*, VII. From these texts it is obvious that Śrī Ranga's stay at Bednūr was for 3 years (1656-59) as he was established at Bēlūr and Hassan by Śivappa in 1659. His period of exile has therefore to be pushed back to 1654-1656 in the light of the Hague Transcripts and Proenza's letter cited above, Cf. Wilks (I, p. 79) placing Śrī Ranga's flight to Bednūr in 1646; Rice (*Mys. Gaz.*, I, p. 356) in 1644; R. Sathyanatha Ayyar (in *Nāyaks of Madura*, pp. 132) after 1653; S. K. Aiyangar (in *Nāyaks of Madura*, pp. 133-134 fn. 60) after 1665, all these require revision.

15. *KNV.*, VII

16. *STR.*, VII, 14.

17. *KNV.*, VIII; *Cikkadēvarāyavamśāvali*, 191; *STR.*, VII, 14.

18. *Sources of Vijayanagar History*, p. 347.

19. *The Nayaks of Madura*, p. 133 fn.

20. *Vij. Sex. Com.* Vol., p. 264.

21. *The Nayaks of Tanjore*, p. 136.

22. *The History of Gingee and its rulers*, p. 173.

name for Bēlūr as occurring in inscriptions is Vēlāpura.[23] Vellore had been twice lost by Śrī Raṅga in 1647 A.C. and 1654 and it was too distant for Śivappa Nāyaka to recover. Bēlūr was also in the possession of Bījāpur since 1640 and on account of its proximity to his own kingdom it was in the fitness of things that Śivappa Nāyaka should recover it for Śrī Raṅga, as an ostensibly loyal feudatory of his. It was, however, not so easy to take the place, for Kṛṣṇappa Nāyaka of Bēlūr and Arkalgud opposed Śīvappa Nāyaka at the head of a vast army.[24] Further Kaṇṭhīrava Narasa Rāja Woḍeyār (A.C. 1638-1659) of Mysore substantially assisted his feudatory Kṛṣṇappa Nāyaka against Śivappa Nāyaka. Śivappa, however, succeeded in thoroughly defeating Kṛṣṇappa Nāyaka in battle and took his son Venkaṭādri Nāyaka, prisoner. This conquest was of far-reaching importance as it restricted the sphere of influence of Mysore up to Bēlūr in the north-west. It also resulted in improving the position of Śrī Raṅga. By 1659 A.C., Śivappa Nāyaka seems to have established Śrī Raṅga at Hassan and Bēlūr, as borne out by inscriptions dated 1659 A.C., which refer to Śrī Raṅga's rûle at Bēlūr.[25] Although according to the *Keladinṛpavijayam* and the *Śivatattvaratnākara,* it was sheer loyalty to the Empire which prompted Śivappa Nāyaka to espouse the cause of Śrī Raṅga, his real motive could have also been self interest. Indeed, by courting the support of the Emperor Śrī Raṅga and by attempting to revive his power and influence, Śivappa Nāyaka evidently hoped not only to re-establish Śrī Raṅga in his suzerainty but also to retaliate and carry on his aggression against Mysore.

Śivappa Nāyaka's relations with Mysore: According to the *Cikkadēvarāyavamśāvali,* Śivappa Nāyaka seems to have proceeded on an expedition to Seringapatam in the early half of 1659 A.C.[26] This expedition is dated in Vikāri (1659 A.C.)

23. See *EC.*, V, Bl. 3, 14, 56, 58 etc.
24. *KNV.*, VII.
25. *EC.*, V., Bl. 81, 82.
26. C. Hayavadanarao: *History of Mysore* (1399-1799) Vol. I, p. 215 and n.

in the *Keladinṛpavijayam*.[27] The event is further said to have taken place in the very year of the accession of Dēvaraja Woḍeyār (1659) and during the period of office of Daḷavāi Hamparājaiya. It may be tentatively fixed between September 1659 and January 1660. S. K. Aiyangar[28] and R. Sathyanatha Ayyar[29] do not take into consideration the contemporaniety of the rulers of Mysore and Bednūr and place the event in the latter part of Devarāja's reign or early in the reign of Cikkadēvarāja. But there is no evidence for that. In furtherance of his own ambition, Śivappa Nāyaka strengthened himself by reinforcing his army by quotas drawn from the Palegars of Sōḍe, Biligi, Tarikere, Harpanahaḷḷi, Cintanakal, Maddagiri and Giduga and by the levies raised by the chiefs of Tulu, Konkaṇa, Koḍagu and Malayāḷa.[30] He then started on his march to Seringapatam, encamped in the neighbourhood of Grāma[31] on his way to the place. Dēvarāja Woḍeyār (1659-1673) of Mysore despatched a large force under Daḷavāi Hamparājaiya. In the battle which followed, Śivappa Nāyaka won a brilliant victory, capturing Hamparājaiya besides sixteen officers, several warriors, elephants and horses belonging to Mysore. He is also said to have taken possession of Grāma.[32]

Accompanied by Lakṣmappa Nāyaka of Hole Narasipur and other Palegars, Śivappa then marched against Seringapatam itself.[33] Bridging up the Kāvērī he crossed the river and encamping near the fort started a regular blockade of the place in October 1659.[34] Meanwhile the authorities in

27. *KNV.*, VII.
28. *Ancient India*, p. 297; *Sources of Vijayanagar History* p. 21
29. *The Nayaks of Madura*, p. 172.
30. *Cikkadēvarāyavamśāvali*, 191, *KNV.*, VIII. See also *Rājāvalikathe*, XII, 476, cited in C. Hayavadanarao—*History of Mysore*, Vol. I, p. 216 n.
31. Grāma is an extant village, the headquarters of a hobaḷi of that name in Hasan taluk.
32. *KNV.*, VII.
33. *The Annals of the Mysore Royal Family*, I, 98; *Mysore Rājāra Caritre*, 25; *Cikkadēvarāyavijayam*, V. 18-19 cited in Hayavadanarao, *op. cit.*, p. 251 n.
34. *KNV.*, VII.

Seringapatam, helpless and unable to withstand the attack, seem to have sought the support of a Bījāpur contingent under Bahlul Khān.[35] Śivappa who had recourse to a diplomatic move made him retire and was about to take the fort. At this juncture according to the *Keladinṛpavijayam* the besieged disheartened, won over by bribe, the officers and agents of Śivappa Nāyaka and had recourse to certain magical rites and ceremonies[36] in consequence of which Śivappa became indisposed. Finding that it was not wise to prolong his stay in the enemies' country, Śivappa raised the siege of Seringapatam and retraced his steps to Bednūr. This retirement however was attended with disastrous results. Dēvarāja Woḍeyār, assisted by the inhabitants of Seringapatam, pursued the retreating enemy and while doing so laid waste Lakṣmappa Nāyaka's territories. Daḷavāi Hamparājaiya meanwhile recovered his lost ground, joined in the pursuit and returned to Seringapatam with considerable spoil.[37] It is stated in the Mysore Archaeological Report for the year 1942 (p. 88) that Śivappa Nāyaka who seiged Seringapatam was defeated by Daḷavai Komarayya, without citing any evidence. The name of Daḷavai Komarayya does not figure in any other source and hence it is doubtful whether Komarayya took part in the campaign. Thus Śivappa Nāyaka's attempt on Seringapatam was foiled mainly due to the treachery and morale of his own men. The relations between Mysore and Ikkēri were thoroughly embittered.

Śivappa Nāyaka and Bījāpur: Bījāpūr and Bednūr were the two powers in the Deccan during the period, having ambitious designs of expansion. Mirjee, a Bījāpur fort, fell into the hands of Śivappa Nāyaka. Sunda, a tributary of Bijāpur was also siezed by Śivappa Nāyaka. Shortly after

35. *Ibid.* The power of Bījāpur in the Karnātak being on the wane about this time it is not unlikely that its generals took part in the local politics espousing the cause of one power against another.

36. *KNV.*, VII. Wilks (*Mysore*, I, p. 69) also refers to the employment of bribery in inducing the Ikkēri army to raise the siege.

37. Chaudapadada Pustaka, fol. V, 7 cited in C. Hayavadanarao, *op. cit.*, p. 218 n.i. *Cikkadēvarāyavijayam* V, 20-24; Mysuru Rajara caritre, *op. cit.*, also Wilks—*op. cit.*

the death of Muhammad Ādil Shāh of Bījāpur, Śivappa systematically carried on his aggressions taking the forts of Ikkēri, Soraba, Udugani, Mahādēvapura and Ambaligolla which had evidently been taken by the Bījāpur Sultan in an earlier expedition.[38]

Minor expeditions of Śivappa Nāyaka: The minor expeditions of Śivappa Nāyaka are passed over by the *Śivatattvaratnākara.* But the *Keladinṛpavijayam* contains some details about them. Śivappa seems to have taken Alave, Katti Kiluru and repaired the forts of Bekala, Cittri, and Candragiri.[39] He is further stated to have taken Nileśvar and erected a pillar of victory there. This expedition brought him into contact with the Kōlattiri family of Malabar. The *Śivatattvaratnākara* says that he built several forts in Keraḷa.[40] He brought under his control the countries of Śivase, Herūr, Karvūr, Biligi,[41] Ayavū,[42] Harnali, Banavāsi and Bodonagaḍa but returned the fort of Śivase to Mahuralinga Nāyaka, its commander. He subjugated queen Annāji of Sōḍe also. Śivappa then took Tarikere and slew its chief Tareguppa Nāyaka. He took Savancir and let it to *Hanavu,* for a fixed quantity of revenue in butter and milk. Timmappa Araśu of Belagutti was also defeated.[43] Śivappa also conquered the territories of the Chautas during Cannammādēvi Chauta's reign and demanded a payment of 3000 *varāhas* per year as tribute.[44] Thus his conquests were wide; and an inscription describes Śivappa Nāyaka as ruling over

38. *KNV.*, VII. As a result of the mistakes in the reports of the English Factory records, the death of Śivappa Nāyaka is placed in 1663 A.C., and many facts that ought to go under his successor's rule have been introduced in his reign. This has led Sarkar to place the invasion of Ādil Shāh on Ikkēri in 1663 during Śivappa's reign. (Sarkar: *Sivaji,* pp. 268-69).

39. *KNV.*, VII.

40. *STR.*, VII, 14.

41. *Mac. Coll.*, 18-15-7, 23-1-48.

42. *Ibid.*

43. *QJMS.*, XII, p. 48.

44. *Mac. Coll.*, 18-15-6.

Āraga, Gutti, Bārakūru Mangaḷūru and other places, his kingdom stretching to the Western ocean.[45]

Śivappa Nāyaka and the Portuguese: Śivappa Nāyaka's expansion wars brought him into conflict with the Portuguese along the coast from Bhatkal to Mangalore. All the Portuguese forts were in a very bad condition, except the fort of Cambolim. The Portuguese had frittered away the best opportunities to befriend the ruler and they fell victims to the wrath of Śivappa Nāyaka and he had little difficulty in driving away these 'Parangis'. The Portuguese did not realise that the destinies of Bednūr were guided by a man of ability, who had mapped out a policy to free his kingdom from any outside influence. They clung steadfast to their old tactics till they found themselves dislodged from Kanara.

Soon after his accession, Śivappa Nāyaka sent an ambassador to Goa to discuss with the Portuguese Viceroy the question of dismantling the fort of Barcelor. The Portuguese, however, wanted that the whole island of Cambolim should be handed over to them if the fortress of Barcelor was to be dismantled and evaded the various other issues[46] raised by Śivappa.

In 1649 Śivappa Nāyaka went on a cruise along the sea coast. This caused greaty anxiety to the Portuguese captain Dom Luces de Souza, who was in charge of the northern fleet at Barcelor and who was instructed by the authorities to make proper arrangements for its defence in case Śivappa Nāyaka was on a voyage and made an onslaught on it.[47]

45. *EC.*, VI, Sg. 11. The relevant portion of the inscription reads:

"केलदीनगराधीशः श्रीमानासीत् सदाशिवः ।
महीपालस्तत्प्रपौत्रः श्रीमान् केलदीवल्लभः ॥
शिवप्पनायकोगुत्ति मंगळूरारमादिकाम् ।
भुवं पश्चिमवार्ध्यन्तं परिरक्षति धर्म्मतः ॥

46. *Instrucoes*, No. 3, 1641-47, Fols. 113-114. For the text of the letter see Appendix A No. 5.

47. *Instrucoes*, No. 3, 1641-47, Fols. 113-114. The instructions were as follows: "You shall start with all vessels of your company and go up the river Sal where you shall find some parangues and units of the

On 1st May 1649 A.C., Antonio Borges da Costa, was ordered to proceed to Bednūr with an elephant as present to Śivappa Nāyaka. The Portuguese further seem to have been anxious to conclude a treaty with Śivappa and also buy the chilleys from his countries.[48] In the earlier half of 1651 Śivappa Nāyaka was particular about having them as his friends, due to the depredations of the Nairs in his territory extending up to Kāsargode. He sent an ambassador to Goa asking for help against the Moors of Malabar, which the Portuguese were willing to give so long as it was not against their ally the Rājā of Cannanore. Fr. Correa was sent along with Śivappa's ambassador to discuss things pertaining to the State and about pepper. He was instructed to take only 200 candies of pepper at the price of 25 *pagodas* per *candy*.[49]

In 1652, the Portuguese fortified Mangalore against Śivappa Nāyaka's wishes. The Nāyaka was shrewd enough to anticipate a clash and so even before the Portuguese sent an embassy to him he declared war against them. On 14th June 1652, the fort of Cambolim was attacked. The attention of the Portuguese was diverted by an attack on Barcelor which was wrenched from their hands with little difficulty. The attack on Mangalore was quick and decisive. The Bednūr troops overpowered the enemy by resorting to methods of mine warfare and breaking up the walls. In spite of reinforcements sent, the Portuguese were not able to cope up with the situation as is evidenced by a letter of the Portuguese Viceroy to the king.[50]

Śivappa Nāyaka concentrated his forces on Cambolim with reinforcements amounting to 80,000 men and ten pieces of artillery and began a regular siege of the place. The war

fleet to whom you shall entrust the guard of the forts of Onor and Barcellor and as I am told that king Sivappa Naique is on voyage, you shall remain in the same fortress of Barcellor till you know with certainty that he goes down with any ruin intended against our forts or go forward in order you may be able to help where necessary."

48. *Instrucoes*: 1647, Folio (none).

49. *Instrucoes*: No. 4, 1647, Fol. 42. For details of Instructions see Appendix A, No. 6.

50. Moncões do Reino, No. 23, Anno de 1653, Fol. 395. For details of the letter see Appendix A. No. 7.

was in full swing and every soldier and mariner that Goa could spare was rushed to the theatre of war. During the siege a Portuguese fleet arrived to relieve Cambolim. After some time another fleet was sighted. By January 1653, a third fleet also arrived. But all these were forced to retire by the thick offensive launched by Śivappa Nāyaka. The Portuguese had to withdraw their vessels. Seventy of the Portuguese were killed, and they withdrew taking with them all they could carry and leaving the fort dismantled.

It may be said to the credit of Śivappa Nāyaka that in spite of the cover given by the guns of the Portuguese fleet, and the isolation of the fort from the mainland, he was able to achieve one of the most spectacular victories in the fort. It speaks of the efficiency of his army whose strength according to Leonardo Paes, amounted to forty to fifty thousand men.[51] The letter of the Portuguese Viceroy at Goa to His Majesty the king of Portugal is descriptive of the efforts made by the Portuguese and the strength of the attack made by Śivappa Nāyaka.[52]

The only fort that had not surrendered was that of Honāvar, defended by Captain Francisco de Souza. It was besieged by Śivappa Nāyaka and the Portuguese were forced to sue for peace. In February 1653, Fr. Gonzalo Martin was entrusted with the mission of making peace[53] and his representations are referred to in a letter of the Viceroy to Diogo de Salazar, Captain General of Kanara, dated 6th March 1654, which speaks of this proposed peace with Śivappa Nāyaka.[54] But the negotiations fell through as the Portuguese did not agree regarding the quantity of pepper to be taken. Meanwhile Śivappa Nāyaka detained some Portuguese personnel as there was a complaint of ill-treatment of Hindus under him by Piexote de Silva, Captain of Barcelor.[55]

51. Rice: *Mysore and Coorg,* p. 159.

52. *Notions of the Reign,* No. 22, Year 1652, Fol. 436. For details see Appendix A, No. 8.

53. *Instrucoes,* No. 4, 1647, Fol. 67.

54. *Ibid.,* Folios 83-84. For details see Appendix A, No. 9.

55. *Instrucoes,* No. 3, 1641-1647. Last but one folio.

Śivappa Nāyaka after defeating the minor palegars of South Kanara attacked the fort of Sao Sabastio, the Portuguese one at Mangalore and captured it. This was the only fort left to the Portuguese. In 1652, the Portuguese had to abandon it for want of garrison and ammunition.[56] This was due to the fact that the authorities at Goa were not able to send reinforcements to the various theatres. The town of Mangalore was also lost after a vigorous and disastrous fight.[57]

The Portuguese were thus crippled and Śivappa Nāyaka became the undisputed master of the coast from Mirjee to Kāsargode. The famous pepper and rice markets of the Kanara coast was left open to merchants, who paid best for it, be it the Portuguese, the Dutch, the English or the Arabs.

Śivappa Nāyaka and the English: The attempts of the English to establish regular trading stations in the west coast, after their failure at Bhatkal were few and far between. Off and on a ship touched the port and took whatever pepper it could get. In 1650 A.C., Capt. Durson came to Bhatkal on his ship the 'Loyaltly'.[58] Previously, towards the end of 1649, Capt. Durson went through a very sad experience. At Mirjee, he was imprisoned and his goods seized on the false pretext that he had tried to pass false *pagodas*.[59] As soon as the news of Durson's imprisonment reached Bednūr, Śivappa Nāyaka sent a Brahmin, Devar Shenoy, to free him and Captain Durson was freed. Later accompanied by Thomas Dey and Hugh Shore, he decided to see Śivappa Nāyaka and express their gratitude.[60]

Śivappa Nāyaka was now fully aware that as a result of his commercial policy the entire pepper trade of the coast was in his hands. He was also aware that the Kanara supplied the best rice and that sooner or later the English, the

56. Souza: *Oriente Conquistade*, III, p. 19.
57. Moraes, *Mangalore*, App. 6, p. 77, *KNV.*, VII.
58. Foster: *English Factories in India*, 1646-50, p. 203.
59. *Ibid.*, p. 306.
60. *Ibid.*, 1651-54, pp. 75-76.

Dutch or Portuguese would compete for the same, thereby fetching him a high price.

Domestic Life: Śivappa Nāyaka had two principal wives, Lingammāji[61] and Śantammāji. By the former he had a daughter named Siddammājī who was married to one Sarabhela Mallikārjunaiya. By Śantammājī he had a son Bhadrappa, who was married to Bommājī, the daughter of one Surirāya Kaḷappa.

Śivappa Nāyaka took three other wives, namely Bhadrammājī, Basavalingammājī and Nāgammājī. By Bhadrammājī, he had a daughter, and by Basavalingammājī a son named Sōmaśēkhara. Nāgammājī, however, had no issue.[62]

Śivappa Nāyaka who was an adept in *yōga* initiated his brother Venkaṭappa in it and entrusted his two sons Bhadrappa and Sōmaśēkhara to his care.

Śivappa founded an *agrahāra* called Śivarājapura, after his own name, on the bank of the river Tungabhadrā. He granted *vṛttis* to Brahmans and caused many sacrifices to be performed. He is said to have made arrangements for worshipping deities at the important shrines of Śiva and Viṣṇu from Rāmēśvara to Kāśi and provided for the feeding of Jangamas.[63] He continued the traditional patronage to Śṛngēri and other *maṭhas*.[64]

Among the ministers of Śivappa Nāyaka were Doḍḍa Tammarasayya, Gauta Basappa Dēvara, and Cauḍappayya; and among his clerks were Kanappayya Venkaṭayya,[65] and Purāṇika Appu Bhaṭṭa.[66]

61. *EC.*, VI, Sr. 4.
62. *KNV.*, VII.
63. *STR.*, VII, 14.
64. *EC.*, VI, Sr. 11, *MAR.*, 1925, No. 35.
65. *KNV.*, VII.
66. *MAR.*, 1916, p. 66 ff.

In a letter of his successor Venkaṭappa II, to the Dutch dated the 3rd January 1661, is mentioned the death of Śivappa Nāyaka.[67] Since the latest known inscription of the Nāyaka is dated 1659 it may be presumed that he could have died sometime between 1660 and 1661. He was buried with his two wives Lingammājī and Nagammājī, in the premises of the old *maṭha* at Bednūr.

67. *Batavia Dagh Register: Extracts in Journal of the Bombay Historical Society,* II, p. 248. The wrong information given in the English Factory Records, i.e., that Śivappa Nāyaka was imprisoned by the Bījāpur forces and that he was released on payment of a ransom of 7 lakhs of pagodas (Foster: *English Factories,* 1661-64, p. 237) has led Sarkar to place the conquest of Bednūr by Ādil Shāh in 1663 in Śivappa Nāyaka's reign (See Sarkar: *Sivaji,* p. 233). The Bombay Gazetteer dates it in 1670 (XV, pt. II, p. 22). All these dates are wrong. The *Keladinṛpavijayam* says that Venkaṭappa Nāyaka, the successor of Śivappa was crowned in Ś. 1583 (1661 A.C.). Further we have the more convincing evidence of the letter of Venkaṭappa Nāyaka to the Dutch cited above. From these we could date the death of Śivappa probably towards the end of 1660 A.C.

CHAPTER IX

VENKAṬAPPA NĀYAKA II (1660-1661) AND BHADRAPPA NĀYAKA (1662-1664)

On the death of Śivappa Nāyaka, his brother Venkaṭappa Nāyaka was crowned at Bednūr. His reign has however been passed over by Buchanan. But the important sources, the *Keladinṛpavijayam* and the *Śivatattvaratnākara* definitely mention his reign. Added to this, the *Batavia Dagh Register* mentions him and speaks of his relations with the Dutch. There are only two known inscriptions of this ruler, both of which are dated in Śaka 1583 (1660 A.C.).[1] Hence his period of rule seems to have been very short, and probably lasted only for a year. Details regarding his short reign are therefore meagre.

Venkaṭappa Nāyaka and the Dutch: From the beginning of the second half of the seventeenth century, the Dutch entered the race for trade along with the English and the Portuguese and directed their attention to the establishment of trading factories in the west coast of India. In 1660 a Dutch Fleet under the command of Roothaes came to Canara for pepper trade. In compliance with the orders from Joan Maetsukyar, the Viceroy of Batavia, Leen dert Leendertz, a sub-merchant proceeded to Barcelor with letters to Venkaṭappa Nāyaka and with a present of 100 nails, 140 nuts, 40 maces, and 24 red clothes. The Dutch governor Ryklof van der Dussen, had also sent his Treasurer with his yacht 'Haogelande' from Colombo, to collect from the area 1500 loads of rice for the Dutch settlement in Ceylon. This was followed by the arrival of *De Gekoonds Leeune* and *Ellurg* and the yacht *De Starre* from the same island. These ships left Barcelor for Batavia and Ceylon after securing a freight.

1. *MAR.*, 1919, p. 37; *Ibid.*, 1916, p. 17.

Venkaṭappa Nāyaka promised the Dutch to prohibit the Portuguese from buying rice on condition that the Dutch bought from Kanara all the rice available for export. He also asked them for convoys to protect their trading vessels against the pirates from Malabar. However, Leendertz, was able to contract only for 1200 loads of rice at 13 Kanarese pagodas, a price that was considered high. Venkaṭappa was on very friendly terms with the Dutch. A letter of Venkaṭappa Nāyaka to the Dutch viceroy, dated 3rd January, 1661 shows the keen interest he took in the Dutch as long as he benefited from them. The letter runs as follows:

> "I have received the letter from your Excellency and am glad to note that you have ordered Mr. Ryklof Van Goens to come to these districts to fulfil the contract closed with Leendertz, but so far he has not been able to carry out his war plan but he promises to do so afterwards. However, the two elephants which your Excellency sent me as present were not necessary considering the good friendship and unanimity that exists between us. However, since your Excellency sends them so cordially I have accepted them with pleasure. I am sending herewith a small counter present."

Bidirur 3rd January 1661. (Sd.) Venkatappa Nāyaka.[2]
Yet Venkaṭappa Nāyaka was anxious to renew his connections with the Portuguese. The Portuguese having been driven away by Śivappa Nāyaka, resorted to dislocate Kanarese trade wherever possible. Leendertz writes in his diary under date 28th December, 1660, that Bernado Coero, the Portuguese Captain, captured a ship at Barcelor which had Venkaṭappa's flag thereon. He took from it two pieces of ordnance, twenty two muskets, all the gun powder, two anchors, eight barrels of red betel, one mast, seven sailors and some cash. Some of the sailors were converted to Christianity. When this news reached Bednūr, Venkaṭappa was so annoyed at it, that he immediately detained an

2. *Batavia Dagh Register*—See Extracts in the *Journal of the Bombay Historical Society,* 1929, Vol. 2, p. 248-249.

European priest, who was on his way from Cochin to Goa. In addition, he did not return the seven war frigates of the Portuguese, captured earlier by Śivappa Nāyaka. The Portuguese represented their case through Ramaji Quothary, who wrote to Kallapa Kalve, evidently a prominent person at the Bednūr court. The priest was thereupon released. The mission of Ramaji Quothary was not, however, fully successful. He was only able to secure the release of the seven ships which could be used only as firewood. His negotiations regarding pepper did not come through as Venkaṭappa insisted that the Portuguese should buy pepper at a fixed price.

Venkaṭappa and Bījāpur: During the reign of Venkaṭappa II, the Ādil Shāh of Bījāpur made an attempt to make Bednūr a tributary state. He arranged with general Salabhat Khān to extort money from Venkaṭappa. But fortunately for Venkaṭappa, Salabhat Khān did not fulfil the wishes of the Sultan.

Venkaṭappa and Mysore: Prospects of war and counter-war between Bednūr and Mysore ever since Śivappa Nāyaka's retreat from Seringapatam, continued to be imminent. For checking any possible encroachments by the Mysore power, Venkaṭappa Nāyaka stationed on his frontiers an army under the charge of Śivalinga Nāyaka, son-in-law of Śivappa Nāyaka.[3] Just as he feared, the Mysore armies resumed hostilities against Bednūr, by laying siege and capturing the fort of Hebbale towards the close of 1661.[4] But it was left to the lot of Bhadrappa Nāyaka, the successor of Venkaṭappa Nāyaka, to retaliate by marching against Hebbale early in 1662 A.C.

End of Venkaṭappa Nāyaka's reign: Venkaṭappa Nāyaka continued the traditional patronage to *maṭhas* and other religious institutions.[5] The *Śivatattvaratnākara* says that he

3. *KNV.*, VII.
4. *Ibid.*, VII.
5. For the various institutions which received patronage see *MAR.*, 1916, p. 67; 1919, p. 37; and *EC.*, VII, Sg. 44.

ruled for some time and crowned his nephew Bhadrappa as king.[6] On his death he was buried with his wife Mallammājī in the old *maṭha* at Bednūr.[7]

Bhadrappa Nāyaka *(***1662-1664***)*: Bhadrappa Nāyaka, like his predecessor, ruled only for a short period. His earliest inscription is dated Śaka 1584 (1662 A.C.)[8] and the latest record known for him is dated Śaka 1586 (1664 A.C.).[9] But these two years were not without important events.

The earlier half of Bhadrappa Nāyaka's reign witnessed a series of reverses at the hands of the Ādil Shāh of Bījāpur. But the kingdom recovered from the blows and continued in peace. Negotiations were set on foot for maintaining good relations with the Dutch, Portuguese and the English. But there were no brilliant undertakings or spectacular achievements. The activities of the Bednūr rulers henceforth were almost to maintain the *status quo*. There were but few attempts at the expansion of the kingdom.

Bhadrappa Nāyaka and Mysore: Soon after his accession, Bhadrappa Nāyaka sent a contingent under Śivalinga Nāyaka against Mysore. Śivalinga Nāyaka marched on towards Bēlūr, where he seems to have met Emperor Śrī-Ranga; and reinforced by the forces of the latter (*Belurgaidi Rāyaram sandhisi tatsainyam verasu*), proceeded towards Hebbale, which had been attacked by the Mysore forces during Venkaṭappa Nāyaka's time, and raised the siege. Marching further, Śivalinga Nāyaka laid siege to Hole Narasipur (Narasimhapura) itself, then in the possession of Mysore. The Mysore forces however took possession of the fort of Konanur, whereupon the Bednūr army marched thither and prepared to bombard and retake the place.[10] At this juncture, Dēvarāya Woḍeyār despatched reinforcements under

6. *STR.*, VI, 15.
7. *KNV.*, VII.
8. *MAR.*, 1916, p. 67; 1919, p. 37; *EC.*, VIII, Tl. 76, 85 & 145.
9. *EC.*, VIII, Tl. 34.
10. *KNV.*, VIII, Konanur is an extant village in Arkalgud Taluk. See *List of villages in Mysore.*

his Daḷavai Kāntaiya of Kalale. In or about March 1662 A.C., Kāntaiya, encamped near the slope overlooking Kanagala.[11] In the action that followed, both sides fought desperately. At length, however, Daḷavai Kāntaiya was defeated and was forced to retreat, while at the same time, Śivalinga Nāyaka himself was struck by an arrow from the Mysore side and fell dead on the battle field.[12]

Nevertheless, Bhadrappa Nāyaka vigorously continued the war, taking possession of Honnavalli, Chikkanāyakanahaḷḷi, Kandi Kere, Budivala and other places on the outskirts of the kingdom of Mysore. Daḷavai Kāntaiya of Kalale was succeeded by Nañjanāthaiya in April 1662. Nañjanāthaiya resumed operations against Bednūr towards the close of 1662. He seems to have strenuously carried on the war, and captured the elephant named *Gangādhara* and the strong and impregnable fortresses of Hassan, and Sakrepaṭṇa with their dependencies Vastare (Vasudhare) and Honnavalli, in December 1663.[13] It was left to the successor of Bhadrappa Nāyaka, to further continue the war against Mysore

Bhadrappa Nāyaka and Bījāpur: Ādil Shāh II of Bījāpur, finding the power of his neighbour increasing, decided to march against Bednūr. The expedition was a short one. But as it was sudden Bhadrappa was unable to check the tide. The Bednūr forces had to withdraw. In alliance with the king of Sōḍe, the Ādil Shāh, sent an advance detachment under Bahlulkhān and Sanjar Khān, consisting of horses, elephants and infantry. Bhadrappa stationed himself at Bhuvanagiri. A battle was fought near Ambaligolla and the Bednūr forces were utterly routed. Bednūr itself was then besieged. The Ādil Shāh himself entered the capital. The

11. *Ibid.*, Kanagala, may probably be identified with the extant *sarvamānya* Karigalale in the Arkalgud taluk. Parts of the present district of Hassan, formed the bone of contention between Mysore and Bednūr, early in the reign of Chikkadēvarāya Woḍeyār.

12. *KNV.*, VIII.

13. *Mysura Dhoregala Pūryābhyudaya-Vivara,* II, 26. *Mac. Coll.*, No. 18-15-37, dates the acquisition in Śobhakrit, Mārgaśira Śu 13 (December 2, 1663). Also *EC.*, III, Sr. 14, ll. 39-41

general Sanjar Khān then besieged the fort of Bhuvanagiri. Bhadrappa, not disheartened by the reverses, rallied forth his forces, blocked the roads, footpaths and passes and cut the lines of communication. The Bījāpur generals had therefore to retire from the battle-field. Later however Bhadrappa sent his envoy Hūvayya to the Ādil Shāh to conclude a peace. A treaty was then signed and the Bījāpur Sultan withdrew. The *Śivatattvaratnākara*, while it omits the above details,[14] agrees with the *Keladinṛpavijayam* in the main outline. The Dutch sources however say that the indemnity was fixed at 1,50,000 *pagodas*.[15] Due to a discrepancy in the English records, all these failures have been attributed to Śivappa Nāyaka, although he had died even in 1660.[16]

Bhadrappa Nāyaka, after the sad experience of the war against Bījāpur, made up his mind to be prepared for any eventuality. So, anxious to cultivate friendship with the Dutch, he wrote to them the following letter:

> "The Happy and very wise king of Keladi writes this letter to Governor of Batavia Joan Maetsukier. This state is in want of some gun powder as your excellency is a friend of the king, we herewith request you to confirm our friendship. You kindly let us have 2000 men or 4800 lbs of gun powder; also 3 metal guns or more. And if I have the honour to receive the above next year, my minister Mallappa Maloe will give you compensation. Please do not wait, but comply with our request if possible."[17]

This letter reveals the shortage of gun powder which Bhadrappa experienced. But the Dutch were too cautious to

14. *STR.*, VIII, 2. *The Kaifiyat of Hole Honnuru* says that the Bījāpur army under Mirza Rustam, Chikka Nabikhān and Danga Kulli Khān invaded and occupied the fort of Hole Honnuru. They appointed *Subedars* for administering the fort. The first *Subedar* was Abdullā Khān. See *Mac. Coll.*, 18-15-39.
15. *Batavia Dagh Register*, 1664, p. 323.
16. See Foster: *English Factories in India*, 1661-1664, p. 237.
17. *Batavia Dagh Register*, 1663, p. 320.

be led away. They had the example of the Portuguese before them and wrote to say that they could not grant his request for guns.

Domestic Life: Bhadrappa had two wives, Bommājī, daughter of Śūrirāya Kāḷappa, and Siddammājī, sister of Gaurammā. Gaurammā was married to Māriyappa Śeṭṭi, whose son Basavappa was later adopted by Cannamājī. After a rule of just over two years Bhadrappa died.[18]

18. The English records mention that Śivappa Nāyaka's son, evidently Bhadrappa, was killed by some Brahmins. (Foster: *English Factories in India,* 1661-64, p. 343). This is confirmed by the Dutch sources that advices from Kanara mentioned that Bhadrappa Nāyaka had been poisoned. (*Batavia Dagh Register,* 1664, p. 325). But the reasons for such an unfortunate end of the Nāyaka are not known. But since there is no grant of Bhadrappa Nāyaka beyond 1664, it may be taken that he very probably died in that year.

CHAPTER X

SŌMĀŚĒKHARA NĀYAKA I (1664-1671)

Sōmaśēkhara Nāyaka was very young when his brother died. On the premature and sudden death of Bhadrappa there were a series of family feuds in the royal house of Bednūr. Mallappa Maloe, the most influential person at the Bednūr court, was then at Goa as Ambassador. The feuds at Bednūr had a bad effect on the negotiations with the Portuguese who refused to deal with any among them seriously. In the end, the court-merchant Narane Maloe was able to assert himself and make things calm and the young Sōmaśēkhara Nāyaka was under his protection. With his guidance and that of Avinahalli Narasappayya, the Bednūr government was carried on.[1]

The earliest known inscription of Sōmaśēkhara Nāyaka is dated Śaka 1586 (1664 A.C.).[2] The latest date known for him from the epigraphs is Śaka 1593 (1671 A.C.).[3] Hence his reign period may be fixed from 1664 A.C. to 1671 A.C.

Sōmaśēkhara Nāyaka and Śivāji: At the time of accession of Sōmaśēkhara, the Deccan and the whole coast of Kanara were enthralled in civil war. In this confusion the great Maratha leader Śivāji, cast his covetous eyes on Bhatkal. In 1664, he fitted out four vessels and sent them to Kanara, while he intended to go overland with an army. He raised Bārakūr by sea, and dismissed the greater part of his fleet at Gōkarṇa, scourged the country and exacted a contribution from Karwar, towards which the English factory paid £112.[4]

1. *KNV.*, Canto VIII, Foster: *English Factories in India* (1661-64), p. 349.

2. *EC.*, VIII, Tl. 92.

3. *Ibid.*, Sa. 39 the following are the dates given by others. Sewell: 1681-1686. (*List of inscriptions in Southern India,* Vol. II, p. 177). Naraharayya—1663-1677 (*QJMS.*, XXII, p. 82). Rice—1663-1671 (*EC.*, VII, p. 43). Mackenzie—1664-1672 (*Rājavamśāvali,* 18-15-15).

4. Grant Duff: *History of Marathas,* p. 91 n. Also see revised edition by S. M. Edwards, I, p. 157.

The idea behind these expeditions was merely to collect booty and Śivāji did not take possession of any territories in Kanara. After Śivāji's raid, the factory at Karwar seems to have been closed temporarily as it is mentioned to have been re-established in 1668.[5] On 8th February 1665, Śivāji with 85 brigades, appeared before Bednūr and before the Bednūr Government could mobilise any defence, he was able to collect a booty of 80,000 guilders and set sail.[6]

Sōmasēkhara and Bījāpur: After some time, Ādil Shāh II of Bījāpur marched against Sōmaśēkhara with a force of 12,000 horses. The expedition was under the charge of two generals, Sheriza Khān and Bābul Khān. Sheriza Khān was able to capture three of the best castles of Ikkēri; and the loss of the Hindus was considerable. This expedition seems to have taken place in about 1668 as an inscription from Tīrthahaḷḷi mentions five villages as paying taxes to the Turukas.[7] The reasons for this expedition are not however known. Soon after the death of Ādil Shāh II, Sōmaśēkhara Nāyaka seems to have joined hands with the Rājā of Sunda and raided the Bījāpur territory across the frontier.

Sōmaśēkhara Nāyaka and the Kōlattiri: At the southern tip of the kingdom of Sōmaśēkhara Nāyaka was Kāsargode, governed by the Nairs. At Kāsargode the Kanarese people necessarily came into contact with the Malayāḷis and with the Kōlattiri family whose territories had been founded by intermarriage with the Zamorins.[8] The Prince Regent had found it extremely difficult to effect the necessary union, among the various branches of his family; and it seems that at the express invitation of one or more of his discontented relatives, Sōmaśēkhara Nāyaka pushed his forces across the Malayāḷa frontier. Prince Rameltiry, who was ill, applied to the Dutch for help for checking the force of the Nāyaka.

5. Bruce: *Annals*, II, p. 202.
6. *Batavia Dagh Register*, 1665, p. 166.
7. *EC.*, VIII, Tl. 98.
8. For an account of the territories of the Kōlattiri Rājas, see *JRAS.*, 1922, p. 167 ff, and *JRAS.*, 1923, p. 81 ff.

But the Dutch declined to help him.[9] Meanwhile Sōmaśēkhara had applied to the Portuguese for help, and got a fleet of ships. The fleet opened fire on the Kōlattiri army, and forced it to retire to Nīlēśvar. This reverse, prompted the Dutch to join the scuffle in order to counteract the Portuguese influence.[10] As a result the Kanarese forces suffered some reverse. The Nairs captured three fortresses belonging to Bednūr.[11] Inspite of the Portuguese aid, the Kanarese suffered a defeat. The Portuguese made use of this failure to advance their own ends and spread rumours that the success of the enemy was due to the aid and advice given by the Dutch. On hearing this, Sōmaśēkhara was naturally dissatisfied with the Dutch. Hence in order to remove any misapprehension and to save their Resident De Bruyn, from difficulties, Huskin instructed M. Coulster to write a short letter to Sōmaśēkhara exposing the calumny spread by the Portuguese and at the same time pointing out that they were at liberty to assist the Malabar prince just as the Portuguese had aided him.[12]

This seems to have been the first clash between the two. Ever after, Bednūr and the Kōlattiris were carrying on regular war. This is borne out by the following information given by the English, who were negotiating for a port for building a factory. When Girby, enquired through a broker, why Āli Rājah had changed his mind regarding Nīlēśvar, the best site for a factory, he answered that he did not think that Baliapatam would be granted. Upon further considerations he judged "the former place (Nīlēśvar) was not so proper, being in a petty kingdom, parting the confines of Kanara and Cannanore who are at war; so that it is apt to be invaded and plundered by either party upon all occasion."[13] The wars against Kanara had been a continual drain on the treasury of the Cannanore king and when Girby urged the cession of Nīlēśvar, he was met with a demand for 2000

9. *Batavia Dagh Register,* 1664, p. 172.
10. *Ibid.,* p. 325.
11. Foster: *English Factories in India,* (1661-64), p. 346.
12. *Batavia Dagh Register,* 1664, p. 43.
13. Foster: *English Factories in India,* 1668-69, p. 264.

seguins 'to assist them in carrying on the wars.'[14] Further the Malayāḷa chief was anxious to draw the English into his dominions from Kanara.

Sōmaśēkhara Nāyaka and Mysore: Sōmaśēkhara Nāyaka was also entangled in a war against Mysore. He resumed possession of Bekkoḍu, Belagoḍu, Kanatūr, Abbina and Bēlūr,[15] which had been taken away by the Mysore forces in the reign of Bhadrappa Nāyaka. The Mysore general Daḷavāi Nañjanāthaiya, pushed on the operations against Ikkēri, carrying fire and sword into Mālnāḍ, passing through Kalaśa, Khandeya, Danivāsa, Hebbe, Sāgara, Bednūr and Honnūr.[16] These activities on the Mysore side seem to have continued up to the latter half of 1664, for, a lithic record dated Śaka 1566 (October 11th, 1664) mentions that Daḷavāi Nañjanāthaiya was sent against Ikkēri and how he was able to win a victory against it.[17]

Being overpowered by force of circumstances, Sōmaśēkhara Nāyaka found it expedient and necessary to sue for peace towards the close of 1664. He sent his ambassador Puruṣōttamaiya to the court of Seringapatam with presents consisting of elephants, horses, robes and jewels.[18] The net result of the war was that by 1665, the sphere of influence of Mysore extended as far as Chikknāyakanahaḷḷi, Hassan, Sakkarepatṇa and Vastare in the north.

Sōmaśēkhara Nāyaka and Tarikere: Sōmaśēkhara Nāyaka, hearing of the maladministration of Tarikere Hanumappa Nāyaka, sent his general Sabbanisa Kṛṣṇappayya to subdue him. The rebellious chief was brought to Bednūr and his son Sītārāmappa was installed in his place.[19] The Nāyaka seems to have also purchased the fort of Hole Honnūru, which was under Muslim occupation for one lakh

14. *Ibid.*, p. 265.
15. *KNV.*, Canto VIII.
16. *Chikkadēvarāya Vijayam*, V, 26.
17. *EC.*, XII, Kg. 46.
18. *Chikkadēvarāya Vijayam*, V, 27-30.
19. *KNV.*, Canto VIII.

of *vārāhas;*. He maintained a small army at the fort and appointed one Śivappa of Mandighaṭṭa as Killedār of the fort.[20]

Sōmaśēkhara and the English: The English found themselves hemmed in between the Dutch and the Portuguese, and in 1664 their trade was not promising. Their only port was Bhatkal. They sent one Vālāji, their broker, with £1500 in gold to purchase 300 tons of pepper from Bhatkal. But unfortunately the ship "Vine" in which Vālāji embarked wrecked and the deal did not fructify. But in October 1664, Taylor, another English merchant arrived at Bhatkal with his ships "London" and "American". He had to wait for the arrival of Narane Maloe, the famous Kanarese merchant and Ambassador at Goa; and when he arrived at Bhatkal on 7th November 1664, Taylor was able to get some pepper from Bhatkal.[21] Scarcity of pepper was to a certain extent due to Sōmaśēkhara Nāyaka's export of the same to Machao, Basra, Persia and Muscat.

Sōmaśēkhara Nāyaka and the Dutch: The Dutch, were making considerable progress in west coast. They had a factory at Barcelor, from which place they were monopolising in the rice trade.[22] An idea of the extent of their trade may be formed from the fact that in the course of May 1664, 102 vessels were filled with rice, cocoanuts, etc., for their settlements in the east.[23]

Narane Maloe, the court merchant of Bednūr was favourably disposed towards the Dutch. He made a representation on their behalf to the Bednūr court for removal of some tolls levied on their goods and was able to get them refund the moneys they had paid.[24] Subsequently, the Dutch under Van Goens tried to secure Mangalore from Sōmaśēkhara. In 1668, Gibert de Bruyn and Jao Cassen brovt were sent to Bednūr with a present and they were

20. *Mac. Coll.*, 18-15-39.
21. Foster: *English Factories in India* (1661-1664), pp. 348-49.
22. Pinkerton: *Voyages,* VIII, p. 364.
23. *Batavia Dagh Register,* 1664, p. 448.
24. *Ibid.*, p. 573.

able to effect a contract and induce Sōmaśēkhara to grant them some concessions.[25]

Sōmaśēkhara Nāyaka and the Portuguese: Sōmaśēkhara who wanted to keep all the foreign powers in good and friendly spirits made new overtures to the Portuguese in 1670. He offered them Mangalore, Barcelor, and Honāvar for the erection of factories under stipulations that the proposed factories should not be surrounded by double walls and that no bastions were also to be erected; no oil mill was to be established; native weights and measures were to be employed and none should be made a Christian.[26] A treaty was concluded between Sōmaśēkhara Nāyaka and the Portuguese in 1671, which allowed them further concessions.[27] According to that the Portuguese were to be given sites at Honāvar, Barcelor and Mangalore for building factories with single walls and without any fortification or erection of oil mills etc., Their boats were to be given free access to the ports of Sōmaśēkhara Nāyaka, king of Kanara. The Portuguese were, however, not to indulge themselves in conversion of the local people as also to help the enemies of the king.

Religious activities, Domestic life and last years of Sōmaśēkhara: Sōmaśēkhara was very liberal in patronising religious institutions and *maṭhas* as is amply testified to by a large number of inscriptions.[28] He also bestowed great attention in improving the good of his subjects. He granted a copper *śāsana* to Harugol Mudalinga and other boatmen of the river Tungabhadrā, lands assessed at 34 *varāhas*, from the

25. *Batavia Dagh Register*: 1668-69, p. 129. The letter of Sōmaśēkhara Nāyaka to the Dutch runs as follows: "Somasecraneyak, of Queldy sends compliments to the Viceroy of Batavia, Joan Maestsukar. The delegates Covert de Bryn and Jao Casesen brovt have been at my court and a perpetual contract has been made between me and the company regarding pepper which contract will last for ever". '(Sd.) Somasecraneyak".

26. *JBBRAS.*, XIX, p. 261.

27. *Pazes-e-Tratados.*, No. 1, 1671, Fols. 57-59. For details see Appendix A, No. 10.

28. *MAR.*, 1916, p. 67; *EC.*, VIII, Tl. 92, 185, 96, 86, 53, 55, 48. *MAR.*, 1943, No. 38, 7, 156, 78, 99, 65, 98, 74, 75; etc. *MAR.;* 1923; 95 and 102.

Korlahalli village in the Gajanūr Śīme.[29] Sōmaśēkhara also patronised dancing. The Court dancing girl was one Puṭṭitāyī Jambhukandi Cennī.[30]

Sōmaśēkhara Nāyaka remained a bachelor for some time; and later married Cannammāji who was destined to become the heroic queen of Bednūr. His last days were rather unfortunate. He was led astray by bad counsel. A wicked person named Barame Mavuta told him that if he took a certain intoxicant, he would improve in his bodily strength. Sōmaśēkhara followed his advice and fell a prey to evil habits and evil company. Further he went mad and committed great enormities. He is said to have ripped up pregnant women with his own hands and found gratification in siezing every beautiful girl that he met. He is therefore known as *huccha* (lunatic) and his effigy is represented in Aghorēśvara temple at Ikkēri as menacled and fettered. Bednūr fell into political confusion and Sōmaśēkhara Nāyaka is said to have been assasinated by one Sōmayya.[31]

29. *EC.*, VII, Sh. 3. The Harigol was a coracle or round basket covered with hides, commonly used in Mysore at the ferries. See B. A. Saletore: *Social and Political Life in the Vijayanagar Empire*, Vol. I, p. 60.

30. *EC.*, VIII, Tl. 71.

31. *KNV.*, VIII. The last date of Sōmaśēkhara Nāyaka I according to the *Keladinṛpavijayam* is 1671 A.C. But there are two inscriptions which furnish him the dates Śaka 1596 (1674 A.C.) and Śaka 1599 (1677 A.C.) (*EC.*, VIII, Tl. 188 and 77). It may therefore be surmised that he lived up to A.D. 1677 though the administration of the kingdom was carried on by Cannammāji, the first queen of the Keladi house, as Sōmaśēkhara had no issue.

CHAPTER XI

CANNAMMĀJĪ (1671-1696)

Early years: During the closing years of her husband's reign, (i.e., during the period when he was mad) Cannammājī was in charge of the government. It was a period of great trouble and confusion in the politics of Bednūr. Probably it started even during the last years of the effective rule of Sōmaśēkhara Nāyaka. According to the *Keladinṛpavijayam* he sent his general Sabnis Kṛṣṇappayya against Hanumappa Nāyaka of Tarikere who had killed his wife and taken to a life of sensuality. The chief was defeated and brought captive to Bednūr.[1] Troubles seems to have started since then. It was probably immediately thereafter that Sōmaśēkhara Nāyaka fell into bad ways having become a victim to the evil effects of an intoxicant; and therefore Cannammājī took over the reins of administration as regent. Taking advantage of this confused state of affairs, the Sultan of Bījāpur sent his general Mujbar Khan and his vakil Jannopant to the Bednūr Court. Some of the wicked men in the Keladi kingdom now joined with the Bījāpuris and conspired to kill Sōmaśēkhara Nāyaka. But Cannammājī was able to thwart their plans and assert herself with courage and ability; and even when she heard of the murder of her husband she bore it with commendable equanimity and prepared to meet the diplomacy of the Bījāpur vakil Jannopant with his own weapons. In the meanwhile, the allies of the Bījāpur Sultan took up arms against the queen and one of them was Kenge Hanumappa Nāyaka, evidently the ruler of Tarikere. In a contest that followed, the Muslim general of Tarikere, by name Sheik Bābā, was killed by the Bednūr forces. Jannopant's diplomacy was successfully counteracted by the Queen. The arch-villain Barame Mavuta was compelled to flee from the country and one by one the conspirators were punished.

1. Canto, VIII.

Among them was the brother-in-law of the Queen, Basavalinga Nāyaka, who was first exiled and then sentenced to death.[2]

A plot to set up a rival claimant to the throne was now hatched by Marebova Lakṣmayya, Vīrabhadrayya and others. Their intention was to set up on the throne an illegitimate son of Andhaka Venkaṭappayya. On hearing this, Barame Mavuta and some others hurried to Biligi, where Kasargōḍu Timmaṇṇa and Sabbanisa Kṛṣṇappayya Nāyaka lived. These officers wove a counter plot on behalf of a son of Bhadrayya. Timmaṇṇa and Kṛṣṇappayya joined hands with the Bījāpur vakil. Jannopant gave battle to the forces of the rival party led by Marebova Lakṣmayya, captured him and had him beheaded.

Queen Cannammāji heard the news of the conflict between the two rival parties, and fearing further trouble, retired with her retinue from Bednūr to the hill fortress of

2. From the letters of the English factors stationed on the west coast, we get some deails relating to the internal affairs of the Keladi kingdom during the period. Caesar Chamberlain, for instance, is one of the factors whose letters (1672 A.C.) are of much value in this connection. "Ceasar Chamberlain, with his three assistants, Bendish, Sherlock and Tores remained in charge of the Karwar factory throughout the year 1672. They had a good deal to report early in the year as to fighting and other troubles in the Canarese territories. Several of the Bednūr Raja's chiefs bearing weary of his rule, conspired to murder him with the help of an envoy from the king of Bījāpur, who had come to collect arrears of tributes. They succeeded in doing this, but most of the mutineers and their abettors were killed by the Rajas's enraged soldiery and a kinsman of the deceased ruler, other than the one intended by the conspirators, was set up as his successor. This led to further conflict and the disturbance was so extensive that for some time it rendered the roads in the whole Canarese country impassable. Naran Malla, the leading merchant of Bhatkal, took up arms in favour of one of the aspirants who at first succeeded and made peace with the king of Bījāpur; but another faction set up a rival and in August, Chamberlain reported that it was feared that this would lead to warfare by the Bījāpur army and further cumbustion." (**Sir Charles Fawcett**—*English Factories in India,* I, pp. 308-9). It must be said here that though Chamberlain was not an eye-witness to the events which he narrates, yet his account is substantially the same as the one given by Linganṇa in the *Keladinṛpavijayam*

Bhuvanagiri. To this place she summoned Kasargōḍu Timmaṇṇa and Sabnis Kṛṣṇappayya with whom she settled her differences. All the three now made common cause and it was unanimously agreed upon that Bhadrayya's son had no claims whatsoever to the throne, and that Queen Cannammājī alone was the legal ruler. Andhaka Venkaṭappayya was exiled to Hosangadi and his illegitimate son beheaded. Cannammājī was now crowned queen at Bhuvanagiri. She later returned with her army and retinue to the capital Veṇupura (Bednūr) from where she began to conduct the administration of the country in the traditional Hindu manner.[3]

The inscriptions of Cannammājī range in dates between Śaka 1594 (1672 A.C.)[4] and Śaka 1617 (1695 A.C.).[5]

Cannammājī's wars: Like her predecessors Cannammājī had to devote her attention to stemming the tides of invasions by her neighbours. The forts of Tavanidhi, Honnali, Jadeya, and Mudoji were taken by Cannammājī's armies. The ruler of Sōḍe, Rāmachandra Nāyaka was prevented from his attempt to extend his power. The Tuḷuva feudatories seem to have captured the forts of Karkala and Mallikārjuna and so the recalcitrant feudatories in the area were subjugated and the forts retaken by Cannammājī.

Cannammājī and Mysore: Cannammājī was also engrossed in military activities against Mysore apparently with a view to improve her position. In them she seems to have

3. *KNV.*, Canto VIII. The coronation of Cannammājī is placed by the work in Ś 1594, Virodhikrit, Phālguṇa bahuḷa 10 (A.C. 1672 March 14).

4. *E.C.*, VIII, Tl. 118.

5. *Ibid.*, Tl. 46. An inscription dated Śaka 1583 records a grant independently made by Cannammājī (*MAR.*, 1927 No. 170). This date, it must be noted, falls in the reign of Bhadrappa Nāyaka, who was the elder brother of Sōmaśēkhara Nāyaka I, and for whom inscriptions supply us with the dates ranging between 1661 A.C. and 1663 A.C. How could Cannammajī, the lawful wife of Sōmaśēkhara Nāyaka I, make a grant under her own authority in the reign of Bhadrappa? It is very difficult to solve this problem unless we suppose that Sōmaśēkhara also began to rule in 1661 A.C. and was co-regent with his elder brother upto 1663 which is the earliest known date for him (*EC.*, VII Sk. 27) and that Cannammājī was associated with her husband in the government of the country from the very commencement of his reign.

been assisted by the Golkonda and Bījāpur forces in the Karṇāṭaka under Hussain Khān and Balbal Khān and by other powerful local chieftains including those of Bēlūr and Arkalguḍ. The leading part however was taken by Kasargōḍu Timmaṇṇa and Sabnis Kṛṣṇappayya and the generals of Cannammājī commanding the large forces of Ikkēri.[6] In 1674 Kumārayya, the Daḷavāi of Cikkadēvarāja Woḍeyār was despatched with an army against them.[7] He won initial successes over local chiefs and took among other places Arkalgud from its chief Kṛṣṇappa Nāyaka of Aigūr; but at Hassan he was defeated and routed by the forces of Cannammājī. Vasudhare and other places were taken by the Ikkēri forces from Mysore.

Cannammājī who was afraid of Mysore seems to have taken Kaḍūr, Bāṇavar (Bāṇapura), Hassan and Belūr and safeguarded her southern frontiers against further encroachments by Mysore between 1680-1681 (Raudri-Durmati). In this series of military campaigns the Ikkēri army was headed by Basappa Nāyaka and helped by the Qutb Shāh of Golkonda and Sāmbhāji. Cannammājī's success was largely facilitated by the absence from Seringapatam of the Mysore army under Daḷavāi Kumārayya, who was then engaged before Trichinopoly in the distant south against the Nāyak ruler of Madura. But Cikkadēvarāja Woḍeyār, the Mysore ruler met the combined army at Bāṇavar and defeated it, and thereby strengthened his position on the borders between his own kingdom and that of Cannammājī. In 1694 Cikkadēvarāja Woḍeyār seems to have started an aggressive policy against Bednūr. Cannammājī, after her return from Subramaṇya about the close of 1694, renewed her fight against Mysore. Among the generals in her army were Daḷavāi Cennabasava Śeṭṭi, Sabnis Bommarasaiyya of Kolivada, Yākub

6. *KNV., IX.* The *Rāmarājiyamu,* however, says that the campaign was led by Kōdaṇḍa Rāma I, nephew of Śrī Ranga III. See S.K. Ayyangar: *Sources,* p. 312.

7. *KNV.* IX, R. Sathyanatha Ayyar places this event subsequent to 1674 (*The Nayaks of Madura* p. 134 n), and the *Mysore Gazetteer* in 1704 (New Edn. II, iii, p. 2414). Both of them require revision.

8. *KNV.,* IX.

Khān, Kṛṣṇappa Nāyaka of Aigūr and the Beda chiefs of Cintanakal (Chitaldrug).[9] The combined forces marched on towards Mysore and laid siege to Arkalgud which, as said earlier, had been taken by Cikkadēvarāja in 1674 from its chief Kṛṣṇappa Nāyaka of Aigūr. Meanwhile the Mysore army under Daḷavāi Timmappayya of Kolala proceeded there. About January 1695, an action took place at Hebbale (Perbale)[10] in the neighbourhood of Arkalgud. Both sides seem to have begun with a volley of arrows, the Mysore elephant Benterāya and the Bednūr elephant Rāmabāṇa taking a leading part in the fight. In the thick of the fight, the Bednūr forces began to feign retreat, only to find themselves overpowered by the Mysoreans. Yet Cennabasava Śeṭṭi and Yākub Khān seated on an elephant turned against their opponents. A bullet shot from the Mysore side struck Yākub Khān as a result of which he fell dead while Cennabasava in panic got down from his elephant and began to flee. The flight of Cennabasava, naturally resulted in general disorder in his ranks. The Bednūr army was split up amidst great slaughter. Rāmabāṇa and other elephants and horses in their camp were captured by the Mysoreans. Bommarasaiya escaped from the battle field; and Kṛṣṇappa Nāyaka of Aigūr lay dead on the ground. It was thus a distinct victory for Mysore.

The repulse of the Bednūr forces was followed by the siege and acquisition of Arkalgud by Chikkadēvarāja between January and February 1695, and of Aigūr, Saklespūr and Kodlipet between March and April.[11] These acquisitions confirmed Cikkadēvarāja's sovereignty in the western part of Mysore. But Cannammājī, who could not put up with her defeat, appears to have renewed her hostilities with Mysore

9. *Apratima Vīra Caritram*, II, 21; III, 80, 140, 146, 169, IV. 5 cited C. Hayavadanarao: *op. cit.*, p. 313, and *n.*

10. *Ibid.*, III, 48. Perbale is the Hala Kannaḍa form of Hebbale, C. Hayavadanarao: *op. cit.*, p. 314 and n. Hebbale may be identified with Hebbale an extant *sarva-mānya* village in the Arkalgud taluk (see—*List of Villages of Mysore*, p. 131).

11. *Mysūru Doregala Vamśāvali*, II, 46-47; Annals of the Mysore Royal Family I, 108 cited in C. Hayavadanarao *op. cit.*, p. 315 and n.

in 1696. According to the *Keladinṛpavijayam* she sent an army against Mysore under the leadership of Sabnis Bommarasaiya of Kolivada. He slew Daḷavāi Timmappaiya, the Mysore general and took his son Kṛṣṇappa prisoner and won a signal victory over the Mysoreans. Kṛṣṇappa was however released later.

Cannammājī and Bījāpur: As Cannammājī had no issue, she adopted one Basavappa, son of Māriyappa Śetti after due consultation with her counsellors. But the people of Nagara, with the aid of the Muslims from Bījāpur, rebelled against her. Cannammājī took shelter in the fort of Kapiledurga and let loose her army to plunder the country. She also guarded all roads leading to her territory, so that no commercial article would enter into or pass out from it. The rebels were thus starved and were obliged to come to terms. Cannammājī also sent Doḍḍabasavappa on an expedition to Sante Bennūr, which he took after slaying Baramaṇṇa Nāyaka, the palegar of the place.[12]

Cannammājī's success against Aurangzeb: The most notable event of her reign was however, the defeat of the Mughal army headed by Aurangzeb in person. The Mughals pursued Rājārām, the son of Śivāji, who had sought refuge in the Bednūr court. Cannammājī treated Rājārām with kindness and promised him protection. Aurangzeb was furious at this and sent her an ultimatum asking her to surrender Rājārām immediately, failing which he threatened to overrun her territories. But great was his chagrin to hear that undaunted, the heroic queen refused to surrender Rājārām and treated his threat with contempt. War ensued and the Mughal Emperor's army was utterly routed and made to flee with great loss. Cannammājī's fame spread far and wide. The Mughal invasion and oppression of the people in the area is borne out by a royal order of Cannammājī, dated 1691 A.C., which refers to the same.[13] Hence this war seems to

12. *Mac. Coll.*, 18-15-7.

13. *EC.*, VII, Sk. 79. The royal order runs as follows: "Kalle Gauḍa of Cikka Jambūr in the Udugaṇi śīme having presented himself stating that in the year Śukla (1689 A.C.), during the oppression of Mughuls, he had paid money from his own hands and erected cattle folds and

have taken place about 1690. P. B. Desai, seems to think that Aurangzeb, impressed by her heroic conduct, honoured her with presents.[14] But it is not known on what evidence he has based this surmise. She also seems to have seized the Mallūr district from the Mughals and included it under Bednūr.[15]

Cannammājī and Malabar: Much information is not available about the dealings of the Queen with the Nairs. Hamilton in his *New Account of the East Indies,* while referring to the Malayāḷis says that the *Rāṇi* kept a standing army of 1,50,000 soldiers to put down the insolence of the Malayāḷis, also mentions that "along the Malabar coast, the Canarese have forts, built of earth wherein are kept two to three hundred soldiers ready to encounter any small party of Malabars that clandestinely come to thieve and rob".[16]

Cannammāji and the Portuguese: After 1671, the relations between Bednūr and the Portuguese continued to be cordial. For according to the terms of a treaty of peace concluded between the queen of Kanara and the Portuguese on 15th December, 1678, the Portuguese were to pay 30,000 *Xerafins* towards the cost of war. The queen was to give them stone and wood for the erection of a factory at Mangalore and to supply annually 1,500 sacks of rice. Besides these, the queen authorised them to erect Roman Catholic churches at Mirzeo, Chandor, Bhatkal and Kalyān.[17] The desire of the Portuguese to continue in amity with Cannammājī is revealed in a letter from the Viceroy of Goa to the queen.[18] In 1687, the Portuguese were very anxious to erect

taken great trouble in laying plans, requested that he might be granted an *umbaḷi* and that an endowment might be granted to his guru Hosūr Lingappadēva and for the Viraktha maṭha erected by his father, Ganga Gauḍa—*umbaḷi* and uttar are granted to him from the village."

14. *Karṇāṭaka Darshana*—Volume presented to Shri R. R. Diwakar on his sixtieth Birthday (1955), p. 366.

15. *Mac. Coll.,* 18-15-15 Section IX.

16. I, p. 287.

17. Danvers: *Portuguese Records,* p. 75, *Portuguese in India,* Vol. II, p. 365.

18. *Riez Viznhos.,* No. 2 Ano de 1681-93. For details see Appendix A. No. 11.

another factory near Barcelor[19] as may be seen from a letter from the Portuguese king. By 1695, they were in possession of Honāvar, Barcelor and Cambolim.[20] As a result of the treaty with Cannammājī they seem to have been able to drive out the Arabs. The Arabs who resented this, returned with a large fleet towards the middle of 1695 to destroy the Kanarese ports. They burnt Mangalore and Basrūr and set sail after gathering a large booty.[21]

During Cannammājī's reign, Dr. Fryer, passed along the Kanara coast, on his way to Bombay. Describing Honāvar, he says:

> "Honavar in hilly barren land, was divided between the Dutch and the Portuguese. It had a castle without soldiers and a town with poor buildings. The castle had been built by the Portuguese and seized by the Kanarese with the help of the Dutch between whom and the Portugals the town was divided; The Naires had no footing in Honavar and the Moors not much. Many of the people had received the Christian faith; those who had not, were the most impiously religious of any of the Indians, being marvellously conversant with the Devil. The people had good laws and obeyed them and travelled without guides on broad roads not along byepaths as in Malabar".[22]

Cannammājī's ministers: Cannammājī was helped in the administration of the country by her chief minister Gurubasappadēva.[23] Her other officers were treasurer Śrīni-

19. *Notions of the Reign*: No. 3, 1685-1698, Fols. 77-78. For details see Appendix A. No. 12.
20. Careris: *Voyages*, p. 220.
21. Pinkerton: *Voyages*, p. 365.
22. Dr. Fryer—*Travels*, p. 57. Between two islands near Bhatkal Fryer saw six skulking Malabar prows waiting their booty. See *East India and Persia*, p. 57. "The Malabar pirate" he says, "are the worst pickeroons on this coast going in fleets. They are set out by great men ashore. At sea, near Goa, Fryer was attacked by a large boat of Malabar Pirates with about sixty fighting men besides rowers who threw stink pots and plied chambers and small shot, flung stones and darted long lances and were with difficulty driven off" (*ibid.*, p. 151, 152)
23. *MAR.*, 1932, No. 39; 1916, p. 67.

vāsayya,[24] accountant Timmayya,[25] and Karaṇika Venkaṭappayya.[26] Among the other important officers during the feuds were Kotepur Siddhappa Śeṭṭi, Bokkasada Siddabasavayya, Kotalda Venkaṭappayya, Kaṇḍācāra Lakṣmayya, Kasaragōḍu Timmappa, Sabbanisa Kṛṣṇappayya, Guru Bhadrappa Devaru, Karaṇika Biligi Subbayya, Venkaṭappayya and Rāyasada Venkaṭappayya.[27]

Cannammājī's patronage to religion and religious institutions: Cannammājī was noted for her keen interest in religion and religious institutions. She continued the traditional patronage of her house to Śṛngēri. Numerous inscriptions testify to her religious bent of mind.[28] She built an *agrahāra* known as Cannammā-agrahāra, probably after her own name, and granted in it *vṛttis* of lands to Brahmans. She also built *maṭhas* for the Jangamas. She is stated to have once fed 1,96,000 Lingāyats.[29] An undated copper-plate grant from Puttūr belonging to Queen Cannammājī's reign registers a grant of land by the queen to the Brāhmaṇa Rāmachandra for conducting worship and other offerings to god Veṅkaṭēśvara of Puttūr.[30]

Domestic life: Cannammājī gave her adopted son Basavappa Nāyaka the necessary education for a prince. After marrying him suitably to two girls, Cannammājī, daughter of Hebbe Mahantayya, and Basavammājī, daughter of Maliga Cenna Vīrappa, the queen went on a pilgrimage to Gōkarṇa. Thereafter she retired from active political life entrusting the kingdom to Basavappa Nāyaka.

Estimate: Though her husband became mad towards the end of his reign and was eventually assassinated, and she had no child of her own, she was able to overcome the

24. *EC.*, VIII, Tl. 180.
25. *MAR.*, 1928, No. 61.
26. *EC.*, VIII, Tl. 161.
27. *KNV.*, IX.
28. *MAR.*, 1916, p. 67; 1923, No. 86; *EC.*, VIII, Sg. 16, 153, Tl. 100, 118, 69, 67, 68, 73, 77, 184, 179, 64 etc.
29. *STR.*, VIII., 8; *QJMS.*, XXII, p. 83.
30. *ARIE.*, 1951-52, C.P. No. 8.

troubulous elements in her kingdom and save her state even from Aurangzeb. Her last words of advise to Basavappa in spite of its convention and poetic embellishment would give an insight into her character—"Do not change the words you once utter and do not neglect your duty anywhere. Take care you ever talk sweet words and disclose not your heart to a dissembling knave. Tread not an unworthy path and make no difference against kinsfolk. Avoid acts of sin, practice noble deeds, and meditate upon the feet of the Almighty. Show mercy to living beings and shield those that seek refuge. Do not speak revilingly of others and do not move in the world without self restraint. Overcome the defects of lust and the like and loathe the cycle of births and deaths. Leave fear in adversity and shun haughtiness in prosperity. Ponder over the basic principles of truth and realise the esoteric *advaita*. Miss not an opportunity and honour those proficient in the Vedic lore. Regard life as but a dream and reflect on the question 'Who am I'. Laugh without making yourself laughable and speak words unsurpassed. Live as an object of people's praise and resort to the path that knows no return. Propitiate Śiva in various ways and enjoy eternal bliss and take care you do not forget this at any time".[31]

The queen seems to have died in 1698 and was buried in Bednūr.[32]

31. *STR.*, VIII, 8.
32. *KNV.*, X.

CHAPTER XII

BASAVAPPA NĀYAKA I (1696-1714)

The earliest inscription of Basavappa Nāyaka is dated in 1697 A.C.,[1] and the latest date known for him from epigraphs is 1714 A.C.[2] According to the *Keladinṛpavijayam*, Basavappa was crowned at Vēṇupura.[3]

Basavappa Nāyaka's reign was full of field actions against the Marathas and Mysore, besides many other minor Chieftains. He clashed with the Marathas who captured the fort of Nevileyagada. He sent an army under his general Cannabasappa, who recaptured the fort, and drove out the enemy and renamed it Basavadurga. Again at Ānandapura a certain Kutsita Śivappa, who was a pretender and who tried to establish his claim to the throne, was beheaded. The Nairs captured the fort of Candragiri but Basavappa soon defeated them. Added to this was the Muslim menace. The forts of Ānegutti, Mahādēvapura, Tadeya Honnali and Mirjan were captured from them. The invasion of the Nawab of Sāvanūr on Kanara was also repulsed.[4] As there are only very meagre sources of information for these campaigns of Basavappa, it is very difficult to verify and date them.

Basavappa Nāyaka who continued the policy of Cannammājī towards Mysore was able to retake Arkalgud from Mysore and restore Aigur and Saklespur to the sons of Kṛṣṇappa Nāyaka of Aigur during the period A.C. 1698-1700. The Bednūr

1. *MAR.*, 1916, p. 67.
2. *Ibid.*, 1923, No. 123, Śaka 1635, Jaya Caitra ba 1. The year Jaya falls in Śaka 1636. The equivalent for the date will be 23rd March 1714 A.C.
3. *KNV.*, X. The following are the other dates assigned to him. Rice A.C. 1697-1714; (EC. VII, p. 4). *Rājavamśavali*, 1713-1731, (*Mac. Coll.*, 18-15-15). Sewell: 1698-1714 (*List of Inscriptions in Southern India* II, p. 177); Naraharayya, 1679-1714, (*QJMS.*, XXII, p. 84).
4. *KNV.*, X.

Commander Garajina Basavappadēva was able to take Vastare (Vasudhare) from the Mysoreans. Ultimately, hostilities ended with conclusion of an advantageous peace by Basavappa Nāyaka with Mysore, through Niyogi Saraja-Nāgappaya by means of a deed of assurance (*bhāṣāpatrike*) in about 1700.[5]

Basavappa and minor chiefs: Basavappa Nāyaka appears to have entered into a treaty with Candraśēkhara Chauta, a neighbouring chief. According to the terms, out of the total revenue of 13,792 *varāhas* from the Chauta territory, 7792 *varāhas* were to be paid to Bednūr as tribute every year and 6,000 *varāhas* were allowed as *umbaḷi* to Candraśēkhara Cikka Rāya Chauta.[6] He also enhanced the tribute to be paid by the Ajilas, to 3,000 *varāhas* during the reign of Śankaradēva Ajila.[7]

Basavappa Nāyaka and the Portuguese: Basavappa continued an active policy against the Portuguese. The Portuguese seem to have been in arrears of payment for the rice taken by them from Kanara. Hence Basavappa promptly wrote to them asking them to pay up the dues early in 1700. The anxiety of the Portuguese to have friendly relations with Basavappa, so that they could have full facilities for getting rice and other provisions is revealed by their letter sent to the king of Kanara. They wrote saying that the price of rice would be promptly paid and assured Basavappa that they would give him necessary help against his enemies.[8]

In March 1702, the Portuguese again wrote to Basavappa Nāyaka that the Arabs had been received in the ports of Kanara and that they would prevent their landing at any cost.[9] To win over the king of Kanara, the factors at Mangalore made presents worth 300 *Xerafins* every year to the king

5. *KNV.*, X.
6. *Mac. Coll.*, 18-15-6; V. Kafiyat of Chauta kings.
7. *Ibid.*, Kaifiyat of Ajilas.
8. *Reis Vizinhos*, No. 5 Fol. 44; see Extracts in *Archivo-Portuguese Oriental;* III, pt. I, No. 95. See Appendix A. No. 13.
9. *Archivo Portuguese Oriental,* III, pt. I, No. 156.

and his servants.[10] In 1704, there seems to have been further cause for friction between the Portuguese and Basavappa for the Portuguese Viceroy at Goa, Castino de Mello de Castro wrote on 1st May 1704, thus: "The king of Canara betrayed me by shutting his ports and refusing cargo of rice and even to prevent any embarking".[11] In December 1704, there seems to have been a skirmish between the Portuguese and the Kanarese. A Portuguese letter, dated 4th December, 1704 gives details about the king of Kanara and the Arabs, who were competing for trade in the area.[12]

In 1707 the Portuguese invaded the territories of Basavappa Nāyaka and attacked the port of Mangalore. But the forces of Basavappa were able to put up a stiff resistence and the Portuguese were compelled to suspend hostilities. Basavappa Nāyaka deputed Dāmarasa Prabhu as his ambassador to Goa with a letter to conclude peace with them.[13] But he had to extend more concessions to the Portuguese. He had for instance to pay 30,000 *Xerafins* and 3,150 bales of rice towards expenses incurred by the Portuguese. Further he promised not to allow the Arabs to trade in Kanara and allow the Portuguese a monopoly in trade, who in return, agreed to help the king in any war in which he may be entailed and promised that every year two Kanarese ships could go to Ormuz and fetch horses.[14] But this friendliness did not continue long.

Soon Vasco Fernandes Cesar de Menzes, the Portuguese viceroy at Goa fell out with Basavappa. He proceeded with a small squadron to Barcelor and having dismantled the fortress at the place, he burnt all the villages on the river banks, and killed all who attempted to offer any opposition. Kalyāṇpur on the same coast suffered a similar fate. Vasco Fernandes then bombarded Mangalore, Kumta, Gōkarṇa and

10. *Ibid.*, III, pt. I, No. 220.
11. *Ibid.*, III, pt. I, No. 252.
12. *Ibid.*, III, pt. I No. 275. See Appendix A. No. 14.
13. *Archivo Portuguese Oriental, III,* pt. II, No. 65. For details see Appendix A, No. 15.
14. *OS. Portuguezės,* VII, pp. 157-167.

Mirzeo, spreading terror, fire and death in every direction. We get details of the attacks in a portuguese document dated the 17th January, 1714.[15] Hostilities however, seem to have ended and there was peace again.

Basavappa Nāyaka's domestic life: Basavappa Nāyaka had four wives, Cannammājī, Vīrammajī, Hebbe Cannammājī and Cannabasavammājī. Cannammājī was the daughter of a certain Basavappa. Vīrammajī was the daughter of Śivayya and grand-daughter of Virūpākṣayya of Hebbekōṭe. Cannabasavammājī was the daughter of Malige Cannavīrappa. By Hebbe Cannammājī, Basavappa had a son named Vīrabhadra and by Cannabasavammājī another son, Sōmaśēkhara. Sōmaśēkhara was married to Vīrammājī and Vīrabhadra was married to Cannammājī, daughter of Cannabasavappa of Sāgar. The prince also had a second wife Mallammājī younger daughter of Sūrirāya Kālappa.[16]

Basavappa's patronage of religion and literature: Basavappa's acts of liberality and mercy were manifold. Like his ancestors he had no bigotry of any kind and favoured alike Jogis, Jangamas, *Paramahamsas* (a sect of *ekadaṇḍins*) and Fakirs. He also bestowed good care on the Śṛngēri math.[17] A copper plate inscription of his dated Śaka 1632 Virōdhin, Jyēstha Śu 5 (June 1, 1709) records the confirmation by deed the gift of lands at Chikkamūḷu Keregrāma and Khaidoṭṭikere grāma in Gājanūru *śime* to the teacher Chārumūrthi Rachavaṭṭidēva, the disciple of Chārumūrthi Kabbinatante Kari Basavarājadēva. The record incidentally mentions the Muslims Burāna Khān, Sābhāsa Khān, Lāḍa Khān and Ālu Khān, from whom the lands in question were purchased.[18]

15. *Archivo Portuguese Oriental*, III, pt. I, No. 65. For details see Appendix A. No. 16.

16. *KNV.*, X.

17. *MAR.*, 1916, p. 67. Other religious institutions also received liberal donations from him, see *Mac. Ins.*, 18-15-6; *EC.*, VIII, Tl. 106, 110, 136 178, 187, etc.

18. *ARSIE.*, 1936-37, C. P. No. 3.

He was a great patron of literature and he himself was the author of many a work. The *Śivatattvaratnākara* is a memorable product of his pen. He is also credited with having written *Śuradruma* in Saṁskrit and *Śūktisudhākara* which is partly in Kannaḍa and partly in Saṁskrit. His patronage of learning was so extensive that he was styled *Śūri-nikara-kalpadruma,* (wish-yielding tree of the poets or the learned). The notable administrators of his reign were Guru Basavappadēva, chief Minister, Sarajina Śāntadēva, Sabbunisa Bommarasa and Siddabasavaiya of the treasury. In the evening of his life he crowned Sōmaśēkhara Nāyaka, his son and died in 1714.[19]

19. *KNV.*, X. It may incidentally be noted that the Keladi kings buried their dead bodies and often queens chose to be buried alive with their lords in self immolation (*sahagamana*).

CHAPTER XIII

SŌMAŚĒKHARA NĀYAKA II (1714—1739)

The earliest record of Sōmaśēkhara Nāyaka is dated 1698 A.C. There are also some *sannads* of his ranging in date between 1698 A.C. and 1706.[1] These dates fall within the reign of Basavappa Nāyaka I. One has to suppose that Sōmaśēkhara Nāyaka II issued the *sannads* during the reign of his father. From the evidence of an inscription of his dated in 1715 A.C.,[2] it may be assumed that he succeeded to the rulership of Bednūr in that year. The evidence of the *Keladinṛpavijayam,* however, makes one think that he ruled from 1714 to 1739 A.C.[3]

The reign of Sōmaśēkhara Nāyaka witnessed a series of wars with the ruling houses of Malabar, the English East India Company, the Dutch, the Portuguese and the Arabs, the reasons for them being mainly commercial. The Nāyakas often used to close the port of Mangalore, which was the main outlet on the west coast for the articles of merchandise and this forced the European and other powers to sue for peace, for fear of being starved to death.[4]

Sōmaśēkhara Nāyaka and his relations with Malabar, English and Dutch: The war between the Kōlattiri family in Malabar and Bednūr was long and continuous. The English interfered in the war. The Bednūr forces were able to rout the prince Regent's army by 1732 and seem to have "gott as

1. *MAR.,* 1916, p. 67.
2. *EC.,* VII, Ṣh. 21.
3. *KNV.,* X.
4. A letter of the English factor at Karwar, reveals the anxiety of the English to make a contract with the ruler of Bednūr for the procurement of rice. "The rice that we have in our warehouse being very old and worme eaten....we have ordered Vincajee to contract for three hundred thousand Bassalore bales of new rice, this year's crops, for our stores."—*Carwar Factory Letter Book,* No. 29-A, Letter No. 21, p. 30 (Nov. 27, 1721).

far as Mount Dilly".[5] The English factors expressed anxiety about their grain supplies usually obtained through Mangalore. Towards the close of January 1732, the region round about River Vaḷarpaṭṭaṇam also became unsettled due to the progress made by the Kanarese army in that area. Adherence to the Prince Regent's cause meant starvation to the English settlements; and so great anxiety prevailed with regard to the provision of grain for consumption in the ensuing monsoon season. The Prince Regent of the Kōlattiri family struck a bargain with the Kanarese on condition that they should help him against the Moplahs of Cannanore. By May 1732, the Kanarese took the fortified peninsula of 'Matame' held by the Moplahs to the north of the River Vaḷarpaṭṭaṇam. They became masters of the whole country up to the very gates of Tellicherry; and by October of the year they had passed to the south of the River Vaḷarpaṭṭaṇam and were thinking of besieging Cannanore itself in aid of the Prince Regent and in pursuance of a treaty with him. The terms of the treaty between the Prince Regent and the Kanarese General Raghunāth were: The Prince was to hold the country north of the River Vaḷarpaṭṭaṇam as far as Nīlēśvaram as a tributary of Bednūr. Bednūr was to have three forts at Madacarro, another at Cavi (Kavvayi) and the third at Nīlēśvaram. The country south of the river was to be under the Prince Regent who was to receive assistance against rebellious subjects, first of whom were the Moplahs of Cannanore.[6]

Shortly thereafter, a dispute arose between the Rājā of Kōṭṭayam, the Rājā of Cannanore and the English regarding the island of Dharmapaṭṭaṇam. The main portion of it, however, was held by the Prince Regent's people and it was quite possible that they might transfer it on to the Kanarese. There was also the fear that the Rājā of Kōṭṭayam might hand it over to the French. The possession of it either by the Kanarese or the French would certainly have hampered very much the English trade, as the country from which their chief pepper supplies were drawn was commanded by this island.

5. Logan: *Malabar,* Vol. I, p. 363. For identification of Mount D'Ely see *JRAS.*, 1922, p. 167 ff., *ibid,*. 1923, p. 81 ff., *ibid.,* 1924, p. 257 ff.
6. Logan: *op. cit.,* pp. 363-64.

But the English were able to win over the Rājas of Cannanore and Kōṭṭayam, mainly through the skill of Stephen Law who had succeeded Braddyl as chief of the Tellicherry factory on 17th December, 1732. But on 3rd January, 1735, a Kanarese army, about 5,000 strong, crossed the River Añjarakandī and encamped on the sandy flats on the east end of the islands with a view to further invasion of the territory of the Rājā of Kōṭṭayam. The English took sides with the Rājā of Kōṭṭayam and demanded the withdrawal of the forces by the Kanarese from Dharmapaṭṭaṇam. The Kanarese general refused to retreat but made an advance towards Agārr, a strongly fortified post built at "Cadalay". On 27th February, 1736, the native levies from Tellicherry—all men of Naranga-purattu Nāyar, the corps of Tīyars and 230 Moplahs, 450 men in all, proceeded to join the forces of the Prince and the Rājā of Kōṭṭayam at Eḍakād.

Two days later open hostilities broke out. The allies were attacked by the Kanarese at Eḍakād, but the assailants were repulsed. Unfortunately, the Kanarese were not able to meet the heavy odds against them. The losses of the Kanarese were heavy. A Kanarese redoubt (Trankier) at the Eḍakād point was taken. The English chief, Stephen Law himself, took the field and tried to intercept the food supplies of the Kanarese. On the 7th March, their Madakara fort surrendered to the English war "gallivats". The fort was about 500 yards in circumference with eight half-moon bastions. On 15th March, Stephen Law concentrated on the isolated position of the Kanarese at Cadalay. The preparations for attacking it were complete on the 17th and on the morning of 18th the first attack was made. The English force secured an eminence with the Nāyars on the right, but the latter fled when attacked by the Kannarese. The English position was next attacked. They were defended with the loss of three men killed and twenty wounded and they had to retreat to a better position.

The incursions of the Kanarese had been disastrous to the Dutch trade at Cannanore. So the Dutch factors at the place were holding aloof from active operations. They were afraid lest the port of Cadalay, if it were taken, would be retained by the English and used to intercept Dutch trade with the pepper country lying up the River Vaḷarpaṭṭaṇam. To remove their jealousy, Stephen Law agreed to give them a certificate renouncing all claim to Cadalay if it were taken. After some more negotiations the Dutch agreed to land 300 men to assist the English.

On 31st March, a council of War seems to have been held and it was agreed to sieze the hill near the Kanarese camp to erect a breast work there, and then to bring canon and mortar to reduce the Cadalay fort.

On the morning of 1st April, this plan was put into operation. An advance guard, half English and half Dutch, siezed the hill. The Kanarese cavalry, made a bold stand, but the Dutch assisted by the English routed them in great disorder, some taking towards the fort and some to the ground below it. The combined forces then made a rush towards the fort; the Kanarese hung out a flag of truce but continued firing. This enraged the assailants and a great slaughter took place at the gate, which was stubbornly defended by the Kanarese. An English Topass, Joan Pichota, scaled the fort wall and discharged his own piece of artillery as well as those of 18 others handed to him, in quick succession. This cleared the wall and the English colours were soon flying on the ramparts. Meanwhile the defence of the gate slackened, the assailants poured in, and many of the Kanarese sought safety by lowering themselves over the walls by ropes. The fort was completely taken amidst great slaughter. Gōpalji, a Kanarese general died in action. A large body (300) of the Kanarese, after giving up their arms and while proceeding to Cannanore were barbarously massacred by the Nāyars. Another body, 200 horse and foot, while trying to escape inland was cut off. The losses of the Kanarese were indeed heavy. The English casualities were five natives killed and eight wounded. The Dutch lost one Ensign and two others burnt by explosion of gun powder. The Nāyars also suffered in their eagerness for plunder for a magazine blew up and killed a hundred of them. Eight canons and one mortar were among the spoils.

The other Kanarese forts Mādayī, Taḷiparamba, Mataḷāy and Ayconny (Ali Kuṇṇu) surrendered one by one. The last one offered stiff resistance. Captain Lane bombarded it at pistol shot from 6 a.m. to 3 p.m. After its surrender, the whole of the garrison, men and women and children were cruelly—most shamelessly and most barbarously and in violation of all laws divine and humane—butchered by the Nāyars.

On 11th May 1736, the English chief at Cadalay, wrote to Sōmaśēkhara Nāyaka detailing the causes of his breaking with him. These were: (1) the factory at Honāvar had to be abandoned in consequence of the oppression of his people; (2) the company's broker at Mangalore had been fined and imprisoned on a false pretext; (3) the promise to respect English trading privileges in the Kōlattiri country had been broken; (4) two English vessels driven ashore in Kanara had been seized and plundered and no redress had been given, and (5) finally the Kanarese general Gōpālayya had created dissensions in the Kōlattiri family and tried to alienate the company's privileges. And the chief followed this up with an offer to negotiate peace between Bednūr and the Prince Regent.[7]

The state of disunion among the petty chieftains of the coast, more so between the different members of the Kōlattiri family, forced the English factors to endeavour to arrange a peace with Bednūr; and after an unsuccessful effort made in October 1736 by Captain Gibbs and Mendonza with 200 soldiers and 180 sepoys to take the Nīlēśvaram fort, the last remaining stronghold of Sōmaśēkhara Nāyaka, the factors sent Lynch to Mangalore to arrange a general peace.[8] The result of Lynch's embassy was a treaty in February 1737, in which the Kanarese Governor of Mangalore, Sūrappaya ratified all former grants to the Company, empowered them to reopen the factory at Honāvar, secured all wrecks from seizure, assigned to the English a monopoly of pepper and

7. *Ibid.*, Vol. I, p. 368.
8. *Public Department Diary*, 1737, No. 10A, 7 Ap., p. 169.

cardamom trade in all the Kōlattiri territory that might be conquered, empowered the Company and their officers to export rice from Mangalore without paying the heavy duty called *Adlamy,* agreed to bar the Kanarese from coming to the south of the River Vaḷarpaṭṭaṇam or erecting strongholds near the Company's fort at Madakkara, and to leave the rest of the Kōlattiri territory to be overrun by the Kanarese as they might think fit; besides damages to the extent of 5,910 *pagodas* were paid for wrongs suffered.[9] On the 16th February 1737, a counterpart agreement was executed by the chief Stephen Law, on behalf of the Company.[10]

Shortly after this, the Kanarese crossed the River Nīlēśvaram and were able to command the Nīlēśvaram portion of the Kōlattiri territory. In April 1737, they advanced as far as Madakkara, farther south, and by August they overran the whole of the country as far south as the River Taḷiparambā; but they could not take the fort of Mādāyi. The Kōlattiris were helpless now and they seem to have approached the English for help. The English factors thereupon negotiated and arranged a treaty of peace between the Kōlattiris and the Kanarese. On 30th August, 1737, the chief, Stephen Law, Lynch, Sūrapaya, the Kanarese general and the Prince Regent met near Madakkara and signed a treaty. According to the terms of the treaty, the territories from the fort of Madday, (Mādāyi), westward to Urbelly, southward, and as the river winds to the foot of the hills, eastward with all the territories, northward, bordering on the river, Kōlattiri resigned to the king of Bednūr to be enjoyed by him in the manner in which he was doing. With what remained to the south, the king of Bednūr was not to pass with an armed force, through the above limits assigned; The Chief and the Council of the English Company were witnesses, as also those by whom the treaty was mediated.[11]

9. *Diary of Tellicherry Factory,* dated 15th February—Extracts in Logan: *A Collection of Treaties, Engagements and other papers of Importance relating to British Affairs in Malabar,* p. 32.

10. *Ibid.,* No. XXXIV.

11. *Diary of Tellicherry Factory,* dated 1st September, 1737. See Logan: *Collection of Treaties,* etc., XXXVI, XXXVII and XXXVIII.

Sūrapaya also gave a counterpart agreement to the same effect on behalf of Sōmaśēkhara Nāyaka. These terms were not, however, acceptable to Sōmaśēkhara Nāyaka, who had more ambitious schemes of conquest in view; and so almost simultaneously he refused the supply of rice to the Company's vessels at Mangalore. By turning off the rice tap, Sōmaśēkhara had it always in his power, to inconvenience seriously the Company's settlements and to cause an artificial famine.

Sūrapaya, was succeeded by Raghunātha as Governor of Mangalore. On 29th December, 1737, he reached the camp at Mādāyi and on 1st January, 1738, wrote to Stephen Law asking him to come forthwith to discuss important state matters. The English sent a deputation, returned and reported that the Kanarese wished the Company to remain neutral in the war about to be commenced with the 'Malabars'. But the Kanarese seized the guns of some English vessels detained at Mangalore in April 1738. Beyond this they did nothing in pursuing their conquests upto October 1738. In that month the Prince Regent gave Rs. 30,000 to the English to prosecute the war and made an agreement with them "to make war against the insolence of Canara" and to "drive out Canara".[12]

About the end of the year hostilities once again commenced; and on 2nd January 1739, there was a skirmish between the English and the Kanarese near Madakkara. The Kanarese were repulsed by the fire of the English troops. By 10th January, prospects of peace began to dawn, but the actual terms were not settled for another 11 months. The chief points in peace were that the English were to be permitted to export a definite quantity of rice without duty from Mangalore and the omission of the clause stopping the Kanarese from making conquests to the south of the River Vaḷarpaṭṭaṇam.[13] In other respects the treaty followed pretty closely that of February, 1737.

After the conclusion of this peace, the Bednūr forces made very little attempt at the extension of their territory

12. Logan: *Treaties*, No. XXXIX.
13. *Ibid.*, XLII, XLIII.

in the Malabar coast. The fact was they had exhausted the resources of the country in this endless war and they found difficulty in maintaining the large force they had, and which was costing them as much as 12,000 *pagodas* per month.

Sōmaśēkhara Nāyaka's other wars: Sōmaśēkhara Nāyaka was also engrossed in other minor wars. Baramē Nāyaka made an alliance with Hanumanta of Guttal and rebelled against the arms of Bednūr. He ravaged the territory of Tarikere and on the appeal of the Lord of the country, Sōmaśēkhara Nāyaka drove back Baramē Nāyaka.[14] In 1720, the pirate Kanhōji Angria landed some men at Mangalore. But he was forced back to his ships and leave the country. Mangalore was at that time a military station under the Nāyakas of Ikkēri.[15]

The relations between Sōmaśēkhara and the Rājā of Sunda were very cordial. The former seems to have sent about 6,000 foot and two hundred horses for help to the Rājā of Sunda.[16] Probably this was sent to him to relieve him of the pressure he had from the onslaught of Bāji Rao, the Maratha Peshwa. Sunda was plundered by the Maratha forces. The people of Sunda and Bednūr fled and both the Rājās agreed to pay *chauth* to the Marathas.[17] This invasion seems to have taken place in 1726-27 A.C

The Bednūr kingdom was subjected to another invasion. Banji Ghorpade allied himself with a Muslim Fatheyallah Khan and entered the kingdom. But he was defeated. Sōmaśēkhara Nāyaka, further helped the minor chiefs like the Nawab of Sāvanūr, chief of Rāyadurga, chief of Budi etc., He is also credited with the conquest of Sira and Ajjampūr from the Mughals.[18]

In 1730 the Amara and Sulia *Māgaṇis* were given to Coorg by Sōmaśēkhara. This was perhaps the result of the

14. *KNV.*, X.
15. Pinkerton: *Voyages*, VIII, p. 365.
16. *Carwar Factory Outward Letter Book*, Vol. 29-A, No. 2, p. 3.
17. *Bombay Gazetteer, Kanara*, p. 136.
18. *QJMS.*, XXII, p. 85.

visit paid by him when he went to Coorg through Subrahmaṇya and made friends with the ruling chief Vīrarājaiya.[19]

Sōmaśēkhara and the Portuguese: Due to the increasing activities of the English and Dutch, the Portuguese do not seem to have had a stronghold in Kanara. But they were very anxious to make peace with Sōmaśēkhara as is evident from their letters from Goa.[20] Sōmaśēkhara did not give elbow room for the Portuguese, and hence in 1719, they were planning an expedition against the army of Kanara.[21] It is not known whether the Portuguese carried out the expedition. In 1727, however, the chief captain of Kanara was asked to please the king of Kanara by paying fully for the rice and helping him against his enemies if the king asked for the same.[22] But in the same year, the Portuguese soldiers seem to have committed depradations in the Hindu temples of Kanara. Sōmaśēkhara naturally protested against this and the Portuguese authorities tried to appease him by promising him that the criminals would be severely dealt with. The Captain of Mangalore was also ordered to offer the king of Kanara artillery and experts to defend his territories when attacked by enemy forces such as from Mysore.[23]

The Portuguese were so particular about getting rice from the Kanarese territory that they were even prepared to concede whatever the Kanarese asked for. Agostinho Machadao, who went on a mission to Kanara in 1728 was instructed to arrange for a deal in rice at a certain price for many years in return for salt at a fixed price.[24] In a letter dated 5th April, 1728, Agostinho Machadao was given directions to act, if the king of Kanara admitted his propositions. "Knowing that rice in Kanara has the same value for our navy as 10 or 12 temples have, they should get for it, 7,00,000

19. *Ibid.*, XII, p. 50.

20. *La Das Moncoes*, No. 80, Fol. 160; *Ibid.*, No. 82, Fol. 106; Extracts in *Archivo Portuguese Oriental*, III, pt. II, Nos. 99 and 133.

21. *La dos Reis Vizinhos*, No. 8, Fol. 80; *Archivo Portuguese Oriental*, III, pt. ii, No. 274.

22. *La dos Reis Vizinhos*, No. 7, Fol. 43, *APO*, III, pt. ii, No. 6.

23. *Ibid.*, Fol. 53, *APO.*, III, pt. ii, No. 27.

24. *La dos Reis Vizinhos*, No. 7, Fol. 60, *APO.*, III, pt. iv, No. 36.

fardos per year and if it costs more, then this should be price they charge to open up their ports; and in proportion to the same price so many measures of salt as correspond to 6,00,000 *fardos* should be given to them."[25] Agostinho Machadao was constantly reminded by the authorities about the imperative need to effect some sort of an agreement with the king of Kanara.[26] In November 1728, the Portuguese factors at Goa felt the dire need for rice.[27] Meanwhile Sōmaśēkhara Nāyaka seems to have asked the Portuguese for a big ship to bring horses to his dominions. But the Portuguese were anxious to have very cordial relations with Sōmaśēkhara and make an alliance of peace and friendship with them. Hence they seem to have written that they could not give him the general right to bring horses but after making a peace, they would allow him such a concession according to fixed terms.[28] Further the Portuguese seem to have helped Sōmaśēkhara in his wars with the Nāyars (Kōlattiris).[29]

By 1733, the Portuguese were able to get from Kanara about 1,900 *fardos* of rice. The factor at Mangalore was also asked to see whether the Kanarese could be persuaded to give at a just price of about 13 or 14 *pagodas* in return for salt.[30]

On 12th May, 1733, Conde de Sandomil, the Portuguese Viceroy at Goa, wrote the following letter to Raghopa Odeyar (Raghunāth), the Kanarese Governor at Mangalore.

> "Received the letter of your Majesty with the news which gave me joy that your Majesty got with my coming over to office. For that I thank you and I hope that you will have always reason to be pleased because always during my tenure, I shall try very willingly to further the mutual interests, the increase of the dominion of the king of Canara, whose friendship I esteem

25. *Ibid.*, No. 7, Fol. 64, *APO.*, III, pt. iv, No. 38.
26. *Ibid.*, No. 7, Fol. 70, *APO.*, III, pt. iv, No. 54.
27. *Ibid.* No. 7, Fol. 73, *APO.*, III, pt. iv, No. 56.
28. *La dos Reis Vizinhos*, No. 7, Fol. 75; *APO.*, III, pt. iv, No. 59.
29. *Ibid.*, No. 7, Fol. 102; *APO.*, III, pt. iv, No. 148; *Ibid.*, No. 150.
30. *Ibid.*, No. 7, Fol. 108, *APO.*, III, pt. iv, No. 157.

very much and wish it may continue firmly. I was pleased with the success of the king of Canara won against the enemies, and that concurs for the benefit the ship that this state sent for help. Now I wished to send others that the king of Canara in his letter asked for and your Majesty also asked for. The maker of Mangalore had written with great emphasis. But as they will come late from north and south and will require some repairs, to be made in summer, it is necessary to keep them so that after repairs they may be sent over in the beginning of winter; this is the time when they can be used as during summer they cannot sail and instead of remaining without use, let them remain here for repairs. Let them go to help well. Let them be useful in everything for the utility of the dominions of the king of Canara and for the pleasure of your Majesty. I am sending through the agents that you sent, my regards to the king and a present in thanksgiving of what I have received.

Goa, 12th May, 1733. Conde de Sandomil".[31]

The Portuguese further seem to have helped the king of Kanara in his wars against the Kōlattiris by supplying him with warships.[32]

In 1734 Sōmaśēkhara sent his ambassador Nāraṇa (Nārāyaṇa) Prabhu to Goa, for asking the Portuguese for help in the shape of army, gun powder, bullets and bombs. The Portuguese however only promised to send the necessary help[33] hoping to contract for a regular supply of rice. The subsequent relations of Sōmaśēkhara with the Portuguese were cordial.

Domestic Life and Religious activities: Sōmaśēkhara Nāyaka married Nīlammāji,[34] the daughter of Nirvā-

31. *La dos Reis Vizinhos,* No. 7, Fol. 121, *APO.,* III, pt. iv, No. 303.
32. *La dos Reis Vizinhos,* No. 7, Fol. 130; *APO.,* III, pt. iv, No. 175, *La das Moncoes,* No. 102, Fol. 710, *APO.,* III, pt. iv, No. 165.
33. *Archivo Portuguese Oriental,* III, pt. iv, No. 176.
34. *EC.,* VIII, Nagar 32.

ṇayya who rose to the position of chief minister.[35] This Nirvāṇayya was a great Saṁskrit scholar and was the author of a Saṁskrit commentary on the work of *Kriyāsāra* of Nīlakaṇṭaśivācārya. He also wrote the *Śivapūjāvidhāna* in Kannaḍa.[36]

Sōmaśēkhara Nāyaka's concern for *maṭhas* and temples is amply testified by his numerous epigraphs which record grants of money and land. He took keen interest in the activities of the Śṛṅgēri *maṭha*. He made an enquiry into the conduct of some servants in it and directed Sacchidānanda Bhārati Svāmi to dismiss the men who were guilty. Further at the request of Sōmaśēkhara Nāyaka, Sacchidānanda Bhārati Svāmi visited Bednūr and was given a hearty reception by the Nāyaka.[37] He also patronised the Kudali maṭha and granted the village of Chennagondanakoppa in Gajanūr śīme to Raghurāja Tīrtha Svāmi of the *maṭha*.[38] He also patronised two Viraktha maṭhas constructed respectively by Keñcuva[39] and Mali Śeṭṭi.[40] For defraying the expenses of the services of the gods Avimuktēśvara and Bindhumādhava set up in the temple newly built by Venkaṭayya in the Malēyāḷa maṭhada grāma in Muttūr śīme and also for the maintenance of the Candraśēkharapura agrahāra erected near the temple, Sōmaśēkhara granted garden land, rice fields, etc., in various villages.[41]

35. This Nirvāṇayya seems to have been in high favour with Sōmaśēkhara Nāyaka for he figures prominently in many of Sōmaśēkhara's inscriptions. See *EC.*, VIII, Tl. 6, 87, 183, 186, *MAR.*, 1923; No. 122, *EC.*, VII, Sh. 7.

36. *MAR.*, 1916; p. 68.

37. *MAR.*, 1928, p. 68.

38. *EC.*, VII, Sh. 98, *EC.*, VI, Koppa 48.

39. *MAR.*, 1927, No. 62.

40. *EC.*, VII, Sk. 42. Many other institutions and *agrahāras* received liberal patronage from Sōmaśēkhara. See *EC.*, VIII, Tl. 6, 186, 87, 183; *MAR.*, 1943, No. 45.

41. *MAR.*, 1933, No. 30. The details of the grant are as follows: (a) Garden consisting of 1,000 arecanut trees producing 2 lakhs of arecanut. (b) Rice field of sowing capacity 5 khandugas, the produce being 25 khandugas of paddy of value 2½ varahas, (c) Land for satra of total revenue value 3 varahas, 9 10/16 hanas, (d) Wet lands in Parusemakki from the uttara lands at Kuruvalli with a total income of

Sōmaśēkhara Nāyaka also erected some public buildings. He built a palace to the west of Vēṇupura on a grand scale surrounded by tanks and gardens. It was named Candraśēkharapura. He also renovated the Nīlakaṇṭheśvara temple, decorated it with metal sheets and presented it with a golden *śikhara*. The fort of Bhuvanagiri was renovated and an upper open *verāndah* was built.[42]

Sōmaśēkhara also paid great attention to the welfare of his subjects. He gave good compensation for any loss incurred by them. To Konaja and Masanoja, two herdsmen from Honnali, he granted rice land in Haranahalli as an *umbaḷi*, in compensation for the death of their father Gauloji in an encounter with a tiger which had been committing ravages in the Balauv pass of the Honnali śīme.[43] A warrior named Basavaiyya was granted some rent free lands in appreciation of his services.[44]

In the evening of his life Sōmaśēkhara Nāyaka undertook a pilgrimage to a number of religious centres nearby and visited Śṛngāpura, Kodiyala, Vasupura, Hosangadi, Śankaranārāyaṇa, Kundāpura, Gōkarṇa, Kollūru, Ānandapura, Mahādēvapura and Shimoga.

Thus Sōmaśēkhara Nāyaka had an eventful reign of nearly 25 years. In 1739 he fell ill and died at Shimoga. His body was brought to Bednūr and buried there.[45]

1 varaha, 7¼ hana, (e) some rice lands in Kuruvalli village of revenue value 6 varahas 2½ hanas, (f) some lands in Nekarikana grāma and Bukkarāyapura, Melubandu, Kalakoppa, Bidirur, Dēvatekoppa, Mangalaguru, forests in Melubanda with their honey wax, etc. Malēyāḷa maṭha was a Maṭha of Smārta sect built at Tirthahalli on the banks of the Tuṅgā. It is said that an ascetic named Gangādharapuri Yōgi set up the god Narasimha at Tirthahalli and he and his disciples resided there and worshipped the god. A spiritual descendant of his named Dēvēndrapura Yōgi set up the god Viśveśvara in the Malēyāḷa maṭha in Śaka 1481. The *gurus* of this maṭha were patronised by early Vijayanagar kings, Harihara II and Dēvarāya I, etc. (See *EC.*, VIII, Tl. 1, 2, 173 and *MAR.*, 1923, No. 69 and 70).

42. *KNV.*, X.
43. *EC.*, VII, Sh. 128.
44. *MAR.*, 1923, No. 122.
45. *KNV.*, X.

CHAPTER XIV

THE DECLINE—BASAVAPPA NĀYAKA II AND CANNA BASAVAPPA NĀYAKA, (1739-1757)

Basavappa Nāyaka II (1739-1755). On the death of Sōmaśēkhara Nāyaka, the throne of Bednūr passed on to Basavappa Nāyaka II, the son of Vīrabhadra Nāyaka II, who was the brother of the deceased ruler. Basavappa Nāyaka seems to have ascended the throne in 1739 A.C.[1] His earliest inscription, however, is dated 1740 A.C.[2] As the earliest known inscription of his successor is dated 1755 A.C.,[3] it may be presumed that Basavappa Nāyaka could have probably ruled upto that year.

Basavappa Nāyaka and the French: During the reign of Basavappa Nāyaka, a new trading company was gaining influence in the west coast. The French East India Company which was the last European trading concern to come to India, were trying to establish themselves in that area. A letter from Tellicherry, dated 7th February, 1740, refers to the French as having started negotiations with the Kanarese. "They (the French) are now gone to the Canarese general at Madday, with a very large present. There arrive daily two ships with a considerable land force from Pondicherry but, what their intentions are, we cannot say".[4] The English, however, were careful to see that the French did not gain any access by helping Basavappa Nāyaka, in his attempts to subdue the princes of Malabar, as they had to depend on his good grace for the pepper and rice from the coast.

1. *KNV.*, XI, states that Basavappa was crowned at Vēṇupura in Śaka 1661, Siddhārti, jyeṣṭha bahula 5. (June 14, 1739).
2. *EC.,* VIII, Ng. 32.
3. MAR., 1927, No. 153.
4. *Secretariat Inward Letter Book,* No. 2/1740.

In February 1740 William Wake, the chief at Tellicherry agreed to pay a duty of ½ *pagoda* per *corge* of rice taken from Kanarese ports for any rice taken above the stipulated quantity of 300 *corge* of rice (42 bales).[5] By March 1740, the English seem to have got from Mangalore 6903 bales of rice and hoped to receive yet another 9000 bales.[6] In 1741, the English made a contract with a notable merchant of Honavar, Har Camatti, for taking pepper. But about the same time the Portuguese also entered the field and succeeded in contracting for 40 *candies* of pepper which prevented the English from getting any quantity of it.[7] Apparently the Portuguese offered a higher price and took away the pepper. In 1744 also the English factor at Mangalore, Charles Crommelin, was not able to buy rice for the settlement due to various reasons, chief among them being the underhand methods of the Portuguese in getting rice for themselves. Further, the Kanarese appear to have insisted on a duty of one *pagoda* per *corge* of rice taken by the English contrary to the previous agreement (i.e. ½ *pagoda* per corge).[8] On 3rd January 1745, the English chief at Tellicherry wrote to Basavappa Nāyaka complaining about the increase in duties. But Basavappa did not take serious notice of it and sent only a very formal reply.[9] The English, however, were forced to be friendly with the ruler of Bednūr. They could ill-afford to incur his displeasure as they entirely depended upon his territories for their supplies of pepper and rice.

Basavappa and the Kōlattiris of Malabar: The Kōlattiri prince Kunhi Rāma seems to have engaged the attention of Basavappa Nāyaka on account of his dilatory policy. In

5. Logan: *Treaties*, No. xlii.

6. *Secretariat Inward Letter Book*, No. 2/1740, p. 168. The selling price of the rice, however, seems to have been Rs. 98 for a *candy* of about 502 pounds and Rs. 115 with all charges. *Secretariat Inward Letter Book*, No. 2/1740, p. 143.

7. *Secretariat Inward Letter Book*, No. 3B/1741-42, p. 336.

8. *Secretariat Inward Letter Book*, 1743, p. 79. The Kanarese were but legitimate in raising the tax, as they had to incur a lot of expenditure in subduing the Malabar chief.

9. *Secretariat Inward Letter Book*, 1744/45.

January 1741, the Kōlattiri endeavoured to regain his lost territories from the Kanarese, which they had taken in the previous war, by negotiating with the Kanarese general at Madday.[10] But he was not successful in his attempts.[11]

Basavappa Nāyaka felt that the enormous cost of maintaining an army in the territories of the Kōlattiri prince was in undue proportion to the revenues which accrued to him from the conquered territories. Hence he seems to have thought of evacuating the territories if the Prince consented to pay him 100 thousand *pagodas* over and above the 7000 which he had paid. However, this did not materialise then.[12] Meanwhile the Prince Cunhi Homo (Kunhi Rāma) sent one of his courtiers to the English with a proposal that they should build a fort at the mouth of the river Ramatilly, and keep a garrison thereon, as it would prevent insurrections in the area besides serving as a check on the Kanarese.[13]

In 1742, the Prince appears to have after all come to an agreement with Basavappa Nāyaka. He promised to pay him 30,000 *pagodas* in return for the withdrawal of the Kanarese from his country. On payment of about 16,000 *pagodas* the Canarese withdrew from Madday and retired to Ai Conny (Alikuṉṉu). This agreement was not however, communicated to the English, who were mediators between the Kanarese and the prince in the last peace between them.[14] The Kanarese hearing rumours that the prince would break the peace after their handing over Madday to him, and that he had twenty to thirty thousand men with him to fall upon them, changed their plans and reinforced the fort and the garrison. Thereupon the prince applied to the English for help in the shape of gunpowder and lead. But the English were diplomatic enough to steer clear of all embroils with the Kanarese.[15] In 1744, also the Prince tried

10. *Secretariat Inward Letter Book* No. 3A, 1741-42, p. 110.
11. *Ibid.*, p. 189.
12. *Ibid.*, No. 3B, 1741-42, p. 552.
13. *Secretariat Inward Letter Book*, No. 3D, 1742-43, p. 126.
14. *Ibid.*, No. 3B, 1741-42, p. 526.
15. *Ibid.*, No. 3D, 1742-43.

to coerce the English to help him against the Kanarese in vain.[16]

In 1747, there was a skirmish between the Prince of Kōlattiri and the Bednūr forces.[17] In March 1747, the prince seems to have finally concluded peace with the Kanarese.[18]

Basavappa and the Portuguese: The document left behind by Marques de Castello Novo e Alorna, the departing Portuguese viceroy of Goa, gives us an account of the state of India, during and at the end of his administration. About the Kanara country the document says:

> "The king of Canara is more rich than powerful. The traffic in rice with the whole of Malabar and part of Muscat is the cause of a great influ of money into his kingdom. We have in his dominions a factory at Mangalor. We have been at peace for some time now with this prince, and it is of utmost importance to us that this peace should be preserved inviolate. It may seem absurd to say this potentate is much more rich than powerful, but such is the case, for the money as fast as it comes into his kingdom is hoarded up in his treasury and no use is made of it at all. He will not permit any fortifications to be erected in his dominions in case they should at any time be invaded and the enemy establish himself in them."[19]

The document reveals the anxiety of the Portuguese to remain on friendly terms with Basavappa Nāyaka.

Other campaigns of Basavappa Nāyaka: In 1740, Madakere Nāyaka of Chitaldrug laid siege to Sānte Bennūr, but the Bednūr army was able to defeat him.

Mangalore was a scene of plunder and loot by pirates. A fleet of about 2,000 men were landed by Tulajee Angria, the

16. *Ibid.*, No. 4A, 1743-44, pp. 142-143 and 186.
17. *Public Department Diary*, 1747, No. 20, p. 62, Letter dated 6-2-1747.
18. *Ibid.*, Letter dated 28th March 1747, p. 138.
19. Danvers: *The Portuguese in Malabar*, Vol. II, p. 423.

notorious pirate and freebooter who plundered the city and the inhabitants had to flee up the country.[20]

The Kanarese had also a skirmish with the king of Nīlēśvar, which involved them in great loss. In 1747, the Marathas under Sadāśiva Rao Bhau, attacked Bednūr and were able to get a tribute of Rs. 12,000 from Basavappa Nāyaka.[21]

In 1748 Bednūr was again at war with Chitaldurg in which the latter was completely defeated. Madakeri Nāyaka of Chitaldurg seems to have been helped by Chandā Sāhib who was entering on a conquest of the Carnatic. A battle was fought at Mayakoṇḍa, a village about 20 miles west of Chitaldurg. The contest was obstinate and sanguinary, but the troops of Bednūr, being superior in numbers, were able to win the day. Madakeri Nāyaka was killed in action.[22] Chandā Sāhib's eldest son, Abid Sahib, also lost his life in this encounter.[23] In 1749, Madakeri Nāyaka's son Kasturi Rangappa Nāyaka with the assistance of Moti Khān, and Muzaffar Jang and an army of one lakh of men laid siege to Sānte Bennūr. But he was repulsed with loss by Basavappa Nāyaka.[24] There was another attack by the Marathas. Nārāyaṇa Rao of Poona invaded the kingdom of Bednūr. Basavappa Nāyaka, had to buy them off by paying five and half laks of *varāhas.* Some time later, Madōji Purandhar of Poona again invaded the kingdom and carried off twelve lakhs of *varāhas.* Basavappa was therefore forced to increase taxes on all lands at the rate of one *honnu* per *varāha.*

20. *Public Department Diary*: 1746, No. 19B, p. 502.

21. *Peshwa Daftar Rumal* (Ruzkird), No. 34, 1747.

22. *MAR.*, 1944, No. 49. An interesting inscription of Basavappa Nāyaka dated in the cyclic year Vibhava, 13th day of the bright half of Phalguna (18th February 1749) refers to the death of Madakēri Nāyaka in the fight. It registers the gift of a silver plate made from the presents submitted by all in connection with the death Madakēri Nāyaka in the fight, to goddess Mūkāmbikā.

23. *KNV.*, XI. This event is also dated in this work in Vibhava, Phalguna (February, 1749).

24. *Ibid.*, This event is dated in this work in Śukla, Jyeṣtha (May 1749). For a general narration of the affairs of Chitaldurg and Bednūr see Burhan's *Tuzak-i-Walajahi,* pp. 136-37.

This naturally resulted in much discontent among the people and so they protested against it. Being pressed from all sides, Basavappa Nāyaka was not able to maintain his own ground. Thereafter one notices naturally a marked deterioration in the fortunes of the Ikkēri dynasty.

Basavappa Nāyaka is also credited with the capture of the forts of Dummi, Nandigave, Hodigere, Moravanji and Chandragiri. He is further stated to have defeated Wazir Venkaṭa Rāya of Kumbhase.[25]

The notable diplomats of his reign were Guruvappa, son of Nirvāṇayya, principal minister, Venkaṭa Maloe, the Governor of Honāvar, Hur Comaty, principal merchant and Subbu Senoy, the customs officer.[26]

Domestic Life: Basavappa Nāyaka had two wives, Cannammājī and Canna Vīrammājī. As he had no issue to succeed him he adopted a boy named Canna Basavappa, this being the second instance of adoption in the dynasty. Canna Basavappa was the son of Guruvappa.[27] Basavappa Nāyaka like his predecessors took interest in the welfare of religious institutions. He nominated the successor to the pontifical seat of Śṛngēri.[28] He made permanent arrangements for the car festival of God Siddhēśvara at Mantrarāja, Ānandapura as also at Subrahmaṇya. At one time he seems to have entertained one lakh ninety six thousand jangamas.[29]

In the evening of his life he undertook a pilgrimage to the shrines at Kollūru, Koṭeśvara, Vasupura, Śankaranārāyaṇa and Mantrarājapura. After a rule of 15 years, he died and was buried in the compound of the Puṭṭedevāru maṭha.[30]

25. *KNV.*, XI.
26. *Secretariat Inward Letter Book*, No. 2, 1740, p. 143.
27. *KNV.*, XI.
28. *QJMS.*, VIII, p. 28.
29. *KNV.*, XI.
30. *EC.*, VII, Introduction, p. 42.

Canna Basavappa Nāyaka *(1755-1757)*: On the death of Basavappa Nāyaka II, Canna Basavappa Nāyaka ascended the throne in 1755 A.C. Only one inscription of this king dated 1755 A.C. is known.[31] Like his adoptive father he had to witness the frequent invasions and plunder of his territories. Even the English who had been allies of Bednūr were not friendly towards him probably on account of his weakness. Further, he had incurred their displeasure by certain indiscreet acts. For example, he seems to have prohibited the export of rice from his territories by the English for they were helping the Muslims and minor chiefs who rebelled against the authority of Bednūr.[32]

Canna Basavappa and Malabar: In 1755, Āli Rājā of Cannanore organised a buccaneering campaign against the Kanara country. He sent 3,000 men with guns in 70 native small crafts to ravage the area. They attacked Manjēshwar and landed their men to the north of Mangalore at Kollūr and carried off booty worth 4,000,000 *pagodas*. In the course of the expedition some Brahmans were massacred and that was greatly resented and mourned by the Bednūr court.[33] Canna Basavappa adopted the readiest means at his command of bringing everybody to his senses, he stopped the export of rice from Mangalore and thus put the English, French, Dutch and others to a serious predicament.

Towards the beginning of 1757, the Bednūr forces made a dash against Nīlēśvar and defeated the chief of the place. The Kanarese army consisted of 12,000 horses and foot.[34] The Dutch seem to have interfered at this juncture and the chief entered into an agreement with them.[35] However, in spite of the Dutch aid to the chief, the Kanarese came out successful.

31. *MAR.*, 1927, No. 153, The *KNV*. dates his accession in Śaka 1677, Karttika Śu (November 5, 1755)

32. *Secretariat Letter Book* No. 14/17, 1754-55.

33. Logan: *Malabar,* I, p. 394.

34. *Public Department Diary,* 1757, No. 10A. 20th January, 1757, p. 37.

35. *Ibid.,* 22nd February, 1757, p. 73

In the pepper trade of Kanara, there was keen competition between the Portuguese and the English. The English stationed a permanent representative at Honāvar to prevent the Portuguese from depriving them of any considerable quantity of pepper, they might be able to get.[36]

Canna Basavappa Nāyaka's rule was only nominal, for the reins of administration were with his adoptive mother Vīrammājī. She was in amours with one Nimbaya, a mean slave, and this had become a public scandal. Canna Basavappa Nāyaka remonstrated against her ways; and for this reason he was caused to be murdered by the notorious queen,[37] by being strangled in his bath by a Jetti, a professional athlete who used to shampoo him.

36. *Secretariat Outward Letter Book*, No. 18, 1757-63, p. 23.

37. Buchanan: *Journey through Madras, etc.*, p. 127. *Public Department Diary*, 1757, No. 30B, p. 453: "The younger Raja of Bednure has been murdered by his mother on the 17th July". The *Haidar Nāmah* states that Canna Basavappa was treacherously strangled by the neck, during the act of shampooing through a professional athlete. Wilks, confirms this (See Wilks: *History of Mysore*, I, p. 503). There is a fine novel in Kannada entitled *Cannabasava Nāyaka* written by Masti Venkatesa Iyengar (Jeevana Publications, Gavipuram, Basavangudi, Bangalore). It brings into prominence the leading characters in the story, Vīrammājī, Canna Basava, Rājā Rāma Candūr and Lingappa.

CHAPTER XV

VĪRAMMĀJĪ AND THE END (1757-1763)

Vīrammājī succeeded in her own name and adopted another lad named Sōmaśēkhara, who was the youngest of the four sons of her maternal uncle, Puṭṭaṇa Śeṭṭi Canna Vīrappa of Bankāpūr.[1] The murder of Canna Basavappa, as also her continued amours with Nimbaya, the mean slave, caused great consternation among all. Disturbances at Bednūr continued till the end of 1757.[2] The adopted son, Sōmaśēkhara III, was however completely under the control of the queen. Vīrammājī is said to have organised a campaign against the Maratha ruler of Miraj and to have captured through her general Vīrabhadrappa, the fort at his very capital.[3]

Vīrammājī and the English: The English were able to get better trade concessions due to the weak position of the queen. In 1758 they were able to bargain in the pepper price and they seem to have declined to take two hundred and fifty *candies* from Ankola, at the rate of 24 *varāhas.*[4] The queen granted a *firman* to the English in 1761, according

1. *KNV.*, XII, Bankāpur is about 60 miles north-east of Bednūr.

2. *Public Department Diary*, 2757, No. 30, p. 38, p. 390. *Secretariat Outward Letter Book*, 1557-62, No. 18. *Peshwa Dafter*, xxviii, 194, pp. 228-229, 9-9-1757.

3. *KNV.*, XII, but the *Peshwa Dafter* (xxviii, 194, pp. 228-229) makes one understand that Mirjan (Miraj) was conquered from Vīrammājī by the Marathas under Balwant Rao Ganapat. The queen had, therefore to impose 50 per cent additional tax to buy him off. But she could not pay the stipulated tribute to the Marathas, who therefore wrote a strong reprimand to the dowager queen calling upon her to pay up the tribute. This completely estranged the sympathy of the people to the royal house and she was not able to control the hostile elements. (See *Peshwa Dafter*, xxviii, 209, 13-1-1758).

4. *Secretariat Outward Letter Book*, 1757-62, No. 17, p. 25.

them permission to build a factory at Honāvar and to mount thereon 21 carriage guns without paying ground rent for any house or houses which they may build within the place. The other articles of the *firman* were:

> "The English and their servants were to have full liberty to go about in her dominions and that all the Rāṇi's officers and subjects must show them respect. Whatever goods or merchandise the English or their brothers shall bring in their factory at Onore, or import into Mirjee river (except horses) they shall pay on the amount they are sold for, only 1½% customs, including officers' fees.
>
> If the English or their servants import any goods at Compta (Kumta) they shall pay one and half per cent except on sugar, dry dates, kismiss, cocoanuts, copra, cholab, mangest, tobacco, opium, cotton, salt, brimstone and toothenague, on which they shall pay customs as other merchants.
>
> If they export any country goods at any place except Mirjee, Compta (Kumta) and Onore, they shall pay customs as other merchants except on gold and silver, on which no customs shall be charged and in case their goods remain unsold, and they choose to export them again, they shall not pay any duties.
>
> If they cannot sell their goods at the places allowed to them, and they choose to carry them inland, they have full liberty to do so and our *killedars* etc., officers, shall not on any account molest or impede them.
>
> After they have paid the customs at the place allotted, if they choose to carry their goods inland, they shall pay 2 pagodas customs, for as much as one man can carry of Broad cloth, cutness, velvets and silks as far as Madura, if they go beyond Madura, then they shall pay the usual country customs, and in case they choose to sell their goods, in the way they must pay the usual

N. 20

customs of the place at which they sell, but on all goods carried directly from Onore to Bringat, they shall only pay the customs of one and a half per cent at Onore and then no further custom till they come to Bringat.

If the merchants or people to whom the English sell their goods shall make any disputes or delays about paying them their money Our Killedars etc., officers must assist the English, all in their power to recover the money, and the English may, if they please, carry the merchants etc., who owe them money and keep them prisoners in their factory, till they have full satisfaction, and our Killedars officers etc., shall not impede or make any disputes with the English on this account.

No body must go into the English factory by force, if they do and the English complain of them, our Killedars must do speedy justice, and punish them and whenever slaves or servants run away all the officers and subjects must secure them and deliver them up again to the English, but they must not cut their heads off.

In a like manner if any of the Rajaha's (Sōma-śēkhara's) people run away they must deliver them up, if they go to the English factory, the Rajah's officers and subjects must assist the English, to secure the thieves and recover what is stolen. If the English import any goods as necessaries they shall pay no customs on them.

The English must not kill cows, oxen or Men in the dominions.

If any ships or Boats belonging to the English are shipwrecked in the Rajah's ports, on his coasts, all the Rajah's subjects and officers must assist the English in saving all the goods and Effects and deliver whatever is found to the English, but the English have nothing to do with any vessels belonging to any other Merchant.

If any oxen with pepper, Betlenut or other goods come down from inland (or any part of our dominions) belonging to the English the customs man should settle the customs immediately.

The English have free liberty to cut out Timber, stones and wood to build their factory and repair their boats etc, but in case they want to cut any masts and Timbers to build ships with, they must first obtain permission. All the ships of war belonging to the English have free liberty to import and export without paying anchorage duties. The English Anchorage duty, *Killedars'* officers perquisites and all fees is included in 1½%.

Whatever pepper the English bring from Bringat, was to pay only ½ a *pagoda* custom.

The English have free liberty to settle their factory at Bringat, and should carry on good friendship according to this firman."[5]

Vīrammājī's patronage of religious institutions: Inspite of her great difficulties, Vīrammājī continued the traditional friendliness to the Śṛngēri maṭha. It is said that she invited to her capital, in January 1758, Abhinava Sacchidānanda Bhāratī Svāmi,[6] and after giving him a rousing reception, presented him with a crystalline image of Śiva (*Spaṭika liṅga*) and an image of Gopālakṛṣṇa set in rubies (ratnakachita Gopāla-Kṛṣṇamurti), together with the gift of a piece of land valued at 74 *varāhas*. She also endowed the *maṭha* with another rent-free land valued at 300 *varāhas* and arranged for liquidation of its debts.[7]

5. *Public Department Diary*, 1761, p. 75, 19th Jan. 1761. *Secretariat Inward Letter Book*, 1761, No. 15, p. 31.

6. The *Guru* of the Śṛngēri maṭha has to be identified with Narasimha Bhāratī, who became *Jagadguru* in 1758, according to inscriptions (see *Mys. Gaz.*, V, 1179). According to the Śṛngēri maṭha list, however, Abhinava Sacchidānanda Bhāratī was Guru from 1741-1767 and Narasimha Bhāratī from 1767-1770 (*Mys. Gaz.*, I, 307). The *maṭha* list and the data afforded by inscriptions do not always tally.

7. *KNV.*, XII.

Hyder and Bednūr: In 1762, Hyder Ali launched on his scheme of conquests in Mysore and the Carnatic. About the middle of 1762, he conquered Chitaldrug and got a tribute of 4 lakhs and a fine of 2 lakhs of *pagodas* from its defeated chief, Madakeri Nāyaka.[8] Madakeri Nāyaka introduced to Hyder, a young pretender to the Bednūr throne, who professed to be the prince Canna Basavappa who had been murdered by Vīrammāji. The pretender was possibly an artificial creation of the Chitaldrug Palegar to wreck his vengeance on Bednūr as both the principalities were fighting often with each other. It was given out that the pretender put up as Canna Basavappa had been saved by an artifice of the Jetti, concealed in his protector's house for five years, with the aid of his neighbours. The crafty Hyder made use of the opportunity and decided to march against Bednūr, ostensibly to reinstate the alleged pretender but really to serve his own ambitious designs. Further, Hyder had for some time an eye on Bednūr in order to extend this influence on that side to the sea and to acquire the hoarded treasure at the city.

Towards the close of 1762, Hyder accompanied by Madakeri Nāyaka of Chitaldrug marched against Bednūr. He sent at first some searching spies to study the situation at Bednūr. Hyder left Chitaldurg, carrying the pretender with him at the head of 6,000 of his best cavalry and some Kaḷḷars. He had also sufficient food supplies and advanced by forced marches towards Bednūr. The English records, however, say that Hyder's force consisted of about 10,000 horse and more than 20,000 foot.[9]

Before the actual expedition to Bednūr, Hyder, naturally made some sort of an agreement with the pretender and the Chitaldurg chief. The terms were that the young pretender was to be re-established at Bednūr, in return for valuable presents and Rs. 40 lakhs towards the expenses besides the

8. Wilks: *op. cit.*, I, p. 502.
9. *Secretariat Inward Letter Book*, 1763, No. 17, p. 21.

Port of Mangalore, together with a stretch of territory connecting it with Mysore.[10] The pretender readily agreed to abide by the terms. The Palegar of Chitaldurg was to supply some troops to Hyder, in return for some remuneration for the help. All the preliminaries over, the combined armies marched towards Bednūr about the end of 1762, moving in four parallel colonnades. Hyder attended to the pretender with much pomp and ceremony, by having him mounted on a caparisoned elephant, in order to attract the attention of the people. This artful design of Hyder attracted the country people and they furnished the necessaries for the armies such as food.

On entering the territories of Bednūr, Hyder skillfully issued a proclamation in the name of the Pretender, requesting the people to give their allegiance to the new ruler. This appeal had the desired effect. Many of the forts received the so-called lawful prince openly. The army then marched through Chitaldurg-Chandagiri-Shimoga road and took Sānte Bennūr. Thence it marched to Benkipūr, the modern Bhadrāvati and finally took Shimoga, a fortified town, 43 miles east of Bednūr. The queen Vīrammājī, realising the impending danger tried to make a compromise by offering four lakhs of *pagodas*, but Hyder brushed aside the offer and marched on to Kumsi. Here, he found Lingappa,[11] a minister of Vīrammājī, who had been imprisoned at Kumsi, possibly owing to differences of opinion between him and the queen on the fate of Canna Basavappa. Thus Lingappa (Linganna?) was waiting for an opportunity to wreak vengeance on Vīrammājī. He therefore ventured to teach her a lesson and volunteered to reveal to Hyder a secret path leading to Bednūr. Hyder continuing his march came to Ayanur, where he encountered some opposition. The

10. De La Tour: *The History of Hyder Ali Khan Nabob Bahadur, or New Memoirs concerning the East Indies* (London, 1784), I, p. 87.

11. "Lingana" of Wilks (*op. cit.*, 1505). He is probably identical with Śivalingappa, mentioned in *KNV.*, Canto XII, as one of the principal officers.

Garrison there was surrounded and taken. Proceeding further twenty-five miles, the armies reached Ānandapura.[12] The queen seeing the danger coming nearer and with anxiety to avert the possible calamity, offered twelve lakhs of *pagodas*, and as Hyder was nearing Bednūr, she raised her offer to eighteen lakhs. But, Hyder having tasted the fruits of victory, rejected the offers of the queen and marched on. This threw Vīrammājī into a dilemma. She negotiated once again for peace, promising to meet the expenses of Hyder as also to pay an annual tribute of a lakh of *pagodas* and a share in the produce of the country pepper, arecanut, sandalwood, etc.[13] But Hyder who was determined on the conquest of the country demanded the immediate surrender of the *Rāṇī* promising to keep her as pensioner in the fort of Seringapatam. Vīrammājī proudly rejected the offer and decided to defend her city with the help of Abdul Hakim Khān of Sāvanūr, a place about 150 miles to the north-east. Abdul Hakīm, sent her 2,000 horses and 4,000 foot, while he advanced and encamped with a strong force near the river Bālā. Hyder was amazed at the courage of the queen and he marched with a body of his infantry and cavalry towards the fort of Bednūr itself with a view to invest it.

At the city's first barrier, Hyder ordered a noisy but feigned attack. He then entered the city of Bednūr through the secret path pointed out by Lingappa. The citadel was invested by Hyder and his men day and night. But Vīrammājī, defended it with remarkable steadiness and courage, and her troops also remained steadfast in their posts. The defensive works at Bednūr were sufficiently strong but there were not enough troops to oppose Hyder's mighty force. However, Vīrammājī and her garrison continued to fight, not minding the calamities and miseries. Many of them were

12. *Haidar-Nāmah* (1784), pp. 27-28. The work has been noticed at some length in *MAR.*, 1930, pp. 79-106.

13. *Mac. Coll.*, 18-15-7, Kaifiyat of Nagar.

killed in action. Abdul Hakim's troops also aided well in the defence of the fort and in attacking the batteries of the besiegers. The siege was very strict and close. When, Vīrammājī found that her position was worsening, she first set fire to her palace, including her ornamental sleeping apartments, which had been built by Sōmaśēkhara Nāyaka, with Chinese bricks and tiles, washed and set in gold, the interstices being gold, while the walls and doors were ornamented with jewels. She also destroyed most of her jewellery and then accompanied by Nimbaya and Sōmaśēkhara III, escaped on foot through a water drain, and went to Kāvalēdurga, (about 15 miles away from Bednūr, a very strong place surrounded by thick forest). She fortified the place still further with her remaining resources.

Hearing of the Rāṇī's flight, Hyder placed a garrison in the fort of Bednūr, and went to Kavalēdurga and besieged it closely. After a time, not without opposition, the garrison surrendered and the Rāṇī was taken prisoner. Accounts differ as to where the Rāṇī was sent as prisoner. One version says that she was sent in a palanquin to Seringapatam by way of Sira, but other accounts make one infer that she was sent first to Bednūr.[14] Hyder seems to have received the Rāṇī, in the most gracious manner and even tried to reconcile her with the pretender.[15] The pretender also seems to have been induced to grant the Rāṇī a considerable pension and also freedom regarding her private life.[16] It is not possible, however, to say whether all this happened or not, but there are grounds for believing that she was treated with the dignity due to her rank.

14. Captain Francis Robson: *Life of Hyder Ally,* (London, 1786), pp. 30-31; De la Tour: *op. cit.*, I, p. 88 presumes that Vīrammājī was already at Bednūr when the insurrection came about.

15. De La Tour: *op. cit.*, I, p. 86. He says that Hyder caused the new king to be crowned, (p. 87).

16. *Ibid.*, De la Tour says that she was allowed "to live with her husband". By this he of course means Nimbaiya.

Thus after a protracted siege, Bednūr fell on January 19, 1763 (Citrabhanu, Māgha śu 5).[17] And this ended the political rivalry between Mysore and Bednūr, which had lasted for nearly a century and a half. Bednūr however, became a scene of loot and plunder by Hyder's men.[18] When the conquest was completed, Hyder thought that he could expose the imposter and assert his own authority. The popular feeling in support of the pretender was easily suppressed.[19]

Vīrammājī and her paramour Nimbaya, and her adopted son were seized and sent to Maddagiri. Here the queen stayed till she was released when the Marathas under Mādhava Rao took Maddagiri in 1764 and accompanied them to Poona, but died before she could reach the place.[20] Sōmaśēkhara Nāyaka according to Rice,[21] ended his days unmar-

17. *KNV.*, XII. The date given in this work tallies with the date given in the *Haidar Namah* (pp. 27-28), Wilks, places the event in the beginning of March 1763. (*op. cit.*, I, p. 506).

18. For a long description of the destruction of Bednūr by Hyder see C. Hayavadana Rao; *History of Mysore,* Vol. II, p. 448 ff. There is also a long account of the conquest of Bednūr in App. V, of the same volume.

19. Michaud J.: *Histoire des Progne's et dela chute de L' Empire de Mysore sous les regnes d'Hyder Aly et Tippoo Saib,* (Paris), Chapter II, pp. 41-42. In this connection the French writer Michaud gives a story about the sweet-heart of the young prince, whom Hyder wanted to have for himself and which resulted in clash of interests and the subsequent overthrow of the pretender.

20. C. Hayavadana Rao, makes Vīrammājī a leading figure in the attempted assassination of Hyder when he fell ill in June 1763, with Malaria. He further says that Lingappa of Mudubidire ex-minister of the queen, with whose help Hyder entered Bednūr, and whom Hyder did not reward properly, bore a grudge against Hyder and wanted to wreak vengeance. Hence he entered into a compact with Vīrammājī to assassinate Hyder by blowing up the palace when he was conferring with his ministers (*History of Mysore,* Vol. II, p. 470 ff.). But this account is based mainly from later sources like De la Tour. We cannot, however, accept that Vīrammājī had a hand in it; until we have more convincing or corroboratory evidence.

21. Rice: *Mysore and Coorg from Inscriptions,* p. 161.

ried. But in the publisher's preface to the *Śivatattvaratnākara,* we are told that "on hearing that Hyder was contemplating an invasion of the Maratha country, he (Sōmaśēkhara) was kept under the protection of the Dēśai of Nargunḍ," and that he married a daughter of Basappa Śeṭṭi at Nargunḍ, where his descendants are supposed to be still living.[22]

Estimate of Vīrammājī and the end of the Nāyakship: The character and achievements of Vīrammājī have been vindicated by later chroniclers. The annalist Kirmani describes the Rāṇī as "a low-minded and fearless woman wearing the dress of a man" exercising unlimited authority over her country,[23] as "dissolute"[24] and as "bad".[25] While it is not possible to uphold every act of Rāṇī Vīrammājī, especially her possible illicit relations with Nimbaya, there is hardly any evidence whatsoever to consider her unpatriotic or even to think that she attempted to sacrifice her own country for mere vice or for personal pleasures. It is very doubtful if she was "geliebte" of Nimbaya, though her intimacy with him was outside the pale of Hindu Marital Law. As the Latin saying goes 'Virtue rejoices in temptation,'[26] Vīrammājī had evidently fallen a victim to such temptation. Even Kirmani, who has depicted Vīrammājī in very dark colours, has praised her for the undaunted fight she put up and the gallant defence of her city, the encouragement she gave to her troops who remained steadfast in their posts and defended themselves bravely and for the manner in which she secured the help of a Muslim ruler against a Muslim leader with a large army, and for the way in which she 'herself behaved with the steadiness and courage of a man.'[27] Such qualities of Vīrammājī must indeed redeem her personal weakness. While she might not have been a saint, it

22. *STR.*, Preface, p. iii.

23, 24 & 25. Kirmani, Mir Hussain Ali Khan: *The History of Hyder. Naik: (The Neshauni Hyduri)*; Col. W. Miles' Translation, London 1842, p. 128.

26. The Latin text is *Gaudet Tentamine virtus.*

27. Kirmani: *op. cit.,* pp. 135-136.

is possible that her free manners with Nimbaya, gave occasion to gossip, which gave her quite an evil reputation. It must be conceded that she was a ruler of considerable talent, brave and daring in action and highly patriotic by temperament. There were some stray attempts to regain the lost power of Ikkēri, but these failed as there was nobody to help them in their endeavour. Thus the strong and influential House of Ikkēri, after a rule of well over two centuries came to a dramatic end and the kingdom of Ikkēri itself became a part of Mysore.[28]

28. The end of Ikkēri Nāyakship in 1763 under pathetic circumstances closely resembles the end of the Madurai Nāyakship in 1739. See T. V. Mahalingam: *The End of the Madura Nāyakship*, in *Indica.* (The Indian Historical Research Institute Silver Jubilee Commemoration Volume, pp. 221 ff.). The last rulers in Ikkēri as well as in Madurai were women, i.e., Vīrammājī and Mīnākṣi respectively. Both the Nāyakships ended due to the interference of enterprising Muslims, that of Chandā Sāhib in Madurai in support of the pretender Bangāru Tirumala and of Hyder Ali in Ikkēri in support of the pretender Canna Baṣavappa. Both the invaders were unscrupulous and the queens were put to much humiliation and suffering. Vīrammājī and Mīnākṣī died under very distressing circumstances. The last queen of Ikkēri was taken prisoner to Maddagiri and subsequently released by Marathas and she died on her way to Poona. Chanda Sāhib imprisoned Mīnākṣī in her own palace at Trichinopoly. The queen however, unable to bear the insult put an end to her life. The manner in which Mīnākṣī put an end to her life is not clearly known. Some chronicles say that she poisoned herself. But Busthan Ibn Hasan, gives the following account. According to him Hasayn Dost Khān, the third son-in-law of Navab Dost Ali went to Trichinopoly in the garb of concluding peace. Swearing on the word of the Allāh, the king, and the Great Knower, he span the thread of relationship of a brother to her, made into a noose of punishment and deceived her. He cut the throat of the times, broke his plighted word, tinged his scimitar with blood. Finally in the Sarai Known as Dalavai mandap (Dalavay Maṇḍap adjoining the fort of Trichinopoly), he broke (his covenant with her) yielding to his prolific vicious nature, took possession of the fort and set the mischief afoot. The Rāṇi became aware of that deceit, being too weak to take revenge as the power went from her hands. Thus wounded in heart and helpless, she burnt herself according to the custom of the Hindus.—M. H. Nainar: *Tuzuk-i-Walajahi* (Eng. Tr.) I. pp. 70-71.

CHAPTER XVI

GOVERNMENT AND ADMINISTRATION UNDER NAYAKA RULE

Administration : The Nāyakas of Ikkēri were technically feudatories of the Vijayanagar kings and their vassalage is proved by their title 'Nāyaka', the term signifying a captain or governor. The Nāyaka who was appointed in those times, not for a fixed term, continued to hold the office so long as he was loyal and faithful to the suzerain power. The office became hereditary in due course. With the appointment of Chauḍappa Nāyaka as the governor of Keladi Mūla Samsthāna by the Vijayanagar king, a hereditary line of governors began to rule over the area. They had to maintain an army for the imperial home and render assistance whenever requisitioned by the emperors, besides making them an annual financial contribution.

Though the Nāyaka was a vassal, yet in his own jurisdiction he was the supreme head of the government and enjoyed sovereign powers. In the Keladi principality, as in others, the king was the head of the administration and occupied a supreme position. He was indeed the pivot of the machinery of administration.

Coronation: The coronation provided the legal sanction to the accession of a ruler and it gave him the title to govern. As other Hindu kings, the Nāyakas of Ikkēri had their coronations duly performed. Unfortunately, we have no information about the details of the ceremony.

The Yuvarāja: In Ikkēri, as elsewhere also, the king appointed his successor and anointed him as *Yuvarāja*. Usually the eldest Prince was chosen as the successor or as an alternative some other member of the royal family who was worthy of the choice. For instance, Bhadrappa Nāyaka nominated the elder of his nephews, Doḍḍa Śankaṇṇa as his successor and the younger Chikka Śankaṇṇa as *Yuvarāja*.[1] During the period of training, the *Yuvarāja* was placed under able teachers and he was taught the śāstras and other sciences, a knowledge of which was essential for a king. He also received training in military arts like the use of the bow, arrow, missile, horse riding, etc. Besides, he learnt the Fine Arts. Co-rulership was also prevalent in Ikkēri kingdom. Rāma Rāja Nāyaka and Chikka Śankaṇṇa Nāyaka ruled their territories jointly up to 1580 A.C.[2]

Abdication: As in other dynasties, some of the ruling sovereigns of Ikkēri abdicated in favour of their sons in the evening of their lives and retired from active politics. According to *Śivatattvaratnākara*, Sadāśiva Rāya Nāyaka entrusted the kingdom to Bhadrappa and retired to the forest.[3] Venkaṭappa Nāyaka gave the throne to Vīrabhadra Nāyaka, his grandson and led a retired life.[4]

Regency: When the occupant of the throne happened to be a minor, a regent was nominated and entrusted with the administration. During the minority of Vīrabhadra Nāyaka, grandson of Venkaṭappa Nāyaka, Śivappa Nāyaka acted as regent.[5] Unlike many who used their regency as an opportunity for self-aggrandisement, Śivappa Nāyaka acted as the real power behind Vīrabhadra Nāyaka and helped him to stabilise himself on the throne against rebellions and attempted usurpations.

Royal duties: The king had certain duties and responsibilities as the custodian of the welfare of his subjects. His first and foremost duty was to afford protection to his subjects and redress their grievances. According to the *Śivatattvaratnākara*, the king is likened to the *Aṣṭa-dikpālas* (protectors of the eight directions) and other demi-gods like Chandra, Sūrya, etc.[6] The king should always protect the

1. *STR.*, V. 5.
2. See *infra*, Ch. V.
3. *STR.*, V. 5.
4. *Ibid.*, VI, 27.
5. See *infra*, Ch. VII.
6. *STR.*, V. 6.

subjects and redress their grievances.[7] There are many instances of the Keladi kings actually putting an end to the oppression experienced by the people. Mention may be made here of some of them. A copper plate record of Śivappa Nāyaka in possession of Kudali Sōma Bhaṭṭa dated 1652 A.C. gives details as to how lands granted to the Śṛṅgēri *maṭha,* agrahara and temples, were utilised by the common people for planting arecanuts and gaining profits without making over the money due legitimately to the *maṭha* and how Śivappā Nāyaka enquired into the matter, put them down and restored the lands to the *maṭha.*[8] Further there are eight letters and *nirupas* (royal orders) issued by Śivappa Nāyaka for redressing grievances and setting things right.[9] A *nirūpa* dated 1657 A.C., addressed to Timmanna Senabova, runs as follows:

> "We hear that you are playing mischief in the matter of paying 125 *varāhas* to the *Mahājanas* of Śṛngapura, which you were ordered to do. Pay this amount to *Kavi* (poet) Tirumala Bhaṭṭa. If you make any further delay you shall be taught a good lesson."[10]

The *Mahājanas* of Śṛngapura and Vidyāraṇyapura went in a body to Bednūr and complained to Śivappa Nāyaka about the non-distribution of lands to them; Śivappa thereupon cleared the debts and refounded the *agrahāras* which had become the property of unworthy people. The above instances reveal the scrupulous interest taken by the king in the maintenance and proper upkeep of orderly government.

In the mediaeval period, the state sometimes encroached upon the private life of the citizens. The kings controlled and patronised maṭhas, not because they wanted to be the ecclesiastical heads but only to maintain the social solidarity of the kingdom.

7. *Ibid.,* Taraṅga 4 for details of the duties of a ruler, see vv. 49-92.
8. *EC.,* VI, Sr. 11.
9. *MAR.,* 1916, pp. 66 ff.
10. *MAR.,* 1916, p. 66.

The Ikkēri rulers were anxious to improve the economic prosperity of the people. Under them, forests were cleared, new villages or *agrahāras* founded and fresh lands were brought under the plough. Irrigation facilities were afforded, and remission of taxes allowed in order to increase the net yield of the land. Trade with foreign nations was encouraged. Immigrants from foreign countries were generally afforded protection and facilities were given to them for trading. The ports in the territory were accessible to them. Trade in a few commodities was monopolised by the state. Pepper and rice were two such items.[11]

Yet another function of the king was the administration of justice. The Ikkēri kings fully realised that the composite social structure depended upon the administration of justice on right lines. They were anxious to redress the grievances of the subjects and mete out justice. Vīrabhadra Nāyaka decided a very difficult case between the svāmi of Umbaḷi *maṭha* and a certain Mitlakoppa Cannavīra Gauṇḍa wherein the accused were absconding.[12]

Checks on royal authority: Though the king was the head of the state, he never tried to be an autocrat. His powers were limited by certain accepted codes and conventions. The administration was generally based on convention and experience rather than on constitutional laws. As in other Hindu kingdoms, the king was led in his actions by a keen sense of moral responsibility to his subjects. Customs contributed its share to check royal authority. Taxation was based largely on custom. Among the visible checks on the powers of the king was the ministerial Council which was consulted by him on matters of State. The ministers rose to great power under weak kings.

The Ministerial Council: The king was advised by a council of Ministers in State matters. It is, however, difficult

11. The trading and commercial relations of the Nāyakas with foreigners have been traced earlier under Political History in every chapter.

12. *EC.*, VIII, Sa. 46.

to determine the number of such ministers but it may be presumed that the number varied from time to time. There are occasional references to ministers and other officers of the king in the inscriptions of the period. A copper plate record issued by Sadāśiva Nāyaka of Ikkēri, now in possession of Cinnabhaṇḍārada Śāma Rao of Tīrthahaḷḷi, mentions a *Pradhāna* (minister) of the king by name Mālappayya.[13] Another record gives us details about a minister (mantri) named Rāmakṛṣṇa who served under Vīrabhadra Nāyaka.[14] He is described as 'the bearer of the burden of his master's affairs; versed in the Vēdas, Śāstras and Fine Arts, skilled in royal policy, a treasury of six qualities, adorated with the three powers of increase, a brother to the wives of others'. He was to king Vīrabhadra like Brihaspati to Śukra. He belonged to the Vāsīṣta *gōtra,* Asvalayana *sūtra* and Baḥvṛica *pravara.*[15]

The Secretariat: The king seems to have been assisted by a secretariat staff, who attended to the dry details of administration. The inscriptions of the period, however, do not throw much light on the organisational and other details of the secretariat even though there are occasional references to such departments as the military and the treasury. As such we cannot definitely know the precise number of such departments or their relations to one another. Peter Mundy who visited Ikkēri in 1637 A.C. gives some details of the Secretariat or the Record room of the kings of Keladi. 'At my beeing', he relates, 'att Eccary I was att the king's Secretaries, where in his house I saw many hundreds (I may say thousands) of those written palm leaves, beeing very long and narrow, handsomely rouled uppe, those againe tied into bundles hung upp in order about his romme or office soe thatt hee may (not improperly) be stiled Master of the Roules'.[16] These records were evidently grants made by the king, and as will be seen later in the sequel, they were sent

13. *EC.*, VIII, Tl. 5.
14. *EC.*, VII, Sh. 2.
15. *Ibid.*
16. Peter Mundy: *Travels in Europe and Asia,* III, pp. 98-99.

to village accountants, in the cases of grants of land for being copied and returned to the palace wherein they were deposited for constant and future reference. For instance, a grant made in 1673 A.C. was again referred to in 1690 A.C. when a mortgage was settled.

There is occasional reference in the literary sources to the office of *Karaṇika.* The *Karaṇika* means Accountant or scribe. The Karaṇikas who served under Śivappa Nāyaka were Apparāya, Tirumalayya, Biligi Kāṇappayya, Venkaṭayya[18] and Purāṇika Appu Bhaṭṭa.[19]

The king had besides, a number of other officers each of whom was entrusted with some work. The Treasury Officer, *Bhaṇḍāra,*[20] *Parapatēgāra,*[21] *Sēnabōva,*[22] and *Nāḍadhikāri*[23] figure prominently in the epigraphs of the period. Besides there were other palace servants like the wet-nurse. A certain Banadamma is mentioned as wet-nurse in an inscription of Vīrabhadra Nāyaka.[24]

Provincial and Local Government: During the days of Śivappa Nāyaka, the Ikkēri kingdom had reached its heyday and extended over the whole of Canara up to Goa and the north-western parts of the Mysore State.

Divisions of the kingdom: For convenient and efficient administration the kingdom was divided into many provinces generally known as *Rājyas* and some times known as *Maṇḍalas.* A portion of the Shimoga and the North Kanara districts constituted the province of Āraga.[25] The Tuḷuva country was yet another province with its capital at Mangalore.[26] The provin-

17. *EC.*, VIII, Tl. 57.
18. *KNV.*, VII.
19. *MAR.*, 1916, pp. 66 ff.
20. *EC.*, VIII, Tl. 60.
21. *Ibid.*, Sb. 301.
22. *MAR.*, 1928, No. 61; *EC.*, VIII, Sb. 232, Nagar 32.
23. *MAR.*, 1923, No. 122.
24. *EC.*, VIII, Tl. 89.
25. *Ibid.*, Tl. 103.
26. *ARSIE.*, 348 of 1930-31.

ces were in turn divided into Districts, Taluks and Villages. The inscriptions contain references to such divisions; but different divisions are mentioned for different purposes. The names of divisions that occur frequently in inscriptions are the *Rāṣṭra, Kampaṇa, Hōbaḷi, Nāḍu, Venthe, Śīme, Sthala, Pēṭhe* and *Grāma.* An inscription says that the district of Keladi consisted of the *Śīmes* of Ikkēri, Yalagalale, Āṭavāḍi, Kalluse-ainūru, Mankasāle, Hebbeyallu, Kesānūru, Sōraba, Andige, Bandalike, Paṭṭanahaḷe etc.[27] Another inscription from Kuruvadagadde in Honnali taluk mentions that Kuṟuvada grāma belonged to the Honnali *Śīme* of the Baḷe-nāḍ in the Haṭṭaṇa *Venthē.*[28] Still another inscription from Kavaledurga says that the Yeḍehaḷḷi and Handiguni *grāmas* were in Dānivāsada *vaḷagaṇa* in Dānivāsada *Hōbaḷi.*[29] Yet another mentions the Asaganakoppa Kummankana *grāma* as included in Kummata *Śīme* of Āruṇāḍa *Hōbaḷi.*[30] We get information about *peṭhes* or market towns from another inscription. Among the market towns in the Ikkēri kingdom were Āraga, Koḍarūru, Yeḍehaḷḷi, Avinahaḷḷi, Karuvūru, Bidarūru, Mosarūru, Mallaṇahalli and 8 *peṭhes* belonging to the Āragada *Venthe.*[31]

These divisions are not, however, mentioned in any order. But it seems that the first among such divisions was the *maṇḍala.* Āraga was one such *maṇḍala.*[32] The *maṇḍala* seems to have been bigger in size than a *rājya,* the regular administrative division in the Ikkēri kingdom. The number and size of the *Rājyas* depended more on historical accidents than any well set principle followed by the Government. When the *rājya* was large in size, or of some special importance it was perhaps called *mahārajya.* Āraga was one

27. *MAR.,* 1928, No. 63; see also No. 65.
28. *EC.,* VII, Hn. 9.
29. *EC.,* VIII, Tl. 50.
30. *EC.,* VIII, Tl. 75.
31. *MAR.,* 1943, No. 41. Another inscription refers to Mōdusura, Kaluvali, Hārōgopa *grāmas* in Akkiya Pēṭhe of Keladi *Śīme.* (*EC.,* VIII, Tl. 181).
32. *EC.,* VII, Sh. 2.

such *mahārājya.*[33] Dr. Mahalingam thinks that the *rājya* was the same as *Pīṭhika.*[34] But the *Pīṭhika* which is frequently mentioned in inscriptions as *Pēṭhe* may have been different from the *rājya* and smaller than it.

The next important division was the *Venthe* otherwise known as *viṣaya.* It was divided into *śīmes.* For instance the Sōrab *śīme* is said to have been in the Eḍe Nāḍ *Venthe.*[35]

Next to the *śīme* was the *sthala* which consisted of a few villages. An inscription of 1589 A.C. from the Hiriyur taluk of Chitaldrug district mentions a few *sthalas* and the number of villages each of them contained.[36] Probably there was no fixed rule regarding the number of villages that should be in a *sthala.* There was another subdivision called the *hōbaḷi.* For instance Asōda grāma is stated to be situated in Bāṭakūra *Hōbaḷi* in the Nalvattunāḍu *śīme.*[37] Perhaps this was a division that took the place of the *sthala* in some areas.

We also come across a division called the *Kampaṇa.*[38] Among other divisions one was the *Māgaṇi,* as for instance the Santalige *Māgaṇi* in the Āraga kingdom.[39] Its real significance, however, is not clearly known. The estate given to an *amara nāyaka* may have been called an *amara māgaṇi.* Sadāśiva Nāyaka of Ikkēri was given Honnali as *amara māgaṇi.*[40] Mention is made of a territorial division called Banavāsi

33. *Ep. Ind.,* III, p. 119; *Ibid.,* XIV, p. 313, *EC.,* VIII, Tl. 206.
34. *Administration and Social Life under Vijayanagar,* p. 180.
35. *EC.,* VIII, Sb. 55.
36. *Ibid.,* XI, Hr. 88.
37. *Ibid.,* VIII, Tl. 92.

38. Regarding the *Kampaṇas* Dr. Fleet says: 'Kampaṇa is a convertible term with "bada" in its second meaning of a circle of towns constituting an administrative post......"bada" is a tadbhava corruption of the Sanskrit (vaṭa), an enclosure of a town or village, fence wall, hedge etc..... *Kampaṇa* is probably another form of the Canarese *Kampala, Kampilu,* a cluster, heap, assemblage, multitude, etc.'. (*Ind. Ant.* IV, pp. 211 *n.* and 329 *n.*).

39. *EC.,* VIII, Tl. 206.
40. *Ibid.,* VII, Hn. 9.

12,000. It is difficult to find out the implication of the numerical appellation. There was no administrative sub-division of this type during the period of the Ikkēri Nāyaks. The numerical suffix was obviously the survival of an old system of reference to political divisions.

Local officers: The village or *grāma* was the smallest unit of administration. Necessarily there were in it some officers to look after the interest of the village. The *Parupatyagāra* was one such. The term means an executive officer or a Superintendent of works. He was generally the representative of the king and carried out the executive functions of the Government. He collected the local taxes and was also in charge of maintenance of forts. Further he was the trustee of the grants made by the king. It was to the *Parupatyagāra* that royal communications were sent; for instance an inscription from Siddahalli, dated Śaka 1502 (1579 A.C.) mentions the *Parapattēgāra* of Sōrab as Virupākṣayya and that of Kuppattūr as Liṅgappayya.[41]

Another important local officer was the *Adhikāri*. He seems to have been appointed in some important cities and villages. An inscription from Hōlatihālu, in Holalūru *Hōbaḷi* mentions a Nāḍadhikāri who made a gift of four paddy fields and four dry fields in Hōlati village free from taxes to a soldier Basavayya under orders from Sōmaśēkhara Nāyaka.[42] From the above instances we may surmise that many important places had each an *Adhikāri*. It seems that grants made by individuals had to be confirmed by him. He could not, however, make grants independently without the consent and co-operation of certain groups and associations. A copper plate record from South Kanara gives interesting details that in 1556 A.C. one Tirumalarasa *alias* Madda Heggaḍe, the chief of Kap, made a grant of land in the village Mailāra with the consent of the assembly (*nāḷinavaru*) communal and professional guilds (*gaṇa paṇa*) and subordinate officers.[43] Thus in

41. *Ibid.*, VIII, Sb. 301.
42. *MAR.*, 1923, No. 122.
43. *ARSIE.*, *C.P.* No. 8 of 1921-22.

localities where communal corporations existed the Adhikāri's powers seem to have been limited.

The *Gauḍike* was another office in the local areas. The kingdom appears to have been parcelled out into *gauḍikes*, which were granted to responsible persons to recover and pay into the State treasury the revenue realised. An inscription of Venkaṭappa Nāyaka mentions that one Bhadrappa was holding the original order for the gauḍike of Kasabe Kuppattūr in the Kuppattūr *śīme*.[44] This office appears to have been made in public, especially in the presence of responsible government officers, obviously to safeguard State interest.

The Sēnabōva was another important official in the village. He usually recorded the grants made by the king in a register maintained by him, and known as the Sēnabōva's *kaḍatta*. This is borne out for instance, by an inscription of the reign of Cannammājī dated 1672 A.C. which registers the grant of some lands in Jambāni *grāma* to a Hālepayikada Jambani Hucca by royal order. This paper was entered in the Sēnabōva's *kaḍatta* and returned to the donee.[45] The Sēnabōva discharged many functions of a local character, like protecting the interests of local institutions. In 1656 Śivappa Nāyaka sent a *nirupa* (royal order) to a Timmaṇṇa Sēnabōva to the following effect, namely since the temple has not been built and the money sanctioned for it misused thus causing unnecessary debt to the *maṭha*, the said Timmaṇṇa and other Sēnabōvas were to be held responsible for all that and that they would have to make good and if they "continued in this course of criminal conduct" they would be severely punished.[46] It was probably the same man who in accordance with the order of the queen granted land of an annual value of 24½ *varāhas* with a house site in the village of Nivane.[47]

44. *EC.* VIII, Sb. 266.
45. *Ibid.*, Sa. 17.
46. *MAR.*, 1916, p. 66 ff.
47. *Ibid.*, 1928, No. 61.

One Mahābalaliṅgasēnabōva of Coliakere made provision for a *chhatra* in the *maṭha* attached to two temples at Kumbākṣi.[48]

Revenue administration: The rulers of Keladi had a good revenue system, which, however, cannot be claimed to be in any way original, for like their overlords, the Emperors of Vijayanagar, they too were followers of the *pūrvamaryāde* (ancient usage). According to an inscription of Bhadrappa Nāyaka dated 1662 A.C., the sources of revenue were *siddhāya, birāḍa, meluvaṇa, habbagaṇike, besta gārike, maḍihaḍike, divagaraka, banadasōge, haravari vartane, udugere, Kāśāvarga, umbaḷi-vartane, menasina-caḍita, kulabirada, sēnabōvana-vrtane, manihadavāra vartane,* etc.[49]

Besides them there were other taxes like *Arēvāśi*,[50] sthala śuṅka,[51] sambhanda gaṇike,[52] fees for executing charter,[53]

48 *SII.*, IX, pt. II, No. 675.

49. *MAR.* 1919, pp. 37-38. *Siddhāya*: fixed rent (*EC.* VIII, Tl. 15); *Birada*: extra cess on garden cultivation of fines (*EC.* IV, Gu. 47, *MAR.*, 1943, No. 31); *Meluvana*: *mēl-haṇa—uparīkara—mēlavaram*: may be the crown's share of tax, a sort of surplus tax. Cf. *JRAS.*, 1931, p. 165. *Hebbakāṇike,* presents for festivals (Kittel—Kannada Dictionary, p. 403). *Besta-gārake,* tax on fishermen, (*ibid.*, p. 1143); *Banada Sōge*—Tax on forest produce and the screw pine, (*ibid.*, p. 1598) *Maḍihadike*—tax on washerman(?) *Dīvagarake*—Tax on torches of the Huriallee grass, (*ibid.*, p. 377), like the leaves of palms, sugar cane; *Haravari-vartane—Haravaḍi*—The State of becoming public (*ibid.*, p. 1633); *Vartanē*—Fees perquisities especially of grain, paid to public servants of a village or town for their support; (Wilson, Glossary of Judicial and Revenue Terms, p. 453). A tax on grains grown in public lands. *Uḍugare*—A present of clothes to a couple at the time of marriage (Kittel, pp. 217-218). *Kāśāvarga—Kasabarige* or *Kasavarige*—a tax on brooms (Kittel *op. cit.*, p. 391)—*Umbaḷi Vartane*—a tax in kind from a grant of land to an individual for his subsistence. (Wilson, *op. cit.*, p. 532) *Menacina Caḍita*—Tax on black pepper; *kula birada*—a family tax on garden cultivation or fines. *Sēnabōvana Vartane*—A tax for maintaining village accountant; *Manihadavara Vartane*—Manija—mānya a tax for superintending temples, maṭhas, etc. (Kittel; *op. cit.*, p. 193).

50. *MAR.*, 1943, No. 31.

51. *MAR.*, 1923, No. 110.

52. *Ibid.*, No. 123.

53. *Ibid.*, 1943, No. 42.

Mūlavīsa (tax in market towns),[54] religious levy[55] and tax on labourers.[56] Further there was the octroi, which yielded quite a large sum to the rulers of Keladi. Pietro Della Valle noticed how this source was tapped. He says:

> "Having pass'd by Banghel (Bhanger) we entere'd into the great Northern River in which on the left hand is a place where passage boats laden with Merchandise pay a toll to the Ministers of Venkatapa Naieka to whom the circumjacent region is subject."[57]

The traveller obviously means by ministers, the customs officers of Venkaṭappa Nāyaka, during whose reign the system of levying toll on each animal load was current. This is supported by many epigraphs; one of them states that in 1606 A.C. having obtained the orders of the king, all the mahānāḍ śeṭṭis gave a *śāsana* granting to a Śaiva *maṭha* a visa on their stock as follows:

> "Throughout the kingdom ruled by Venkaṭappa Nāyaka, above the Ghats, on all roads for all animals, at the rates of one *visa* for each animal, we agree to give as Dharma, visa by visa, in all the *thānas*".

There were besides Ikkēri the following stations where octroi duties were levied.[58] Sadāśivasāgara, Sirivante, Kesanūr, Tavanidhi, Gutti, Jaḍeya, Kuppattūr, Sōrab, Tagarasi, Kabur; Udugani, Jambūr, Mahādēvapura, Kumbāsi, Haraṇahaḷḷi, Ānandapura, Mosarūr, Pombucca, Dānivāsa, Āraga, Durga, Agumbē, Kovi, Bagunji, Belare, Kalasa, Magunda, Kiga; Nemmāru, Muttūru, Mudekāru, Bidirūr, Hulikallu, Hannava, Karūru, Sauḷanāḍu, Sāvantanakaṭṭe, Bharangi and Avinahaḷḷi. Likewise there were below the ghats many *thānas* where octroi was collected. It is said in an inscription of 1641, for

54. *Ibid.*, No. 41.
55. *Ibid.*, 1927, No. 57.
56. *EC.* VIII, Tl. 95.
57. Travels, II, p. 305.
58. *EC.*, VIII, Sa, 123, See also *Ibid.*, Tl. 49, 42 and 68 as also *MAR.* 1928, No. 58, 1943 No. 45 for a mention of the octroi.

instance, that the tax was collected for the benefit of a *maṭha* on all articles except tassels, silks, arecanut, pepper, cocoanut kernels and wood, paddy, ragi, salt, jaggery, oil, ghee and such other articles which were permitted to be stored by the *maṭha* authorities for the benefit of the six *darśanas*.[59]

Trade in spices prospered well during the rule of the Nāyakas of Keladi. The English carried on trade with the rulers of Keladi at Bhaṭkal on terms of barter exchanging pepper for Arabian or Persian horses and commodities of value like coral, silk and pearls for pepper and money. Peter Mundy gives interesting details of a commercial agreement between the English and the Nāyak of Ikkēri.[60] It is interesting to note that in the trade that was carried on by barter if the value of an article was greater than

59. *EC.*, VIII, Tl. 49; See for a few other instances *Ibid.*, Tl. 42, 68 and *MAR.*, 1928, No.. 58 and 1943, No. 45.

60. Travels, III, i, p. 91. His narrative runs as follows: "And likewise that he (the officer) see to the delivery of 300 candees (kandis) pepper in trucks of the load which you are to deliver at the rate of 22½ *pagodas* the candee. And for the surplus arising from the price of the pepper 7½ *pago(das)* upon the *candee,* I have enordered Mange Naig to buy commodities of you for it if you can agree on the price or else money .... If you bring good horses of Persia or Arabia I will buy them and paie you in pepper. Likewise if you bring corall silke, perle or anie other good commodities of value, I will paie you for them in pepper and money." (Travels, iii, i, p. 92). Mundy further records: 'For pepper he (the king, assured us that we might finde yearlie between 1500 and 2000 *candilles* in the port besides the trade of the whole coast each candill conteynainge about 4 *kintalls* Portuguez (Khandi Candill—Candy was 20 man—lbs.) and that he would both incourage his subjects in manuring the trees, which of late, in the dead times of trade, they have neglected, and would likewise publish an edict through out his countrie that all the pepper should be for us and none to be exported either by sea or land. For aloath, lead, corall or any other varieties out of Europe, he will take them of in barter of pepper and paie us the overplus in money. From England and China he desireth all varieties for which we shall receive satisfaction to our own content, but chieflie (and which for the future we have promised him) horses from Persia and Arabia to which end a shipp from that port may yearlie be sent thither in September or October or retaine againe in March the following or soone and to good benefit.'

the value of the one exchanged for, it was made payable in money.

Boundaries of land were usually marked out with stones engraved with the figure of the Liṅga in the presence of the people of the neighbouring villages to avoid any dispute.[61] The revenue income from a village was estimated and the items of expenditure laid down.[62] Taxes were remitted for valid reasons like havoc done to lands by floods, dilapidation of villages, etc.[63] Delinquency in the payment of taxes was taken serious notice of by the rulers. This may be seen from the fact that Śivappa Nāyaka enquired of his *aḷiya* (son-in-law) Keñcaṇṇa in writing, how he had received information that some tenants of the Śṛṅgēri *maṭha* in the Mangaḷūru *śīme* were 'playing mischief' without making due payments and ordered him to send for them and see that the due amount was paid.[64]

Lands were usually granted by the kings as *uttar* but when they lost their owners they reverted to the State, which alone could regrant such lands.[65] They were also granted for certain services as the maintenance of boats by boatmen for crossing rivers,[66] or the creation of cattle folds or the laying of plans to protect the people from foreign oppression,[67] or the maintenance of religious institutions like *maṭhas*.[68] Transfer or exchange of lands had to be done with the knowledge of the Government.[69] Private ownership of land was recognised in the Keladi kingdom as may be seen from instances where the kings purchased lands. For example in 1631 A.C. during the rule of Vīrabhadra Nāyaka the palace authorities "took

61. *EC.*, VIII, Sb. 354.
62. *Ibid., Nr.*, 79; also Sa. 157, Tl. 40, 62, 81, 94, etc., *MAR.*, 1923, No. 28.
63. *EC.*, VIII, Tl. 44, 67, *EC.*, Sh. 3 etc.
64. *MAR.*, 1916, p. 66.
65. See for instance *EC.*, VIII, Tl. 53.
66. *Ibid.*, VII, Sh. 3.
67. *Ibid.*, VII, Sk. 79.
68. *Ibid.*, VIII, Tl. 60.
69. *Ibid.*, VIII, Sa. 16, 17; Sb. 548, etc.

the estate of an individual in an agrahāra village, paying him a sufficient sum for his maintenance in exchange and paying to the same agrahara some compensation; and out of the land thus acquired in the village by the palace authorities they made a grant to a Tirumala Bhaṭṭa free of taxes besides some rice lands, a garden and a house.[70]

The way in which the Keladi rulers brought about the settlement of a mortgage is also interesting. A grant of land made was sold by Cannammājī in 1690 A.C. to Manōhara Jaṭā Śankaradēva's disciple, Manōharamahatta Mallikārjunadēva's disciple, Kampaṇa Manōharadēva as follows:

> "Whereas formerly in the year Pramathin (A.C. 1673) we (the government) received 300 *varāhās* and granted to Siddha Basavaiya of the Customs in the Hombucha *śīme* a property rated at 40 *varāhas,* 1 *haga* as *uttar* and his son Nañjaṇa for his livelihood obtained a loan of 300 *varāhas* from Keñcaṇṇa, mortgaging it with the *śāsana*—and the principal and interest having mounted up to so that he could not levy the sum, and he having given permission to sell the property and repay herself, and he having agreed to sell it for 400 *varāhas* to repay the principal and interest, and having applied that the 400 *varāhas* may be taken to the palace and in lieu of the mortgage *śāsana,* a *śāsana* in our own names should be given for the property, we have received the 400 *varāhas* for the palace and grant you by *śāsana* the land in Hondiga village rated (as specified) with all rights."[71]

From this grant it appears that the lands granted as *uttar* could be mortgaged with the *śāsana* pertaining to the particular land, the mortgagor in such a case retained his right in his mortgage regarding ownership, if he was unable to repay the principal and interest, he could permit the mortgagee to sell the plot of land, even such a mortgagee could sell to the State his plot of land and the State could again grant by *śāsana* this land as a gift.

70. *MAR.,* 1929, No. 89.
71. *EC.,* VIII, Tl. 57.

Right of succession: From the grants issued from time to time by the Keladi rulers some details regarding the right of succession as it prevailed during this period may be ascertained. One of the few inscriptions of the founder of the dynasty Chauḍappa Nāyaka reveals how, in the disposal of wet land granted to the children of Vīrappa, a stone carver (*Kālukuṭiga*) of the village Kalise, the right of succession was to be from females to males (*Aḷiya Santhāna kaṭṭu*).[72] This practice by which the sister's son becomes the heir, is still prevalent in parts of Mālnāḍ and the adjoining Kanara district.

In case a person died without issue his property was disposed of by the State. On the 3rd August 1573 A.C., Rāma-Rāja Nāyaka issued the following proclamation to some of his merchant subjects of the village Kalase in Keladi district for among them some had died leaving no heirs. "In order" runs this edict, "that our ancestors might obtain spiritual merit and attain the region of Śiva, we have granted with pouring of water the right of *aputrikē* to all the śeṭṭis, *paṭṭaṇasvāmis* and merchants of the *peṭhē* of Kalase in the Keladi *śīme*, which has been conferred on us. In case the deceased have elder or younger brothers or kinsmen, etc., they might enjoy the estate. If none such is forthcoming the widow of the deceased might take the estate and that which is left, might be given away for a tank embankment or a temple. But it will not be taken to our palace. In case any of the rulers of the Keladi *śīme* seize the same by greed, they will go to the region of Yama and hell."[73] Such a proclamation must have gone a long way in endearing the rulers to the hearts of the subjects.

In addition to the land revenue which formed the bulk of the resources of the Keladi Nāyaks there were other miscellaneous sources of income like levies, fees and contributions. Among such may be mentioned the religious levy, *Mulavīsa*

72. *MAR.*, 1930, No. 65.
73. *MAR.*, 1930, No. 60. For other instances regarding succession to property See *MAR.*, 1943, No. 31 and 1944, No. 47.

tax, tax on labourers and *sambhanda gaṇike* (fee for transferring rights). An inscription dated 1726 A.C. informs us that religious levy in cash as the *kappa* and *kāṇike* were collected from people other than Jīyas, gold-smiths, kōmaṭis, Bhūsuras, Tigalas and Mēdars residing in Ānandapura, Sadāśivapura etc.[74] The *Mūlavisa* tax was levied in the eight market towns of Āraga, Kodanūr, Karūru, Bidarūru, Mosarūru and Malēnahaḷḷi and remitted to the palace. The amount of tax was 1/16 *visa* per load. In the *thāne* at Āraga a tax of ¼ *haṇa* for 1 lakh arecanut was levied. Further all loads taken through Kalise road, Jambur road and the road between Sorab and Gutti were taxed at 1/16 *visa* per load.[75] During the time of Basavappa Nāyaka, a fee for transferring rights (*sambhanda gaṇike*) seems to have been levied. According to an epigraph dated 1714 A.C., one Padmanābha bhaṭṭa belonging to the Chitpavan community of Brahmins applied to Basavappa Nāyaka for employment as an *arcaka* (priest) of the Veṅkaṭēśvara temple in the place of the previous *arcaka* who died issueless. He stated that he was doing similar work in another temple Chennasōmēśvara shrine, at Sorab. The king, after receiving from the applicant fee for transferring the rights (*Sambhanda gaṇike*) directed by a *nirup* his officer Rāmappa to hand over the lands of the said temple yielding annually the sum of 24 *varāhas* 1 *haṇa* to the applicant, and to install him as the *arcaka* for conducting the worship in the temple with permission to receive the usual presents made by the devotees and enjoy his post as *arcaka* as a hereditary estate.[76]

Basavappa granted to Mahāmahattu Mullājisvāmi the Mīraṇaghaṭṭa village in the Gājanūr *śīme* altogether rated at 1338 *varāha* 2 *haṇa* 3 *haga* 1 *beḷe* with the tax on certain newly come labourers.[77] Details are not available about this tax in the epigraph. Further there was a fee collected for executing charters. An inscription of Cannammājī records the gift of land to Vīrūpākṣadēva, a disciple of Kambala Sītārāmadēva

74. *MAR.*, 1927, No. 57.
75. *MAR.*, 1943, No. 41.
76. *MAR.*, 1923, No. 123.
77. *EC.*, VIII, Tl. 95.

of Āraga after taking 185 *gadyāṇas* as price and 15 *gadyāṇas* as fee (*kāṇike*) for having got the charter executed.[78]

The amounts collected from these various sources must have contributed to the financial stabililty of the Keladi kingdom.

Judicial administration: The inscriptions of the Keladi Nāyaks furnish some details regarding the administration of justice to the subjects. As seen earlier the king was the highest authority and judge in the country. An inscription dated 1582 A.C. during the reign of Rāmarāja Nāyaka informs us as to how injustice done to a particular individual by the state was compensated by it. Rāmarāja Nāyaka granted to Puṭṭanahaḷḷi Bhadra Gauḍa an umbali as follows: "As we had your eyes put out we grant you 5 *khandugas* of lands in the fields in front of Puṭṭanahaḷḷi."[79] Mention has been made earlier how Vīrabhadra Nāyaka disposed of a civil case between the svāmi of the Umbaḷi *maṭha* and one Mitla Koppa Cannavīra Gauḍa.[80] In 1652, Śivappa Nāyaka enquired into a case of non-payment of dues to the Śṛṅgēri *maṭha*, by the common people, confiscated their lands and handed them over to the *Maṭha*.[81] An inscription of the time of Sōmaśēkhara Nāyaka dated 1718 A.C. furnishes interesting information as to how the king compensated for loss of life of a certain herdsmen Gauḷōji of Honnali fort, who died after killing a tiger, which was committing ravages in the neighbouring territories. Sōmaśēkhara Nāyaka wrote and despatched an order to Rāyappa as follows:

> "The herdsmen Gauḷōji of Honnali fort, when a tiger had been committing ravages (*rāuda*) for many days in the Balaur pass of the Honnali *śīme*, cut down the tiger and died. His sons Kānōja and Masanōja having applied for an *umbaḷi* as recommended by our son-in-law....we grant them rice lands in Haranahaḷḷi as an *umbaḷi*."[82]

78. *MAR.*, 1943, No. 42.
79. *EC.*, VIII, Sb. 232.
80. *EC.*, VIII, Sagar 46. See under section settlement of disputes.
81. *EC.* VI, Sr. 11.
82. *EC.* VII, Sh. 128.

Yet another record dated 1757 A.C. refers to one Kōdihaḷḷi Basavappa who seems to have beheaded one Mancha Barama, who was committing lawless acts and for whose arrest orders were issued. It appears that he was put into confinement pending the enquiry and he claimed compensation for the time his land was thrown out of season. A refusal given on this petition was now confirmed with a remark that petitions of this kind from the country for payment of money was not to be made.[83] But next year Sōmaśēkhara Nāyaka III, on the advice of Śivaliṅgappa, probably his guru, granted him an *umbaḷi.*[84]

The *Śivatattvaratnākara* gives some details regarding procedural method in *judicial* administration. According to the work, the king should decide cases impartially in consultation with learned Brahmins. When he cannot do so in person, one of the Brahmins must be made to preside.[85] The work goes on to a detailed account of methods of finding out the guilty party, deciding cases where witnesses were not available and about cases concerning property, boundary disputes and punishments. But as the accounts given in the work are purely conventional and traditional, they cannot be taken to present the correct picture.

Military system: In the mediaeval period a strong army was an essential feature of a stable kingdom. And it was with the aid of such a force that the small principality of Ikkēri expanded its sphere of influence and extent of territories. We do not get any information about the military organisation of the Nāyakas from the epigraphs of the period. As in other kingdoms the army of Ikkēri appears to have been divided into infantry, cavalry, artillery and elephantry. The later rulers of Ikkēri were dependent on the Portuguese and other foreign traders for their supply of gunpowder. According to Leonardo Paes, Śivappa Nāyaka possessed enormous wealth and maintained a standing army of forty to fifty thousand

83. *EC.*, VII, Sk. 209.
84. *Ibid.*, Sh. 210.
85. Kallola, VIII, Taraṅga 1.

men.[86] The Nāyakas also seem to have constructed strong fortresses and they depended on them for the defence of their frontiers.

The sources of information at our disposal relating to the military organisation of the Nāyakas are very meagre and hence it is not possible to sketch the details in broad outline. However, it may reasonably be assumed that it was largely modelled on the organisation under the Vijayanagar Emperors themselves.

86. Rice: Mysore and Coorg from Inscriptions, p. 159.

CHAPTER XVII

SOCIAL LIFE, RELIGION, LEARNING, ART AND ARCHITECTURE UNDER THE NĀYAKS

Social Life

Society: Castes and communities in the kingdom: In the kingdom of the Nāyaks of Keladi lived a large number of communities and social groups, the traditional four castes having multiplied into various sub-castes and communities. The caste of an individual was generally found out by his calling, which however was usually determined by the community to which he belonged. Some of the Keladi inscriptions mention 101 kulas and the 18 *jātis*.[1]

As in ancient India so in the period under study the Brahmins were a much respected community. Though members of the sacerdotal class, they were found in different walks of life. A few of them were priests and were attached to temples. Some were owners of estates and lands. A few others took to trade and settled down as merchants while still others remained as monks or sannyasis. Some were active politicians, administrators and generals. Rāmakṛṣṇa for instance was a Brahmin minister of Vīrabhadra Nāyaka.[2] Many Brahmins occupied positions of importance in the state. A few of them that may be mentioned are Rāyasam Timmarasayya, Karnaṇika Venkaṭappayya, Purāṇika Appu Bhaṭṭa, etc. Most of the ambassadors of the Keladi court were Brahmins. Viṭhula Sinay was one such. The observations of Van Linschoten about the Brahmans is worth citing here:

> "The Brahmans are the honestest and most esteemed Nation among the Indian Heathens for they doe alwaies serve in the chiefest places about the king as Receivers, Stewards, Ambassadors and such like officers. They are of great authority among the Indian people, for that the king doth nothing without their counsell and consent."[3]

1. *EC.*, VIII, Tl. 15, and 84.
2. *EC.*, VII, Sh. 2.
3. Purchas—His Pilgrims, X, p. 255-56.

Grants were made to them, fresh agrahāras formed by each ruling sovereign for them and they were held in very high respect.[4] According to Della Valle the Brahmans, dedicated wholly to learning and the service of the temples, were the most noble of all the races.[5]

Among the other important communities in the Ikkēri kingdom were the Jīyars, goldsmiths, Kōmaṭis, Bhūsuras, Tigaḷas and Mēdars.[6] There were separate quarters for each of them. The Sadāśivapura agrahāra is said to have consisted of 15 divisions each for a community.[7] An inscription of Sōmaśēkhara Nāyaka mentions Brahman quarters (*Brāhmanavāḍa*) and quarters for the Śūdras (*Śūdravāḍa*).[8]

Corporate activity: Professional and merchant guilds also flourished during the period. We get details about an agreement of several śeṭṭis, and others of the mercantile guild of Bidure from an inscription of Vīrabhadra Nāyaka dated 1640 A.C.[9] The inscription records an agreement given in the presence of Narasiṁha Oḍeya who was holding the *mudra* of Mangaḷūru by Cikka Rāya Oḍeya of Puṭṭige belonging to the Chauta family to Abhinava Cārukīrtti Paṇḍitadēva and the several śeṭṭis and others of the mercantile guild of Bidure, undertaking not to encroach in future upon the civic rights and privileges hitherto enjoyed by the latter and to preserve in tact the property of gods and the priests since the excess of his subordinates had resulted in their abandoning their homes and settling elsewhere. Thus we get glimpses about the prevalence of various castes and communities in Keladi kingdom.

Social Institutions: Among the social institutions marriage was of great importance. The Keladi kings seem to have married at a comparitively early age. Plurality of wives was prevalent and most of the kings had more than one wife.

4. See for instance *EC.*, VIII, Tl. 110; Tl. 156, Tl. 7; *EC.*, VII, Sh. 2, *MAR.*, 1923, No. 80, No. 110.
5. Della Valle: Travels, I, p. 88.
6. *MAR.*, 1927, No. 57.
7. See infra, Chapter III.
8. *EC.*, VIII, Tl. 48.
9. *ARSIE*, C.P. No. 8 of 1940-41.

Sati: Another equally important social institution in the Keladi days was that of *sahagamana* or sati. There are a large number of Mastikals in the Kannaḍa districts with sculptured representations of the women committing sati. A Mastikal inscription from Keladi refers to one Rāmakka, wife of Keladi Kariya Tumme Gauḍa, who became a mahāsati, on the death of her husband.[10] Foreign travellers like Pietro Della Valle give very vivid and realistic pictures as to how sati was performed. He describes "As we return'd home at night we met a woman in the city of Ikkēri, who her husband being dead, was resolved to burn herself as it is the custom with many Indian women. She rode on horseback about the city with face uncovered, holding a looking glass in one hand and a lemon in the other, I know not for what purpose; and beholding herself in the glass, with a lamentable tone sufficiently pitiful to hear, went along, I know not whither speaking or singing certain words which I understood not; but they told me they were a kind of farewell to the world and herself; and indeed being uttered with that passionateness which the case required and might produce they moved pity in all that heard them, even in us who understood not the language. She was followed by many other women and men on foot, who, perhaps, were her relations; they carried a great umbrella over her, as all persons of quality in India are wont to have, thereby to keep off the sun, whose heat is hurtful and troublesome. Before her certain drums were sounded, whose noise never ceas'd to accompany with her sad Ditties or songs; yet with a calm and constant countenance without tears, evidencing more grief for her husband's death than her own, and more desire to go with him in the other world than regret for her own departure out of this: a custom indeed cruel and barbarous, but withall of great generosity and virtue in such women and therefore worthy of no small praise. They said she had to pass in this manner about the city I know not how many days, at the end of which she was to go out of the city and be burnt, with more company and solemnity. If I can know when it will be I will not fail to go to see her and by my

10. *EC.*, VIII, Sa. 35.

presence honour her funeral with that compassionate affection which so much great conjugal fidelity and Love seem to me to deserve."[11]

The traveller describes her as being "cloth'd all in white and decked with many necklaces, bracelets and other ornaments of gold; on her head she had a garland of flowers, spreading forth like rayes of the sun; in brief she was wholly in a Nuptial dress and held a lemon in her hand, which is the usual ceremony. She seemed to be pleasant enough, talking and laughing in conversation as a bride would do in our countries."[12]

11. Della Valle—Travels II, pp. 266-67.

12. *Ibid.*, p. 273. Della Valle visited her house and was engaged in a conversation with the widow about to burn herself. "We discours'd together, standing, for a good while. She told me that her name was *Giaccama* of the race of *Terlenga* that her husband was a drummer, that it was about nineteen dayes since her husband's death, that he had left two other wives, elder than she, whom he had married before her, (both which were present at this discourse) yet neither of them was willing to dye, but alleg'd for excuse that they had many children. This argument gave me an occasion to ask *Giaccama* (who shew'd me a little son of her own, about six or seven years old, besides a little daughter she had) how she could persuade herself to leave her own little children; and I told her that she ought likewise to live rather than to abandon them at that age. She answere'd me that she left them well recommended to the care of an uncle of hers there present, who also talk'd with us very cheerfully, as if rejoycing that his kinswoman should do such an action, and that her husband's other two remaining wives would also take care of them. I insisted much upon the tender age of her children to avert her from her purpose by moving her to compassion for them, well knowing that no argument is more prevalent with mothers than their love and affection towards their children. But all my speaking was in vain, and she still answer'd me to all my reasons, with a countenance not only undismayed and constant, but even cheerful, and spoke in such a manner as shew'd that she had not the least fear of death. She told me also, upon my asking her, that she did this of her own accord, was at her own liberty and not forc'd or persuaded by any one. Whereupon, I inquiring whether force were at any time us'd in this matter they told me that ordinarily it was not, but only sometimes amongst persons of quality when some widow was left young, handsome, and so in danger of marrying again (which amongst them is very ignominous) or committing a worse fault, in such cases the friends of the deceas'd husband

Though women of some classes performed *Sati* by burning themselves some others, particularly the Lingayats performed it by being buried alive with their dead husbands.[13] This kind of *Sati* is also mentioned in inscriptions.[14]

were very strict and would constrain her to burn herself even against her own will, for preventing the disorders possible to happen in case she should live (a barbarous, indeed and too cruel Law); but that neither force nor persuasion was used to *Giaccama,* and that she did it of her own free will; in which, as a magnanimous action, (as indeed it was), and amongst them of great honour, both her relations and herself much glory'd. I ask'd concerning the ornaments and flowers she wore, and they told me that such was the custom in token of the *Masti's* joy (they call the women, who intends to burn herself for the death of her husband, *Masti*) in that she was very shortly to go to him and therefore had reason to rejoyce; whereas such widows as will not dye remain in continual sadness and lamentations, shave their heads and live in perpetual mourning for the death of their husbands. At last Giaccama caus'd one to tell me that she accounted my coming to see her a great fortune, and held herself much honor'd, as well by my visit and presence as by the fame which I should carry of her to my own country; and that before she dy'd she would come to visit me in my house, and also to ask me as their custom is, that I would favour her with something by way of Alms, towards the buying of fewel for the fire wherewith she was to be burnt. I answr'd her that I should esteem her visit and very willingly give her something, not for wood and fire wherein to burn herself (for her death much depressed, and I would gladly have diswaded her from it, if I could) but to do something else therewith, that herself most lik'd, and I promised her that, so far as my weak pen could contribute, her name should remain immortal in the world. Thus I took leave of her, more sad for her death than she was, cursing the custom of India which is unmerciful to women. Giacamma was a woman of about thirty years of age, of a complexion very brown for an Indian and almost black, but of a good aspect, tall of stature well shap'd and proportion'd. My Muse could not forbear from chanting her in a sonnet which I made upon her death and reserve among my poetical papers." From the interesting conversation cited above it may be surmised that sati was voluntary and not compulsory.

13. Even though there is no contemporary description of it in Ikkēri Nuniz's description of this in Vijayanagar may be found interesting. He says: "These go with much pleasure to the pit inside of which are made two seats of earth, one for him and one for her, and they place one in his own seat and cover them in little by little till they are covered up and so the wife died with the husband" (Sewell: A Forgotten Empire, pp. 392-393). Again Barbosa describes

Generally the classes of people who performed *Sahagamana* came from the nobility of the kingdom like the king, great lords, knights and the fighting classes. According to the epigraphs which are numerous, the classes of people called the Gauḍas and the Nāyakas also performed *sahagamana*.[15] It is interesting to note that many of the queens of Keladi committed Sati or Sahagamana.[16] According to an inscription in the Sorab taluk in the Shimoga district, the wife of one Bomma Gauḍa performed Sahagamana with great desire.[17] Again another inscription records Sati by a certain Mēchigauḍi on the death of her husband Hariya Gauḍa of Keladi.[18] The edification of a dead person might have been another cause for the wide prevalence of Sati. The performance of Sati was commemorated by the erection of Satikals on which are seen sculptured representations of the widows who committed Sati.

it as follows: "They dig a great hole deep enough to come up to her neck, and place her in it alive, standing on her feet and begin to shovel in the earth around her trampling it down with their feet until she is covered to the neck with well trodden earth. Then they place a great stone over her and there she stays dying alive and walled up in clay and they carry out other ceremonies for her." (Barbosa, I, pp. 218-219).

14. *EC.*, VIII, Sb. 496, 165, etc.

15. *EC.*, XI, Dg. 116, *EC.*, VII, Sk. 302, *EC.*, VIII, Sa. 8 etc. It is very interesting to note that Sati seems to have largely prevailed in the Shimoga district.

16. *KNV.*, VI and VII.

17. *EC.*, VIII, Sb. 495.

18. *MAR.*, 1930, No. 58. Though Sati was voluntary, it is not easy to account for its popularity, Hervey's remarks on this question are worth citing "Excessive jealousy of their female connections, operating on the breasts of Hindoo princes, rendered those despots regardless of the common bonds of society and their incumbent duty as the protectors of the weaker sex, and in so much that with a view to prevent every possibility of their widows forming subsequent attachments, they availed themselves of their arbitrary power and, under the cloak of religion, introduced the practice of burning widows alive under the first impressions of sorrow or despair, immediately after the demise of their husbands. (Some Records of Crime, II, p. 506 quoted by Thompson, *Sutte*, p. 45).

Women: In any particular age, the status of women could be considered conveniently by dividing them into two classes. They may be called ordinary family women and the dancing girls or public women. Family women, were generally of a retiring nature and did not take active part in social festivities. It was only the dancing girls who took part in them. No Foreign traveller who visited Ikkēri has left any descriptions of the family women. But the dancing girls have attracted the notice of the travellers. Della Valle gives some information about a dancing woman in Ikkēri, who was sent along with others, to lead the traveller to the royal court.[19] From the observations of this traveller it may be surmised that dancing girls were skilled considerably in acrobatics.

19. He writes: "With those that come to fetch him, came also a publick Dancing Woman, who performed a pretty piece of agility in his presence; for standing, upon one foot, when the drums and other instruments sounded, with the other she swiftly turned round the Air a large iron Ring, about a span in Diametre, without letting it fall off her great toe, and at the same time with one hand toss'd two hollow brass balls, catching one in her Hand whilst the other was aloft and so alternatively and very humbly without letting them fall; which indeed with great dexeterity to be imploy'd at the same time with foot and the hand, standing firm all the while on the other foot without support and yet attending to the Musick and this for a good pace together during which an old man with a white beard and bald head who brought her stood behind her, crying all the while Abud, Abud, Abud, which in their language signifies 'yes' and in this instance as much as Good, Good, Good, Good." (Della Valle, *op. cit.*, II, p. 263).

In another place Della Valle describes the Dancing girls as follows: "On the fifteenth of the same month came first in the day time and afterwards at night to our House, Twelve or Fifteen, publick Dancing women, who, by consequence are also publick strumpets, although very young, being conducted by certain of their men. In the day time they did nothing but talk a little, and some of them made themselves drunk with a certain wine made of dry'd Raisins or a sort Aqua vitae and other mixtures call'd in India Nippa, I say some of them because certain others of less ignoble race as they are more abstinent in eating so they drink not any thing that inebriates. At night they entertained us a good while with Dancing after their modes accompany'd with singing not unpleasant to behold; for they consist of a numerous company of women, all well cloth'd and adorn'd with gold, jewels and Tresses of several fashions, who sing and strike their wooden instruments. They begin all their dances slowly and by degrees growing to a heat, at last end with furious and quick motions which

The Dancing girls were interested in religious activity also. An inscription dated 1673 A.C. refers to a dancing girl Puttitāyi Jambhukhaṇḍi Cenni, as the builder of Mahattu Maṭha at Jenni.[20]

Court Life: Life in an Oriental Court is attractive and interesting. The grandeur of the Court, the method of doing homage to the king, the pastimes of the sovereign, the method of transacting business by him—these form a very interesting study.

The Keladi kings lived in great pomp and splendour. Pietro Della Valle gives vivid details of the pomp and splendour at the Ikkēri Court. The kings of Keladi seem to have used only cushions for sitting while they held their court. For instance Venkaṭappa Nāyaka "was seated in a kind of porch on the opposite side of a small court, upon a kind of pavement somewhat rais'd from the Earth cover'd with a canopy like a square Tent, but made of boards, and gilded. The Floor was cover'd with a piece of Tapistry something old and the king sat, after the manner of the East, upon a little quilt on the out-side of the Tent, leaning upon one of the pillars which upheld it on the right hand, having at his back two great cushions of fine white silk."[21]

appear well enough. Amongst their dances two pleased me well, one in which they continually repeated these words....and another wherein they represented a battel and the actions of slaughter. In the conclusion, the Master of the Ballet, who directs all and was one of those that brought them, danced in the midst of them with a naked Ponyard, wherewith he represented the actions of slaughter as the women did with short sticks. But the end of this shew was most ridiculous, for when they were dismissed they not only were not contended with the largeness of the Ambassador, although I added as much of my own to it, but went away very ill satisfied, testifying the same by cholerick yellings, which to me was a new comedy." (*Ibid.*, II, pp. 272-273).

From the statement of Della Valle it is known that there were also groups of ballet dancers in the Keladi kingdom.

20. *EC.*, VIII, Tl. 68.

21. Della Valle, *op. cit.*, II, p. 251.

The king seems to have presided over important religious festivals in temples. In the Ikkēri temples, festivals were held at night every Monday and every New and Full Moonday and the king himself was usually present at them. Della Valle who saw some of them describes the king's participation in them.[22]

The pagentry and the pomp of the Keladi court, as of all other oriental courts, rested largely on the number of retinues and captains employed in the palace to maintain the dignity of the court. Pietro Della Valle gives a vivid picture of the pomp of the royal Court. He observes:

> "The pomp proceeded in this manner. Many horsemen went foremost, who were followed by divers foot, arm'd with Pikes and other weapons some of them brandishing the same as they went along; then march'd certain Musketiers with Drums, Trumpets, pipes and cornets sounding, these cloth'd all in one colour after the Portugal manner, but with coarse stuff of small value; and

22. "In the great temple, not only the inside in the middle whereof is a very high and slender cupola, but also all the outer walls and all those round about the Piazza which lies before it, as also the Houses on the adjacent sides were all full of lights. The concourse of the people of all sorts and degrees, both men and women, was very great and they appeared to go about visiting all temples. When it was late the king came to the great temple, accompanied onely by his two grandsons, to wit Seda Siva Naieka (whom I had formerly seen) son of one his daughters and Virabadra Naieka, a young boy, his son's son whom he designs for his successor, of his other kindred elder than he, to wit the above said Seda Siva and two of Venkatapa's nephews by one of his Brothers, whom he keeps prisoner, do not disturb him. The king came in a Palanchino at a great pace, his two nephews on horse-back and so did Vitula Sinay, who rode by the king's side with appearance of a great favourite. Likewise Putapara (Puttapayya) came in a Palanchino and other of his Grandees come on palanchinos and some on horse-back, following him at a great distance with some number of soldiers and servants on foot, but in sum, the whole train was not very considerable. The king stay'd in the Temple about an hour, being entertained with Musick, Dancing and other things which I could not see. At length he came forth and with the same company, and running in as much haste as he came return'd home." Della Valle, *op. cit.*, II. p. 284

amongst them rode a servant of the Ambassador's, better clad after their fashion, as Captain of the Guard. Then followed the Ambassador in the middle, between Vitala Sinay and Muse Bai, and after him we have his retinue to witt the chaplin Sig: *Gonsalvo Caravalglio* and *Sig Francesco Monteyro* .... After us came the other Horsemen."

He further adds:

"On the right hand and behind the king, stood divers courtiers, one of whom continually waved a piece of fine white linen, as if to drive away the flies from the king. Besides the king there was but one person sitting, and he the principal favourite of the Court, call'd Patapaia, and he sat at a good distance from him, on the right hand, near the wall."[23]

From the extracts quoted we get an idea of the pomp of the Court and Court etiquette in Ikkēri.

Habitation, Food and Dress

Habitation: The foreign travellers who visited Ikkēri and other places have left accounts of the size of the cities and the palaces and houses in them. But they have not left accounts of the villages in the empire. For a description of the city of Ikkēri, the writings of Della Valle are indispensable. The Italian traveller says that:

"The city of Ikkēri is seated in a goodly plain, and as we entered we pass'd through three gates, with small forts and ditches, and consequently three inclosures; the two first of which were not walls, but made of very high Indian canes, very thick and closely planted, instead of a wall and are strong against Foot and Horse in any case, hard to cut and not in danger of fire, besides that the herbs which creep upon them, together with their own leaves make a fair and great verdure and much shadow. The other inclosure is a wall, but weak

23. Della Valle: *op. cit.*, pp. 250-252.

and inconsiderable. But having passed these three we pass'd all. Some say there are others within, belonging to the citadel, or Fort, where the palace is, for Ikkēri is so good largeness, but the houses stand thinly and are ill built, especially without the third inclosure, and most of the situation is taken up by great and long streets, some of them shadow'd with high and very goodly trees growing in Lakes of Water, of which there are many large ones, besides Fields set full of Trees, like Groves, so that it seems to consist of a city, Lakes, Fields and woods mingled together and makes a very delightful sight."[24]

Again the same traveller describes the palace in Ikkēri thus:

"In this manner we rode to the Palace, which stands in a fort, or citadel of good largeness, incompass'd with a great ditch and ill built bastions. At the entrance we found two very long, but narrow, Bulwarks. Without the citadel are many houses, and I believe there are shops also in several streets, for we pass'd through two Gates, at both of which there stood Guards, and all the distance between them was an inhabited street. We went through these two Gates on Horse back; which, I believe, was a privilege, for few did so besides ourselves, namely such onely as entered where the king was; the rest either remaining on Horseback at the first Gate, or alighting at the entrance of the second. A third Gate also we enter'd, but on foot, and came into a kind of Court, about which were sitting in Porches many Prime Courtiers, and other persons of quality. Then we came to the fourth gate, Guarded with soldiers, into which onely we Franchi or Christians and some few others of the country, were suffer'd to enter, and we presently found the king."[25]

24. Della Valle—*op. cit.*, pp. 244-245.

25. *Ibid.*, p. 251. For detailed descriptions of other towns like Mangalūr, Barcelor. Bhatkal, Honnali, Uḷḷal, Onor (Honavar) see Della Valle, p. 301, 297, 390 n., 234, 303, 202-3 n. etc.

The subjects of Keladi, lived in fully equipped and well provided houses. Della Valle describes the city of Sagar, which was built by Venkaṭappa Nāyaka, thus:

"It is called Saghar and is already pretty well inhabited, with houses all made of Earth after their manner. The palace is finished and Venkatapa frequently goes to it; as also a temple built upon a great Artificial Lake, and a house for his Nephews and other grandees with all conveniences thereunto, particularly great stalls for Elephants, of which he keeps above eighty; we saw many of them here, some for war of large and handsome. A market was kept this day in Saghar, as it is the custom every Sunday and at Ikkēri every Friday. There was a great concourse of people, but nothing to sell besides necessaries for food and clothing. The way between Ikkēri and Saghar is very handsome, plain, broad, and almost always direct, here and there beset with great and thick trees which make a shadow and a delightful verdue."[26]

Large towns seem to have had special amenities which smaller towns and villages could not have enjoyed. The foremost among them was a pleasure garden or park. Further there were pleasure resorts like swimming pools. For instance Venkaṭappa Nāyaka built a city called Sadāśivasāgara with a palace and a swimming resort and another called Viśvanāthapura on the Varadā.[27] Śivappa Nāyaka built a large pond in a place about two miles to the north-east of Ānandapura for purposes of recreation. The pond is said to have been fed by a tank situated about a mile and a half away.[28]

Food: The articles of food grown in Keladi kingdom were mainly rice, besides grains and corn. Kanara was the granary of the west coast for the best rice during the period

26. *Ibid.*, II, p. 265-66. The flooring of many houses was of mud. But it was kept neat and clean by smearing cow dung and water. The contemporary practice was well noticed by the traveller. (See pp. 230-31).

27. *QJMS.*, XXII, p. 77.

28. *MAR.*, 1941, p. 72.

and all the foreign settlements on the west coast depended on the supply of rice by it.

When Della Valle and others visited the Ikkēri court he says they were supplied with "sugar canes, fruits, sugar and other things to eat, but not any animal and, if I was not misinform'd he excus'd his king's not sending him sheep or other animals to eat, by saying that he was a Lingayat (Lingayat) or Noble Race, who neither eat nor kill any creatures, as if he should have sinn'd and defil'd himself by sending any to the Ambassador, who would have eaten them."[29]

There appear to have been also sweet meat shops (*miṭāyi aṅgaḍi*) also in certain places of the kingdom.[30]

Dress: The Keladi kings seem to have spent considerable sums on their dress and ornaments. Describing his audience with king Vīrabhadra Nāyaka, Peter Mundy writes:

"We were admitted to the presence of Beere Budra (Vīrabhadra) Naique, king of Mollinare (Malnad). It being a great festival of jentures (himself being one) he sate in state, soe having kissed his hands and Delivered our present, Hee caused us to come uppe and sitt by him. I dare say there

29. Peter Mundy and the other English Ambassadors were entertained to supper by king Vīrabhadra Nāyaka. Mundy gives details about it as follows:

"On 28th February, 1637 the king invited us for supper, where out table cloth and dishes were of plantaine leaves sowed together. We had at least 20 severall sorts of Achare (achar), to say, pickled fruits as Mangoes, Cardamum, Green pepper, etts to relish Meates, as we use cloves, capers, cowcumbers etts. In our Dishes wee had milk both sweet and sower and sirruppes of several sorts. Rice was dressed in sundry manners all spread in Divers parcells on the plain leaves, as was the achare. The king himselffe sate by us with a rod in his hand, pointing to this or that he would have us eate, being desirous wee should taste of all. Our Drinke was such as he himselffe dranck, even perfumed water. We sate on the ground. They neighter eate flesh nor fish nor Drinck, strong; besides our touching any of their implements is odious to them and that vessell, etts held unclean." (Peter Mundy, Travels, III, pp. 81, ff.).

30. Narasimhachar: Karnataka Kavicarite, II, p. 336.

is hardly such another grossee proportionable Man to be found in all his owne Dominiones, off about 30 yeares of age. Hee hath many wives and women, never a child. Hee sate after the Indian manner with well nigh a pecke of sweet flowers strung and hung over Necke and shoulders, some as belts, others as collars. These at tymes were taken away and others fresh broughtt, as it were every quarter of halffe hover; his neck and arms laden with ritch ornaments of gold sett with pretious stones. One of his ears hung great pearles as bigge as pretty fine hazel nutts.

He sate foremost on an elevated place like our theatres on stages, his greatt ones behind or within him, all besett allsoe with jewells, chaines, collars, bracelets, arme bands, etts of gold with stones of great price. Their haire (which they lett grow) is bound up in a fine large kerchiefs hanging in a lumpe or bunche on one side of their heads. This is the usual fashion, from the king to the common, the women in the same manner but withoutt a cloath, soe heare the kerchieff, and the women none."[31]

The captains and other important dignitaries in the state also wore ceremonial and rich costume. Della Valle gives vivid details of the dress worn by the courtiers. Describing the dress of the Muse Bai, a general of Venkaṭappa Nāyaka, who had been sent to conduct the Portuguese embassy Della Valle observes:

"Another great person sent by the king to accompany him, he was a Moor by sect, but of Indian race, very black, and Captain General in these parts of Banghel from which charge he was lately returned and his name was Muse Bai. With these came also a son of his, a youth of the same colour, but of a handsome race, and cloth'd oddly after the Indian fashion, that is naked from the girdle upwards, having onely a very thin and variously painted cloth cast across one shoulder, and another of the same sort of girt about him, and hanging down loose; he had a little bonnet upon his head,

31. Peter Mundy, Travels III, p. 81 ff.

like those of our Galley slaves, but wrought with diverse colours; his hands, arms, Neck and Nose, were adorn'd with many ornaments of gold, and he had a guilt Ponyard at his girdle, which shew'd very well. His father was cloth'd all in white, after the manner of India, to wit of such as wear clothes and go not naked from the waste upwards, upon his white vestment he had a shorter sur coat of velvet, guarded with gold at the bottom, loose and open before, which is the custom onely in solemnities. He had no sword, but onely a Ponyard on the rightside, the hilt and chape gilded and as I believe of silver. Upon his head he had a little cap of the same form, made of cloth of gold, for in these countries it is the fashion for Men to cover their Heads either with such caps or with white Turbans, little and almost square. Vitula Sinay and some other personages who came with them to accompany the Ambassador were all cloth'd with white garments of very fine silk or other rich silken sur coats upon the same, to honour the solemnity and upon these they had such colour'd clothese as in Persia they call scial and use for girdles, but the Indians wear them across the shoulders, cover'd with a piece of very fine silk, so that the colour underneath appears or else wear white silk alone."[32]

The women's attire seems to have been very colourful. Della Valle describes their dress as follows:

"We saw going along the streets several companies of young girls, well cloth'd after their manner, with some of the above mentioned wrought and figur'd silk from the girdle downwards and from thence upward either naked, or else with very pure linens either of one colour or strip'd and wrought with several besides a scarf of the same work cast over the soulder. Their heads were deck'd with yellow and white flowers form'd into a huge and large diadem with some sticking out like Sun-beams, with others twisted together and hanging down in several fashions, which made a pretty sight.[33]

32. Della Valle: Travels, II, pp. 247 ff.
33. Della Valle—*op. cit.*, II, p. 258.

The dancing girls were adorned "with girdles, rings upon their legs, Necklaces and other ornaments of Gold, and with certain pectorals, or breast plates, almost round, in the fashion of a shield and butting out with a sharp ridge before, embroyder'd with gold and stuck either with jewels or some such things, which reflected the sun-beams with marvellous splendour; as to the rest of their bodies they were uncover'd, without veil or Head Tire."[34]

Amusements: Among the amusements and games in the Keladi kingdom may be mentioned wrestling, duelling, the theatre, dance and music. These seem to have given considerable pleasure and entertainment to the people. Venkaṭappa Nāyaka built a *Nāṭyaśāla* to encourage the double arts of Dance and Drama. In the inscriptions also we get occasional references to the *mēḷa*[35] and musicians.[36] During religious festivals in temples there used to be dancing. Della Valle again gives a colourful description of dances.[37] Allied to the dance was the kōlāṭṭam or the stick play. Young girls trimly clad used to go round the streets in small batches "all of them carrying in each hand a little round painted stick, about a span long or a little more, which they struck together after a musical measure, to the sound of drums and other instruments and one of the skilfullest of the company sung one verse of a song, at the end of which they all reply'd seven or eight times, in the number of their metre with words cole, cole, cole. They went to the temple followed by other women, and used to dance in circles in the temples, till late in the night."[38] Pietro Della Valle who observed the custom says that this was a festival which they celebrated for three days at the end of a certain feast in honour of Gaurī, wife of Mahōdaka and hence it was celebrated by girls.[39]

34. *Ibid.,* p. 269.
35. *EC.,* VIII, Tl. 68, 69, 71 and 85.
36. *Ibid.,* Tl. 182.
37. Della Valle—*op. cit.,* II, p. 258 ff.
38. Della Valle—*op. cit.,* II, pp. 258-259.
39. *Ibid.,* p. 259.

Among the musical instruments, we get reference to *Mahāmuraja,*[40] *viṇa*[41] and the *tambūru*[42] from inscriptions.

Religion: During the rule of the Keladi kings, all the religious sects in South India such as the Śaiva, Vaiṣṇava, Muslims and even the Christians were living side by side. The Nāyakas of Keladi generally tried to patronise all religions in the kingdom without any distinction.

Śaivism: Among the Hindu religious groups in the Ikkēri kingdom, the Śaivas appear to have constituted the majority. They may be classified under two small groups (1) Advaitins or Smārtas and (2) Vīraśaivas. Vīraśaivism was the faith to which the Nāyakas adhered. The mode in which the kings subscribed their grants give some idea about their faith. Almost all the kings bore the titles *"Viśuddha Vaidīkādvaita Siddhānta Pratiṣṭāpaka"* and *"Śivaguru bhakti Prayāṇa"*, which bear proof of their devotion to Śiva. The founders of the Ikkēri dynasty were reared in the atmosphere of Śaivism. An inscription of 1577 A.C. speaks of Rāmarāja Nāyaka holding faith in Śiva as his chief aim.[43] They were great devotees of the Advaita *maṭha* at Śṛṅgeri to which institution they made several grants. For instance an inscription dated Śaka 1542 (1621 A.C.) states that Veṅkaṭappa Nāyaka I re-established Śṛṅgēri.[44] Yet another records the restoration of the endowment of Śṛṅgēri *maṭha* by Śivappa Nāyaka.[45] There are numerous other grants of the Nāyaks to this *maṭha,* which we shall discuss in the sequel under the section on *Maṭhas.*

The Vīraśaivas were an influential religious sect in the kingdom. Vīra Śaivism as a religion was given a popular impetus by Basava, a minister and contemporary of the Kalachūri king Bijjaḷa. The way had however been prepared for him, by a succession of Śaiva teachers. They did not concern

40. *EC.*, VIII, Sb. 153.
41. *Ibid.*, Sb. 258.
42. *Ibid.*, Sb. 379; *EC.*, XII, Gb. 29.
43. *EC.*, VIII, Sb. 475.
44. *EC.*, VI, Sg. 5.
45. *Ibid.*, Sg. 11.

themselves very much with the philosophical doctrines of the Vēdāntins. "What philosophy the Jangamas professedly have is Vēdāntic, but in fact they are deistic (not pantheistic) disciples of .... Basava who taught Śiva worship in its grossest form, the adoration of the Liṅga (phallus); while his adherents who spread all over India under the name of Jaṅgamas, 'vagrants or Liṅgāyats (Phallus wearers) are idaltrous deists with but a tinge of Vedantic mysticism."[46] They are staunch Śaivas, reject the authority of the Vedas, do not have belief in the doctrine of rebirth, object to child marriage, approve remarriage of widows; they constitute even now a very powerful community in the Kannaḍa country, particularly among the trading classes.

The Nāyaks of Keladi were never inimical to religious institutions propounding faiths other than the Vīraśaiva cult. They gave liberal patronage to the Dvaita maṭhas at Uḍipi and Kūḍali. Rāmarāja Nāyaka for instance, made a grant of land in Śaka 1493 (1571 A.C.) to the celebrated Dvaita teacher and scholar Vādirāja Tīrtha for worship in the temple of god Kṛṣṇa at Uḍipi.[47] It is interesting to observe that this gift was made in order that Sadāśiva Nāyaka may obtain re-union with Śiva. At the time of the re-installation (*punaḥ pratishṭhā*) of god Kṛṣṇa at Uḍipi by Vēdavedyatīrtha, disciple of Vādirāja Tīrtha in Śaka 1536 (1613 A.C.) Venkaṭappa Nāyaka granted to the temple the village of Huvinakere in Bārakūru-rājya.[48] He made endowments not only to Hindu institutions but also to mosques. As an example of this may be cited a grant of land made in Śaka 1550 (1627 A.C.) by Venkaṭappa Nāyaka I to a mosque built at Bhuvanagiridurga.[49] Though no gift is known to have been made to any Christian institution it is believed there were more than thirty thousand Christians among the subjects of Śivappa Nāyaka.[50]

The Nāyakas even though they were nurtured in the ideas of pure Śaivism adopted a liberal attitude towards other faiths.

46. Hopkins: Religions of India, p. 482.
47. *EC.*, VIII, Sb. 55.
48. *SII.* Vol. VII, No. 297.
49. *EC.*, VIII, Tl. 38, also *EC.*, VIII, Sa. 108.
50. Rice: Mysore and Coorg from Inscriptions, p. 159.

The Vaiṣṇava influence was on the ascendant during the reign of Kṛṣṇa Dēva Rāya of Vijayanagar. Veṅkaṭādri, the brother of Rāmarāya conferred on Sādāśiva Nāyaka the governorship of Bārakūr rājya. Under Veṅkaṭa II, Vaiṣṇavism found patronage in Vellore, Ikkēri and even in Uḷḷal. However, the Nāyakas of Ikkēri championed the cause of Śaivism. It is certain that the faith of the monarchs and the faith which was making giant strides in the empire, must certainly have exerted some influence over them. This is evident from some of the inscriptions and grants of the Ikkēri kings. In 1577 A.C. an inscription of Rāmarāja Nāyaka which opens with the usual obeisance to Gaṇādhipati and to Śaṁbhu also contains salutation to the boar.[51] The boar can be traced to the Vaiṣṇava influence. In 1616 Venkaṭappa Nāyaka granted lands for the maṭha of the Rāmanuja sect at Ikkēri and for the god Venkaṭēśvara.[52] In 1630, Vīrabhadra Nāyaka gave a gift for perpetual lamp for god Venkaṭēśvara.[53] In 1640 again he granted land yielding 80 *varāhas* for the expenses of gods Lakshmīnarasimha and Sacchidānandēśvara.[54] In 1665 a grant of Sōmaśēkhara Nāyaka contains an invocation to the boar.[55] In an inscription dated 1666 A.C. there is an invocation to Gaṇēśa along with one to Varāha (boar). The epigraph ends with '*Śrī Kṛṣṇa*'.[56] In 1674 a grant to Basavaliṅga ends with '*Śrī Rāmakṛṣṇa*'.[57] In 1702 there is again an invocation to the boar.[58]

From the fact that the whole South India was permeated with ideas of Vaiṣṇavism it is evident that the Ikkēri rulers who in spite of the fact that they were nurtured in the ideas of pure Śaivism, must have for some reason of state rather than of conviction followed a liberal attitude towards other faiths.

51. *EC.*, VIII, Sb. 475.
52. *EC.*, VIII, Ng. 79.
53. *EC.*, VIII, Sr. 157.
54. *Ibid.*, Tl. 3.
55. *EC.*, VIII, Tl. 7.
56. *Ibid.*, Tl. 56.
57. *Ibid.*, Tl. 188.
58. *Ibid.*, Tl. 208.

A notable feature of the religious movements of the period was the holding of religious controversies between eminent religious teachers. There were two such scholars of rival faiths during the latter half of the sixteenth century. Bhaṭṭōji Dīkshita was a strong *advaitin* with a partiality for Śiva, while Rāmānuja (not the founder of the faith but another learned scholar) was a devout Vaiṣṇava. Bhaṭṭōji Dīkshita seems to have challenged Rāmānuja in a religious controversy and defeated his opponent, whence Rāmānuja had to relinquish all his honours. Bhaṭṭōji Dīkshita earned the title of Viśiṣṭha-Vaidīka-advaita-Siddhānta-sthāpanācārya besides other marks of honour and court presents from Venkaṭappa Nāyaka I.[59] In spite of these controversies, and strong feelings as between members of one faith against another, it is indeed remarkable that there was no persecution in the kingdom.

The temple and the Maṭha: The temple and the *maṭha* were two important institutions which moulded the religious life of the people. The temple was the symbol of the expression of religious impulse of the people. The *maṭha* existed to propogate certain schools of thought and literature. The temples were maintained either by royal benefaction or by private patronage. The kings built temples and endowed them with lands or money or made remissions of taxes in their favour. For instance Sadāśiva Nāyaka made a gift of sarvamānya land yielding produce worth 4 *varāhas* to the god Mallinātha of Aḷahaḷḷi.[60] In 1553 A.C. the village Hattya Kūḍūru was granted to the temple of Tirumaladēva by Koṇḍappa Voḍeya under the orders of Śankaṇṇa Nāyaka.[61] Yet another epigraph dated 1536 A.C. records the gift of land and gold to god Kōṭināthadēva and goddess Sankamadēvī of the temple of Kōṭēśvar.[62]

59. *QJMS.*, XXII, p. 78.

60. *MAR.*, 1923, No. 120.

61. *ARSIE.*, 422 of 1927-28.

62. *SII.*, IX, pt. ii, No. 578. There are numerous other grants to temples by private individuals as well as by public. See *ARSIE.*, 385 of 1926-27. *EC.* VII, Sk. 255, *ARSIE.*, 283 of 1931-32, etc.

The goddess Mūkāṁbikā was the tutelary deity of the Nāyakas. The temple of Mūkāṁbikā at Kōllūr, South Kanara, received liberal impetus and patronage at the hands of the rulers. Vīrabhadra Nāyaka granted the income from two villages Koḷambaḷike Rāḍigrāma in Kabu nāḍa śīme and Valarūra[va]ṭa in Nirulanda *śīme* for worship, offerings and lamps to the goddess Mūkāṁbikā and the subsidiary dieties in the temple at Kollūru.[63] An inscription on a step leading to the *Navaraṅga* of the temple records the visit of the Keladi queen Cannammājī. The inscriptions reads "*Keladi Cannammājī sēvē*" meaning that Cannammājī did pious service to the goddess.[64] Vīramma, the wife of Venkaṭappa Nāyaka I, gifted two *dvārapālaka* images weighing 17½ maunds and 13/8 seers each for the service of goddess of Mūkāṁbika.[65] Cannavīrammājī, the queen of Basavappa Nāyaka granted a silver pot weighing *la* 7½ and *ga* 2 to goddess Mūkāmbikā.[66]

A few of the pilgrimage centres of the period in and around the Ikkēri kingdom were Uḍipi, Kollūru, Śankaranārāyaṇa and Mangaḷūru.

Maṭhas: The *maṭhas* in mediaeval South India were important religious institutions receiving the benefactions from State, and maintained themselves with the wealth they possessed and the endowments made to them. They were primarily educational seminaries and encouraged learning and spread secular knowledge as well.

One comes across many such maṭhas in the Keladi kingdom. The foremost amongst them was the Śṛṅgēri maṭha. Originally founded by Śrī Śankara, the great Advaitin and philosopher it was presided over by a regular succession of pontiffs. The *maṭha* beginning as a centre of religious and and philosophical education, became an institute of organised temple worship and of feeding crowds of pilgrims thronging

63. *ARSIE.*, C.P. No. 3 of 1927-28.
64. *MAR.*, 1944, No. 53.
65. *Ibid.*, No. 52.
66. *Ibid.*, No. 48.

to it. From the inscriptions of the period we can say that the following pontiffs of Śṛṅgēri lived:

Vidyā Tīrtha.
Vidyāraṇya Tīrtha.
Bhārati Tīrtha.
Narasiṁha Bhārati.
Rāmachandra Bhārati.
Śankara Bhārati.
Chandraśēkhara Bhārati.
Purushōttama Bhārati.
Rāmachandra Bhārati.
Narasiṁha Bhārati.
Immāḍi Narasiṁha Bhārati.
Abhinava Narasiṁha Bhārati.
Sacchidānanda Bhārati.

Each of them bore such titles as *Paramahamsa Parivrājakācārya* (chief *ācārya* of the *paramahamsa sanyasis*) *Padavākya pramāṇa pāravara parīṇa* (who has seen the farthest point in grammar, philosophy and logic) devoted to Yama, Niyama, and others, the eight branches of Yōga, establisher of the pure *Vaidīkādvaita siddhānta*, etc. They were, as they are even now, taken in palanquins carried crossways blocking the entire road and preventing anything else passing.[67] There is a work in Sanskrit verse called *Guruvamsamahākāvya* (the History of the successive teachers of Śṛṅgēri Maṭh) a biographical work composed by Lakṣmaṇa Śāstri, son of Viśvēśvara Śāstri under the orders of Sacchidānanda Bhārati, disciple of Narasimha Bhārati. The author mentions the names of Cannammāji and Somaśēkhara Nāyaka but not either of Vīrammājī or Haidar Āli. This shows that he was a contemporary of Sōmaśēkhara Nāyaka II (1714-1739) when Sacchidānanda Bhārati, disciple of Narasiṁha Bharati adorned the pontifical seat at Śṛṅgēri. Lakṣmaṇa Śāstri, the author of the work seems to have been a good Sanskrit scholar as he composed the work under the orders of Sacchidānanda Bhārati, it may

67. *Mys. Gaz.*, New Edn. V., pp. 1174-1181.

be assumed that he must have incorporated all the available traditional information about the successive teachers of Śṛṅgēri. Though the information recorded by him about the earlier gurus is purely legendary his account of the latter gurus contemporaneous with the Keladi kings contain some historical information.[68] Venkaṭappa Nāyaka is said to have invited Abhinava Narasimha Bharati to his court and presented him with his green flag as a badge. He was the author of a commentary of the Śivagīta and an expert in Tantras and mantras. At the invitation of Venkaṭappa Nāyaka I Abhinava Narasimha Bhārati and Sacchidānanda Bhārati visited Ikkēri. Sacchidānanda Bhārati made discourses in *Tarka, Mimāṁsa* and *Vēdānta* in the court of Venkaṭappa and was admired for his learning by the Court Pandits. After spending a few days in Ikkēri and Sagara, the Guru with his disciple returned to Śṛṅgēri. On the demise of Abhinavanaṛāsiṁhabhārati, Sācchidānanda Bhārati succeeded him. At the request of Venkaṭappa, he visited Ikkēri and Kollūru where he worshipped Goddess Mūkāṁbikā. During the reign of Vīrabhadra Nāyaka, the chief of Kalasa, Bhairava invaded the territories of the Keladi state and took possession of some part of the territories measuring six *yōjanas* (24 miles), Śṛṅgēri being situated within it. Bhairava sent some of his officers to bring Sacchidānanda Bhārati to Kalasa, his capital. Without fearing him the Guru went to Kalasa and was lodged in a tent on the bank of the Tuṅgā. After going through his usual religious duties the Guru went to see Bhairava in his palace and having praised the good qualities of Vīrabhadranāyaka, his enemy and having blessed Bhairava boldly sat before the greedy chief. Intent on taking away the wealth of the Śṛṅgēri maṭh, Bhairava marshalled his warriors with drawn swords before the Guru. Sacchidānanda Bharati showed no signs of fear and began to discourse on spiritual subjects in a dignified tone. Thinking that the ascetic was no timid man to surrender the wealth of the Maṭh to him,

68. *MAR.*, 1928, pp. 15 ff. For a detailed account of the successive teachers of Śṛṅgēri maṭh upto the time of Venkaṭappa Nāyaka I, see *MAR.*, 1928, pp. 15-20.

Bhairava presented the Guru with silk clothes and sent him back to Śṛṅgēri. No sooner had the Guru reached Śṛṅgēri, than came Bhairava to Śṛṅgēri with his army. Having been frightened at the sudden arrival of the plunderer most of the inhabitants of Śṛṅgēri left for a neighbouring village for safety. Having won over the treasurer of the *Maṭh* Bhairava carried away the money of the *Maṭh*. Having made a ditch around Śṛṅgēri, as a protective measure against the enemy, Bhairava went before the Guru and fearing his spiritual powers returned to Karkala without making any attempt to pacify him. The army of Vīrabhadra Nāyaka, however, followed the chief and surrounding Karkala interrupted the movements of Bhairava.

With a view to see Sacchidānanda Bhārati, Vīrabhadra Nāyaka went to Tīrthahaḷḷi, where he learnt that Bhairava had won over his armies and was again marching against Śṛṅgēri. Sacchidānanda Bhārati was about to leave the town for engaging himself in penance elsewhere. Meanwhile Vīrabhadra sent a Paṇḍit to tell the Guru that he was prepared to put down Bhairava and that there was no necessity for the Guru to leave the Maṭh. Accordingly the Guru blessed Vīrabhadra and performed penance in Maṭh for the king's victory. In the battle which ensued Bhairava was defeated and surrendered himself to Vīrabhadra, who pleased with his submission allowed him to go back to his capital and keep peace. Hearing this the Guru was immensely pleased and narrated the stories of Bhārata and Rāmāyaṇa to Vīrabhadra. It is at this time that the Guru composed a kāvya called *Rāmachandramahōdaya.* But the Guru's peace was shortlived, for a few days after, Bhairava plundered the maṭh for a second time and made the Guru "as emaciated as the crescent moon after the loss of his wealth." The Guru left the empty Maṭh and lived somewhere outside Śṛṅgēri. Hearing this, Vīrabhadra stationed some of his army on a mound near Śṛṅgēri to guard the town and persuaded the Guru to return to the Maṭh. Śṛṅgēri now became partly a military station and partly a sacred place of gods and saints. After receiving the blessings of the Guru, Vīrabhadra returned to Ikkēri.

Enraged at this, Bhairava sent his army for a third time and besieged the town. The commander of Vīrabhadra's army was a man of low character and having been bribed by Bhairava, began to retreat. The inhabitants of Śṛṅgēri were frightened and appealed to the Guru for help. The author of the *Guruvaṁśamahākāvya* seriously narrates the story that the Guru saw in his dream that at his fervent prayer the Gods and Goddesses of the Maṭha attacked Bhairava's army and put it to flight and that as the Guru dreamt there was no army besieging the town the next day. The Guru is said to have composed in memory of the victory, his three minor works called *Guru Śataka, Mīnākshi Śataka* and *Kovidāshṭaka* and lived in peace for the rest of his time.

During Śivappa Nāyaka's time Sacchidānanda Bhārati proceeded to Bidure (Bednūr) the capital, where he was received with due honours. The Guru built a temple in Śṛṅgēri and set up the goddess Bhavyāṁbikā. As one Narasiṁha Yōgi, the successor of Rāmachandramuni did not behave well towards Śṛṅgēri maṭh, he was driven out of Bidure and ordered to reside in a maṭh at Sangama. The lands and other properties of the maṭh were handed over to Śṛṅgēri by Śivappa Nāyaka. After the demise of Sacchidānanda Bhārati, Nṛsiṁha Bhārati ascended the pontifical seat of Śṛṅgēri and at the invitation of Cannammājī went to Bidure. Having stayed there for a few days, he returned to Śṛṅgēṛi. During the great famine in the year Akṣaya (1686 A.C.) Nṛsiṁhabhārati was so liberal as to feed daily more than a thousand people. His successor was Sacchidānanda Bhārati and he was duly anointed as the Guru on the third lunar day of the dark half of Phālguna of the cyclic year Pārthiva in Śaka 1627 (1705 A.C.) and was greatly honoured by Basava, Cannammāji's successor. At the invitation of the Nāyak the Guru proceeded to Bidure and returned to Śṛṅgēri with honours. Some time after the Guru proceeded on a pilgrimage to Subrahmaṇya where his procession with all honours is said to have been carried out in spite of the powerful opposition made by the followers of Mādhvācārya. The Guru bathed in *Kumāradhāra* and worshipped Subrahmaṇya in the cyclic year Ananda (A.C. 1734). From Subrahmaṇya he proceeded to Vēlāpura at the request of the Nāyak of the place and his ministers. Then he went to Uppinaṅgaḍi and from that place he passed through Kōṭīśvara and Honavar to Gōkarṇa where the Guru took necessary measures to guard the wealth of Maṭh against a pirate chief, who failing in his attempt to steal the valuables of the Maṭh directed his attention to the wealthy inhabitants in Gōkarṇa and Uḍipi and carried away both their wealth and women.

From Gōkarṇa the Guru went through Manōjña-nārāyaṇapura to Śṛṅgēri. On his way to Śṛṅgēri he proceeded to Bankipur at the request of Hanuma, pālaygar chief of the place. From Bankipur he passed to Tārikere, the stronghold of another Pālaygar chief called Paṭṭābhirāma, who presented the Guru with an elephant to carry the victory drum in addition to large sums of money. After reaching Śṛṅgēri and spending some time there Sacchidānanda Bhārati proceeded again to Gōkarṇa on the occasion of the solar eclipse. From Gōkarṇa he went to Biḷige at the request of the chief of the place. From Biḷige he went to Banavāsi and received from Sadāśiva, the chief of Banavāsi, large sums of money as presents to the Maṭh from Banavāsi; he returned to Keladi and visited Sagar and Ikkēri halting for a few days at Tīrthahaḷḷi; on his way back again at the request of Sōmaśēkhara Nāyaka, Sacchidānanda Bhārati went to Bidure and was given a hearty reception by the Nāyak accompanied by his ministers and army. Having spent a few days there, he returned to Śṛṅgēri.

Such is the brief biographical sketch of the successive gurus of Śṛṅgēri given by Lakshmaṇa Śāstri in his *Guru-vaṁśaparaṁpara.* It is also to be noted how the life of the Gurus of the Śṛṅgēri maṭha had taken a quite different turn with Bhāratīkrishṇatīrtha under the influence of Vidyāraṇya. From Surēsvarāchārya onwards to Vidyāśaṅkara, the chief avocation of the Gurus was learning, spread of learning and penance. They had no jaghirs or land endowments to manage, no rituals to observe except self-realisation and no tours to make with elephants, camels, palanquins, flags and other paraphernalia of titles and honours. With the arrival of Vidyāraṇya at Śṛṅgēri everything changed. With the money and materials secured by Vidyāraṇya for the Maṭh, Bhārati Kṛshṇatīrtha caused the temples of Śāradā and Vidyāśankara to be constructed. Besides the daily worship of the gods and goddesses and saints, special worship on the occasion of *Navarātra* in September and October, *Śivarātri* in February and other religious festivals on other occasions began to be performed and such performances required the expenditure of large sums of money. With a view to meet the expenditure of money necessary for worship and for feeding large numbers of Brāhmaṇas gathering from all quarters on the festive occasions, Vidyāraṇya got from the Vijayanagar emperors rich land grants and honours.

Thus instead of remaining a calm centre of study, contemplation and penance, the Maṭha became a small state with officers to collect its revenue and spend it, with priests to carry on the daily and special worship and with a huge body of servants to take care of the honours of the Maṭh. The Gurus from Vidyāraṇya onwards seem to have been termed *Rājahaṁsās* or royal saints consistent with the stately rank of the Maṭha. The other Maṭhs established by the followers of Rāmānujāchārya and Mādhvāchārya followed suit and vied with each other in securing from different kings extensive land grants and titles for their respective maṭhs. Thus beginning as centres of religious and philosophical learning, Maṭhs became institutes of organised temple worship and of feeding crowds of pilgrims thronging to them.

The Nāyaks of Ikkēri had very intimate connections with Śṛṅgēri. Almost all the Nāyakas made municificent gifts to the Śṛṅgēri *maṭha* for its maintenance and support. Venkaṭappa Nāyaka I, built a *maṭha* for the accommodation of the venerated Svāmi Abhinava Nṛsiṁhabhārati, presented an *agrahāra* to the Brahmans and earned the title *Re-establisher* of Śṛṅgēri.[69] Śivappa Nāyaka issued a number of *nirupas*

69. *EC.*, VI, Sr. 5.

(royal orders) relating to the affairs of the Śṛṅgēri *maṭha*.[70] One of them dated 1653 A.C. addressed to Sacchidānanda Bhārati informed him that in accordance with his request during his visit to Bidarūr that the people who had usurped the lands formerly granted by Harihara II for the worship of Mallikārjuna, Vidyāśaṅkara, Sarasvatī and other deities, for the upkeep of a feeding house and for *vṛttis* to the Brahmans, and had appropriated all the additonal income derived from the areca plantations made by the *maṭha* at considerable expense, and that they should be put down and the lands restored to the *maṭha* for carrying on religious duties and charities intended by the donor, he held an enquiry into the matter, punished the usurpers, and ordered the restoration of the lands. He also requested the svāmi to see that the worship of the above mentioned deities were conducted regularly and charities managed properly according to the scale fixed by him.

Another dated 1656, addressed to Aḷiya Keñcaṇṇa conveyed to him the information received about some tenants of the Śṛṅgēri *maṭha* in the Mangaḷūru *Śime* playing misçhief without making due payments and ordered him to send for the tenants and see that the amount was duly paid.

Another of the same date, addressed to the svāmi, informed him that he had sent the draft of the Śṛṅgēri and Vidyāraṇyapura grants drawn up by one Purāṇika Appu Bhaṭṭa and requested him to have the boundary stones set up for the lands proposed to be granted to the Brahmans and to return the grants by a Tatam Bhaṭṭa. He also asked the Svāmi to pay personal attention every now and then to the conduct of the worship of the deities and the management of the *maṭha* charities.

A *nirupa* dated 1657, addressed to Timmaṇṇa Sēnabōva runs as follows: "We hear that you are playing mischief in the matter of paying 125 *vārahas* to the Mahājanas of Śṛṅgāpura which you were ordered to do. Pay this amount

70. *MAR.*, 1916, pp. 61 ff.

to *Kavi* (Poet) Tirumala Bhaṭṭa. If you make any further delay, you shall be taught a good lesson."

Yet another *nirupa* dated 1660, addressed to one Narasa, ordered him to make over to the Svāmi of Śṛṅgēri certain villages that had been originally granted to Aṇṇāji Svāmi of Kūḍali Śṛṅgēri *Maṭha* but subsequently resumed on the death of his disciple Vidyāraṇya as the svāmi said that the *maṭha* was connected with Śṛṅgēri *maṭha.*

A *nirupa* addressed by Sacchidānanda Bhārati of Śṛṅgēri dated 1654 to the Mahājanas of Śṛṅgāpura and Vidyāraṇyapura, who had gone in a body to Bednūr to make a complaint to Śivappa Nāyaka about the non-distribution of lands to them states that Śivappa Nāyaka had cleared the debts of the *maṭha* and refounded the *agrahāra* which had become the property of unworthy people either through mortgage or through sale; that as desired by him, the copper plates recording the new grants had been sent to him, and that if they returned to Śṛṅgēri, the lands would be distributed to them according to the grant.

Śivappa Nāyaka enquired into the mis-management of lands granted to the *maṭha,* put down the mischief makers and set things right.[71] He also granted certain fields, house sites and *vṛittis* to the *maṭha* in the Vidyāraṇyapura *agrāhāra.*[72] The above instances reveal the scrupulous interest taken by Śivappa Nāyaka in the maintenance and proper upkeep of the *maṭha.*

Venkaṭappa Nāyaka II (1660-61) continued the traditional patronage to the *maṭha.* He granted a village in the Mukkara nāḍu *sīme* to the Śṛṅgēri svāmi on the occasion of his visit to Bednūr.[73] A *sannad* of Bhadrappa Nāyaka dated 1662 says that at the request of Sacchidānanda Bhārati during his visit to Bidarūr, the village Kerehaḷḷi Gāvatūru, was granted in the presence of the god of the place, on the occasion of

71. *EC.,* VI, Śṛṅgēri 11.
72. *MAR.,* 1925, No. 35.
73. *Ibid.,* 1916, p. 67.

Makara-samkramaṇa or winter solstice.[74] A *nirupa* of Somaśēkhara Nāyaka dated 1664, addressed to Tirumala directs him to grant lands of the revenue value of 300 *varāhas* in the village Erehaḷḷi for the worship of the deities Chandramauḷīśvara and Śāradāmbā of Śṛṅgēri. Another *nirupa* dated 1667 addressed to Mallaṇṇa directing him to utilise 100 *varāhas* sent to employ masons for carrying out repairs to the Mallikārjuna temple at Śṛṅgēri.[75]

Cannammājī continued the traditional patronage to the Śṛṅgēri *Maṭh.* One of her letters addressed to Nārasimha Bhārati svāmi of Śṛṅgēri orders the customs officers to pass all goods free of all duties which were intended for the *maṭha.* Through four *nirupas* all dated 1697 A.C. Basavappa Nāyaka I called upon a number of local officers to help the Śṛṅgēri authorities in their enquiries regarding religious duties and contributions due to the *maṭha* in Bārakūru *hōbaḷi śīme,* Arvattagrahāra *śīme,* Kumbaḷa *śīme,* Bhaṭṭakala, Baggavāḍi *hōbaḷi,* Gersoppe, Sirāli, Chandāvara, Karkala *hōbaḷi,* Basarūru, Śankaranārāyaṇa, Belatangāḍi, Mogaranāḍu, Gājanūru, Keladi *hōbaḷi,* Dānivāsa, Kandya, Garaje, Gōnibīdu and Jāvamge. Those who disregarded the decision of the representatives were to be summoned and forced to abide by it.[76] The above instances, amply reveal the deep and abiding interest taken by the Nāyakas in the affairs of the Śṛṅgēri *maṭha.*

Besides, the Śṛṅgēri *maṭh,* other religious institutions received encouragement at the hands of the Nāyakas. The Mulavāgil *maṭha* was one such. This was one of the two *maṭhas* of Bhāgavata sampradāya in the Mysore State, another being at Talakāḍ Tirumukudlu, in Narasapur taluk. The svāmis of both the *maṭhas* claim spiritual descent from Padmapadācārya the immediate disciple of Śaṅkarācārya who was appointed as the head of the *maṭha* at Dvāraka by Śaṅkarācārya himself. According to tradition, Agnimūrdha Kṛṣṇānanda

74. *Ibid.*
75. *Ibid.*
76. *Ibid.*, 1916, p. 67.

svāmi, the 27th spiritual successor to Padmapadācārya of the Dvāraka *maṭha* came to the south and stayed at Mulavāgil in the Kolar district. On the invitation of Bhadrappa Nāyaka of Ikkēri, he went to Tīrthahaḷḷi and founded a *maṭha* named after Mulavāgil at Bhadrasamudra, an *agrahāra* granted to him by the king. Before leaving Tīrthahaḷḷi he founded a *maṭha* at Talakāḍ and appointed a svāmi to it.

The Mulavāgil *maṭha* claims that the *maṭhas* at Dvāraka and Talakāḍ are its branches. Some papers in the possession of the *maṭha* show that its claim was admitted by an assembly of disciples and scholars who met at Surat about 35 years ago. Kṛṣṇānanda svāmi figures as the donee in four copper plate grants—two issued by Śrī Raṅga III in 1660 and 1661, one issued by Bhadrappa Nāyaka in 1662. The svāmi is described as the promoter of the doctrines Viṣṇusvāmin, who was the immediate sucessor of Padmapādācārya. Both the *maṭhas* at Mulavāgil and Talakāḍ are named after Kṛṣṇānanda svāmi and the deity in both is Gōpālakṛṣṇa. The *maṭha* at Talakāḍ is known also as the Koppala *maṭha* from the name of a village of the same name. A record of the *maṭha,* said to be a copy of stone inscription registers a grant of Agnimūrdha Kṛṣṇānandasvāmi by Mādhava Mantri in Śaka 819. But this date is clearly wrong. It may be concluded that the *Maṭhas* at Mulavāgil and Talakāḍ came into existence about the middle of the 17th century.[77] Bhadrappa Nāyaka granted lands in Muttūr and Sitūr in Madhuvankanāḍ to Yōgi Kṛṣṇānanda, head of the Mulavāgil *maṭha*. The svāmi is therein described as the chief of the *Paramahaṁsa sanyāsins* of the world, the *Advaita Siddhāntin,* expounder of faith laid down by Viṣṇusvāmi and master of tantras.[78] Venkaṭappa Nāyaka II granted certain villages in the Madhuvankanāḍ *śīme* and Sitūru *śīme* of revenue value 259 *varāhas* 1½ *haṇas* to *Paramahamsa parivrājakācārya pada-vākya prāmaṇa paravara parīṇa yamaniyamaddhy = aṣṭāṅga yōga nirata* and promoter of the

77. *Ibid.,* 1919, p. 38 ff.
78. *E.C.,* VIII, Tl. 156.

doctrines of Viṣṇusvāmi Kṛṣṇānandasvāmi of Mulavāgil, for services in the *maṭha* at Munivṛnda.[79]

The tolerant attitude of Nāyakās of Keladi is amply borne out by a number of epigraphs which record grants to institutions propagating faiths other than Śaiva. A copper plate inscription dated Śaka 1479 (1557 A.C.) registers a grant of land made by Sadāśiva Nāyaka to Dharmanātha, the 15th Jaina Tīrthankara. The gift was made at the instance of the Jaina teacher Dēvachandradēva for the spiritual welfare of his guru Munichandrādēva, the disciple of Abhinavadēva Kīrtidēva.[80] Venkaṭappa Nāyaka I made a grant of the Tivati village in Haralatu *śīme* to a *maṭha* of the Rāmānuja sect (Vaiṣṇava) and the god Venkaṭēśa.[81] It is also interesting to note that Venkaṭappa patronised a Muslim mosque in Bhuvanagiridurga.[82] Though no gift is known to have been made to any Christian institution "there were more than thirty thousand christian subjects among the subjects of Śivappa Nāyaka."[83]

The Nāyakas also gave liberal patronage to the Dvaita maṭhas at Uḍipi and Kūḍali. Rāmarāja Nāyaka, for instance, made a grant of land in Śaka 1493 (1571 A.C.) to the celebrated Dvaita teacher and scholar Vādirājatīrtha for worship in the temple of god Kṛṣṇa at Uḍipi.[84] This gift was made in order that Śadāśiva Nāyaka may obtain reunion with Śiva. At the time of the reinstallation (*punaḥ pratishṭhā*) of god Kṛṣṇa at Uḍipi by Vēdavēdyatīrtha, disciple of Vādirājatīrtha in Śaka 1536 (1613 A.C.), Venkaṭappa Nāyaka granted to the temple the village of Huvinakere in Bārakūru *rājya*.[85] Cannammājī granted land for charities of the Rāmajikūṭada *maṭha* in Kōṭipura of Anale Koppada *Śīme*.[86] Sōmaśēkhara Nāyaka III,

79. *MAR.*, 1919, p. 37.
80. *Ep. Ind.*, XX, pp. 89-90.
81. *EC.*, VIII, Ng. 79.
82. *Ibid.*, Tl. 38.
83. Rice: Mysore and Coorg form Inscriptions, p. 159.
84. *EC.*, VIII, Sb. 55.
85. *SII.*, Vol. VII, No. 297.
86. *MAR.*, 1938, No. 82.

made a grant of the village Savagoṇḍanahalli to Raghurāja Tīrtha of the Kūḍali *maṭha*.[87]

The Mahattu *māṭha* at Campakasaras of Ānandapura was another institution which received patronage. Venkaṭappa Nāyaka I granted the village Taralagere of revenue value of 84 *varāhas* with freedom from toll on 12 bullocks for service of the Mahattina *maṭha* of Campakasaras.[88] Vīrabhadra Nāyaka granted to the same *maṭha* some wet lands.[89] In 1662, the village of Madaravalli was granted as *uttara* rent-free land to the *maṭha*.[90] There were numerous other Mahattu and other *maṭhas* also which received munificent donations from the Nāyakas.

Festivals: The celebration of festivals was an important aspect in the religious life of the people. The festivals though religious in significance were conducted on elaborate scales with spectacular effect.

One such festival which was celebrated in the Nāyak Court was the Divāli or the festival of lights. The festival celebrated in honour of Kāḷi (otherwise called Bhavāni) wife of Lord Śiva and Lakshmī, wife of Viṣṇu, goddess of prosperity and abundance, on the last two days of the dark half of the month of Āshāḍa and at the new moon and four following days of the month of Kārttika (October) when all the houses of Hindus were illuminated with rows of lamps. The use of lighted lamps in this festival is to commemorate the slaying of the giant Nārakāsura.[91]

87. *EC.*, VII, Sh. 98.

88. *MAR.*, 1923, No. 108. For other grants to the *maṭha* see *EC.*, VII, Sagar 111, etc.

89. *MAR.*, 1928, No. 108, III-B.

90. *EC.*, VII, Sk. 27.

91. Della Valle, *op. cit.* II, pp. 206-7. There are numerous explanations about the significance of Divāli (1) Viṣṇu apportioned four chief holidays between four varṇas. The Brahmans were to observe the *rākhipūrṇima* or the full moon day of *Śrāvaṇa* (July-August). To Kṣatriyas Viṣṇu gave the Dasara holiday, to the Vaiśyas or traders the Divāli when they are expected to worship goddess Lakshmī, who presides over wealth, and to the Śūdras the *Hōḷi* festival. The second expla-

The festivals in the temples were celebrated with great pageantry and colour.[92] The festivals usually began with the

nation claims Divāli as the day on which Rāja Bali was deprived of his empire on earth. In Mahārāshṭra, women prepare effigies of Bali, and worship them. Another explanation is but a variation of Lakshmi worship in which Bengalis bring clay figures of Kāḷi and worship them in place of Viṣṇu, represented by heaps of rupees placed in trays.

It is said that king Vikramāditya of Ujjain was crowned on this day, the 16th Ashvin, and counted his era accordingly. Thus it is held to be a new year's day.

Yet another explanation is that Rāma after his return from Lanka was crowned on this day! (Rai Bahadur B. A. Gupte: *Hindu Holidays and Ceremonies,* pp. 36 ff.)

92. Pietro Della Valle gives us a graphic account of the festivities held in Aghōrēśvara temple at Ikkēri. "After the people were called together by the sounding of the several trumpets a good while without the temple, they began to make the usual procession within the yard or Inclosure with many noises of their barbarous instruments as they were wont to do here every evening, which after they had done as often as they pleased they went forth into the street, where much people expected them, carrying two idols in procession, both in one *Palanchin,* one at each end, small and so deck'd with flowers and other ornaments that I could scarce know what they were. Yet I think that in the back end was *Agoresourer* (Aghōrēśvara) to whom the temple is dedicated, and the other *Parvati* or some other wife of his. First marched the trumpets and other instruments of divers sorts, continually sounding, then follow'd amongst many torches a long train of Dancing women, two and two, bare headed in their dancing dress with many ornaments of gold jewels. After them came the *Palanchino* of the idols, behind which were carried many Lances, spears with silken streamers and many umbrellas garnished with silken tufts and fringes round about, more stately than those used by others, even the king himself, for these are commonly the ensigners of Grandeur. On each side of the *Palanchins* went many rows of women either publick Dancers or prostitutes but because these were not to dance, they were bare-fac'd indeed, but with a cloth bound about their heads and hanging down behind upon their shoulders and before upon their breasts. Some of them next to the *Palanchino* carry'd in their hands certain little staves either of silver or sliver'd over at the end of which hung thick long and white tufts of hair of horse tails with which they went fanning the Air, as a piece of Grandeur. Neither were there wanting about the idols many of their priests or Ministers of the Temple who accompany'd them; particularly one who seem'd the chief and *Archimandrita* of the rest; besides abundance of Torches whose light dispell'd the darkness of Moonless night. In this order they came to the

sounding of several trumpets (for summoning people together) and then the idols were taken out in procession first within the enclosures of the temple and then outside through

Piazza and there, after they had made a large ring, the dancing began; first two Dancing women, one from one side of the circle and another from another, yet both with their faces always turn'd towards the idols, walk'd three steps forward and then three backward; and this they did innumerable times. After the said two Dancers alone had done thus two others from the several sides joyn'd with them, and they did the same again, three and three. This salutation or preamble of the ballet, being many times repeated, they began to dance, namely, two that danc'd better than the rest, one on the right side of the circle and the other on the left, both with their faces, never with their backs, towards the *Palanchino* of the idols. Though often in the dance they retired backwards as well as went forwards. Their dancing was high with frequent leapings and odd motions, sometimes inclining their haunches as if they meant to sit down, sometimes rising very high and causing the skirt wherewith they are cover'd from the girdle downwards to fly out, and always holding one arm stretch'd out before them, wherewith they now and then made as if they were thrusting or fencing; besides other mad gestures which were all accompany'd by words which they sang, and sometimes with cries more apt to give horror than delight. Hence, while all other Dancing women (that is those who were uncover'd and loosed for dancing) danced all in a company together further distant from the idols, striking their little sticks and singing, being guided by a man who danced with them and was their Master, the other dancers who were cloth'd stood about the idols, but danced not, nor ever mov'd from their place; onely they accompanied the show, very fine with ornaments of gold and jewels, and some of them having flowers other leaves of betle or other odoriferous herb in their hands.

This Dance being ended, the procession went forwards with the same pomp and a numerous train of men and women of all sorts. They went not round the great Piazza in front of the temple but within the outermost walls of the Temple, which is surrounded by very large streets, inhabited for the most part by the said dancers, or publick strumpets. The circuit of the Procession began with from the right hand as you come out of the Temple, which comes to be the left when you enter in; and in the same manner I saw the Procession begin at the Temple of the Town *Ahinela;* this procession stop'd at several places in the streets thro' which it pass'd; and at every such stopping, the above mention'd Dancings, perambulations and other performances were again repeated; whence the show lasted a good while and concluded at length with the last Dance in the Piazza before the

the important streets. The idols for the procession were taken in a palanquin, decorated for the purpose. The procession consisted of a large train of men and women, chief among them being the priests of the Temples. The Palanquin was taken round in a way through the important streets to the accompaniment of Dancing, Music, and bright torches. At the end, the idols are taken back to the temple and replaced with proper ceremonies. On every new and full moon day, certain other extraordinary solemnities were celebrated. The king himself took part in the festivities.[93] The whole city including the temples, houses and streets were illuminated with torches. There was also dancing and singing by women which preceded the processions of the idols in the temples.

Temple-Gate, which ended the procession with the idols re-entered the temple, where it being replaced according to their accustomed ceremonies, the solemnity ended and all the people departed."

(Della Valle—*op. cit.* II, pp. 279 ff.)

93. Describing the festivities on the new moon day, Della Valle writes: "This night an infinite number of torches and candles were lighted not only in all temples but also in all streets, houses and shops of Ikkēri, which made a kind of splendour over all the city. In each of the temples was its idol, which in some was a serpent, and they had adorned the outward porches not onely with lights, but also with certain contrivances of paper on which were painted men on horseback, elephants, people fighting and other odd figures behind which paper lights were placed in certain little porches, like those which we make in our sepulchres; these with other gay ornaments of silk hung round about made a sufficiently pretty show. In the great temple not only the inside, in the middle whereof is a very high and slender cupola; but also all the outer walls and all those round about the Piazza which lies before it, as also the houses in the adjacent sides, were all full of lights. The concourse of people of all sorts and degrees, both men and women, was very great and they appeared to go about visiting all the temples. When it was very late the king came to the great temple, accompanied onely by his two grandsons, to wit Seda-siva Naieka, son of one of his daughters, and Vira-badra Naieka, a young boy, his son's son, whom he designs for his successor. The king stay'd in the temple about an hour, being entertain'd with Musick, Dancing and other things. At length he came forth, and running in as much haste as he came return'd home. After the king was come out of the Temple they carry'd the idols a while in procession about the Piazza but with small pomp and company." (*Ibid.*, pp. 283-4).

The festivals in the temple were generally concluded by a car festival.[94] A copper plate inscription dated 1669 A.C. records the grant by Sōmaśēkhara Nāyaka, of land in village Siruvalige and appropriation of its revenue for expenses of the *Rathōtsava* (car festival) in the temple of Gaṅgādharēśvara at Siddāpura.[95]

There must have been a number of other festivals celebrated during different seasons such as for instance the festivals on the first day of the month, the full moon, Pañcaparvams,[96] Śivarātri,[97] Daśamī, ēkādaśī, dvādaśī and so on to which however there are no direct records from Ikkēri.

Education and learning: In mediaeval India each caste or community had its own educational system. The extent and content of their education were determined by the nature of their occupation. The state, however, did not interfere with the educational system that obtained during the period. It did not maintain schools for the people.

But each village or group of villages had a school in which the teacher taught the three R's to children. The school was either held in the pial of the house of the teacher or in an open space. Della Valle gives us interesting information about the working of these schools and the method of teaching followed in them. He writes "They (the boys) were four,

94. Della Valle gives a description of a chariot belonging to one of the temples; "Moreover, in a close place opposite to the temple, I saw one of those very great carrs or chariots wherein upon certain feasts they carry their idols in procession, with many people on it and Dancing-women who play on musical instruments, sing and dance. The four wheels of this carr were fourteen of my spans in diameter, and the wood of the sites was one span thick. At the end of it were two great wooden statues, painted with natural colours; one of a man, the other of a woman, naked, in dishonest posture; and upon this carr which was very high was room for abundance of people to stand and in brief, it was so large that scarce any but the widest streets in Rome as Strada Giulia or Babuino would be capable for it to pass in." (Della Valle, *op. cit.* II, p. 260).

95. *ARSIE.*, C.P. No. 12 of 1939-40.

96. Asiatic Researches, XX, p. 30.

97. *EC.*, V, Bl. 4; XII, Mi. 20.

and having taken the lesson from the Master, in order to get the same by heart and repeat likewise the former lessons and not forget them, one of them singing musically with a certain continued tone (which hath the force of making a deep impression in the memory) recited part of the lesson; as for example, 'one by itself makes one', and whilst he was thus speaking, he writ down the same number; not with any kind of pen, nor on paper, but (not to spend paper in vain), with his finger on the ground, the pavement being for that purpose strewed all over with very fine sand after the first had writ what he sang all the rest sang and writ down the same thing together. Then the first sang and writ down another part of the lesson; as for example, 'two by itself makes two' which all the rest repeated in the same manner, and so forward in order. When the pavement was full of figures, they put them out with the hand, and if need be strewed it over with new sand from a little heap which they had before them wherewith to write further. And thus they did as long as the exercise continu'd, in which manner likewise they told me, they learnt to read and write without spoiling paper, pens or ink which certainly is a pretty easie and secure way of learning."[98] Thus the pial school served as places where the young boys learnt the three R's. Besides these the *maṭhas* and temples disseminated religious and secular knowledge as well by being centres of education. From the inscriptions of the period we learn that there were certain endowments for the conduct of six *darśanas* of the *maṭhas*.[99]

Literature under the Nāyaks: The Nāyaks of Keladi gave much encouragement to literary men and impetus to literature. Venkaṭappa Nāyaka I encouraged works on *kāvyas, Nāṭakas, Dharma Śāstras* and the like. He patronised the twin arts of music and Dance (*nāṭyaśāstra*) and built a *nāṭyaśāla* to encourage them. He caused a number of works to be written by his court Pandits. Among them were (i) a

98. Della Valle—Travels, II, pp. 227-228. See also Ancient Indian Education by Keay pp. 149-152. *JRAS*., 1834, pp. 15 ff for an article on the school system of the Hindus.

99. *MAR*. 1943, No. 37; *EC*. VIII. Tl. 73, 89 and 184.

metrical translation in Kannaḍa of the *Śivagīta,* consisting of 18 *adhyāyas* in the Uttara Khaṇḍa of the *Padmapurāṇa* by the poet Tirumala *Bhaṭṭa.* (ii) *Śiva aṣṭapadi* in Saṁskrit by the same poet. (iii) a commentary on the *Āgama* work *Tantrasāra* was written by Raṅganātha Dīkshita. (iv) a large work called *Mānapriya* relating to horses, was written by another scholar Āśvapaṇḍita.[100] Bhaṭṭōji Dīkshita was another scholar who was author of the *Tattva-Kaustubha.* The opening verses of the work reveal that the author wrote it at the instance of Keladi Venkaṭēndra who may be identified with king Venkaṭappa. Bhaṭṭōji Dīkshita calls himself the son of *Śrīmad Vidvān maḳuṭa māṇikya* Lakshmīdhara Bhaṭṭa in the *Tattva Kaustubha.* He may be assigned to the last quarter of the sixteenth century or the first quarter of the seventeenth century.[101]

It is said that one staunch *Viśiṣṭādvaitin,* Rāmanuja Śṛṅgin lived in Venkaṭappa's Court.[102] He was famous far and wide as an exponent of *Viśiṣṭādvaita* and won many titles and marks of honour. Bhaṭṭōji Dīkshita had two grievances against the Śrīvaiṣṇavas. First, a Śrī Vaiṣṇava author (Raṅganātha) had written a criticism of his work *Manōrama* giving it the indecent name of *Manōrama Kucamardana* and secondly the same person had heaped insults on the great Appayya Dīkshita whom he would refer to by nicknames such as *Lambhakarṇa* etc. He seems to have challenged Rāmanuja and prevailed in a controversy that followed and Rāmanuja had to relinquish all his honours in favour of his adversary. Venkaṭappa bestowed on Bhaṭṭōji Dīkshita the title of *Viśiṣṭha-Vaidikā-advaita-siddhānta-sthāpanācārya,*

100. *JRAS.,* 1911, p. 190.

101. Karnataka Historical Review, Vol. IV, p. 97. For a new approach to the date of Bhaṭṭōji Dīkshita see Annals of the S. V. Oriental Institute, Vol. I, p. 117 ff; also P. K. Gode—Studies in Indian Literary History, Vol. II, (Singhji Jain Series No. 38; Bombay 1954), p. 65 ff. For a list of works ascribed to Bhaṭṭōji Dīkshita see P. K. Gode, *op. cit.,* Vol. II, p. 75 n 3.

102. *KNV.,* Canto V, p. 88.

besides extending to him other usual marks of honour and court presents.[103]

Venkaṭappa also afforded patronage to the Mādhva scholars like Vādirāja Tīrtha and his disciple Vēdavēdyātīrtha.[104] Basavappa Nāyaka, the adopted son of Cannammāji wrote the *Śivatattvaratnākara* (an encyclopaedic work), which gives also the history of this dynasty up to his own time. The work consists of 108 *taraṅgas* and is the essence of all sciences of knowledge coming within the purview of the *Vēdas* and the *Āgamas.* The subjects dealt with in the 108 *taraṅgas* are of varied interest and are mostly presented from the viewpoint of the Śaivite *Purāṇas* and *Āgamas.* Some are of scientific and historic interest and as such are valuable, e.g. the motion of the planets described in the 19th *taraṅga,* religious laws and social ethics common to humanity in 28th *taraṅga,* the history and life of Liṅgāyat reformer Basava, the origin of the kings of Vijayanagara in 34th *taraṅga,* and of the chiefs of Keladi country. Chapters 36, 37, 39, 41, 43, 62, 76, 90, 93, 96 and 99 deal with a brief history of the Keladi kings, beginning with the founder Chauḍappa up to Sōma-śēkhara and Cannammāji, the parents of Basavarāja. Other chapters of general interest are 23 and 24, which deal with geographical divisions of Bhāratakhaṇḍa, 40 which deals with qualifications necessary for kingship, 44 and 50 about Town planning, Architecture and Iconography, 47 about music, 48 which treats of battles and the manouvering of the army, 51 of the theatres and curtain painting, 52 and 57 of dancing and action on the stage, 84 of Hōra Śāstra 87-89 of Elephants, horses and cows and 107 and 108 of Liṅga worship obtaining among the Vīra Śaivas.

The 108 *taraṅgas* are arranged in Nine *Kallōlas.* At the end of each *Kallōla* the author indicates briefly the subject matter of the *kallōla* and gives the sources from which he collected the information. At the end of the first *Kallōla,* the following works are stated to have been consulted: *Vīra-*

103. *QJMS.*, XXII, p. 78.
104. *EC.*, VIII, Sb. 55, SII, VII, No. 297.

śaivasikhāratna, Śaivāmṛtapurāṇa, the prose work *Dāśāṅga-sṛushtyuddharana* and the *Vīraśaivācārasaṁgṛaha.* This *kallōla* contains 509 *ślōkas.* The second *kallōla* contains 641 verses, the books consulted being *Mahābhārata,* the *Varāha, Kūrma* and *Skanda pūraṇas* and the Śaiva work *Kumārī-khaṇḍa.* The third *kallōla* has 645 verses and collates matter from the same sources. The fourth contains 1142 verses and is based on the *Purāṇas, Smṛitis, Siddhāntas* and the Itihāsas and Vidyāranya's *Pitāmahasaṁhita.* In the fifth *kallōla* are 1005 *ślōkas,* based on the polity of Kāmandaka, Bṛihaspati and Śukra, the *Tantrakhaṇḍa* of Uḍḍamarēśvara, the *Sahyādri-khaṇḍa, Nidhipradīpika, Jyōtishārṇava,* the *Āgamas, Śilpa-śāstra* and the works on omens. In the sixth *kallōla* are 722 verses in which is collected information on Dancing and Music, the works consulted being those of Dhattila, Nandin, Bhṛiṅgin, and Kōhalaka, Ādibhārata, Gītaratnākara, *Uppalaparimaḷa* of Sārngadhara, Viśvakarmmamata, Māyamata, Varuṇārgala, Vātsyāyanīya, Nandīśamata, Gauṇakāputramata, Śukramata, Bṛihaspatimata, Ratraśāstra, Nalamata, Gaurīmata, Dhan-vantarīmata, Āśvinīmata, *Rasaratnākara, Rasādihridaya, Khaniśāstra, Mantraśāstra, Yogaratnāvali, Prayōgasāra* and *Vihagēndrasamhita.* The seventh *kallōla* which deals with the yōga system of philosophy is based on *Haramēkhalīkatan-tra, Mērutantra, Mānasōllāsa, Kautukachintamaṇi, Vāgbhata, Amṛitānandakhaṇḍa, Daśarūpaka, Purāṇasamuccaya* of *Vidyā-nātha, Samudratilaka, Hōraśāstra, Varāhasaṁhita, Bārhas-patya, Sālihōtra, Garuḍa, Nalamata, Nakulamata, Parāsāra-mata, Śivayōga, Śivalōka* and *Haṭhayogapradīpika.* It contains 2481 verses. The eighth *kallōla* is based on the works of Parā-śara, Manu, Yājñavalkya, Drōnācārya and *Varāhasaṁhita,* the *Vātlāgama* and the *Paramēśvara Saṁhita, Jābalyupaniṣad* and *Śaivāgama,* and deals with state affairs, construction of forts etc., and contains 1011 verses. The ninth and the last *kallōla* consists of 1125 verses and is based in the works, *Śarīrōpaniṣad, Garbōpaniṣad,* the *Purāṇas, Śaivasiddhānta dīpika, Mimāmsa, Nyāya, Yōga, Vēdānta* and their branches, the works of Siddha and Jainācarya and all the *Āgamas.* It deals with spiritualism and the religious systems current.

The exact date on which the *Śivatattvaratnākara* was finished is given as Śaka 1631, Sarvadhārin, Friday, the full moon day of Śrāvaṇa (1709 A.C.) at the end of the work.

Being a quasi-historical work the *Śivatattvaratnākara* is very valuable. A research scholar will find plethora of material in this work and has only to choose his favourite in the galaxy of fascinating subjects.

Basavarāja was also the author of another Saṁskrit work named the *Subhāshitasuradruma.* This work is still in manuscript stage and is in the Government Manuscripts Library at Bhandarkar Oriental Institute, Poona.[105] The manuscript contains 293 folios, 13 to 15 lines to a page and 40 to 43 letters in a line. The manuscript contains only skandhas I, II, and IV, the III being missing. Each skandha is separately numbered and contains folios as under:

Skandha I	1 — 84 folios.
Skandha II	1 — 183 ,,
Skandha IV	1 — 26 folios (folio 1 is missing).[106]

He was also the author of a Kannaḍa work called *Sūktisudhākara.*[107] His patronage of learning was so extensive that he was styled *Suri-nikarakalpadruma,* a wish yielding tree to the group of poets (or the learned).

Appayya of Bhaṭakala, who composed many songs in Kannaḍa and to whom R. Narasimhacarya assigns the date Circa 1705 A.C. seems to have been a protege of Basavappa Nāyaka.[108]

Nirvāṇayya, a minister of Sōmaśēkhara Nāyaka II, wrote the *Śivapūjāvidhāna* in Kannaḍa.[109]

105. A portion of the manuscript has been edited by Mr. E. D. Kulkarni in the Bulletin of the Deccan College Research Institute, Vol. XI, March 1951, pp. 379 ff.

106. For a detailed analysis of the contents of the work see Bulletin of the Deccan College Research Institute, Vol. XI, pp. 382 ff.

107. *KNV.,* X.

108. Lives of Kannada Poets, Vol. II, pp. 1-2.

109. *Ibid.,* p. 28.

Basavappa Nāyaka II, even in the midst of his difficulties found time to encourage learning. It was during this reign that Shaḍakshari, one of his ministers wrote a chronicle '*Vīraśaivadharmasirōmaṇi*' trying to make Basavappa Nāyaka the natural son of Sōmaśēkhara Nāyaka.[110] Another Vīraśaiva poet was Maritoṇṭadārya who wrote the *Vīra Śaivānanda Candrikā.*

Thus the Nāyaks of Ikkēri were not only scholars well versed both in Saṁskrit and Kannaḍa but were also patrons of many learned men and poets.

Art and Architecture: The contributions of the Nāyaks of Ikkēri to art and architecture were considerable. The architectural features of the secular and religious buildings of an age or region are not the same as those of another age or region, the difference being due not only to their growth and development but also to local influence and peculiarities. Architecture under the Ikkēri Nāyakas represented not only the culmination of the Hoysala style of architecture in the Karṇāṭaka but also its harmonious blending with the Dravidian style of architecture. Many of the buildings are representative of the Malnad style of architecture.

For convenience of study the Keladi monuments may be classified under three groups:

1. Temples.
2. Civil architecture like palaces, ponds and irrigation projects;
   and
3. Military architecture.

1. *Temples*: Among the temples constructed by the Nāyakas, the Aghōrēśvara temple at Ikkēri is one of the earliest. The temple is to the north-east of the town of Ikkēri i.e., about 1½ miles from the roadside and about 2 miles from Sagar. Probably built by Sadāśiva Nāyaka in the early sixteenth century it is a very beautiful temple in mixed style

110. *JRAS.*, 1910, pp. 149-50.

and is unique in conception and treatment. It is a combination of Dravidian and Hoysala styles of architecture with some features of the Indo-Saracenic style too.

The temple consists of a *garbhagṛiha,* an open *śukhanasi* and a big *mukhamaṇḍapa* of 25 *aṅkaṇas.* There is a narrow passage leading from the *Sukhanāsi* all round the *garbhagṛiha* for purposes of circumambulation. The roof of *mukhamaṇḍapa* is unusually high being about 16′ 6″ and the pillars are beautifully carved; the four central ones being more ornamented than the rest.

The outer wall is not over-wrought with carvings as in other Hoysala buildings. But there are features of Hoysala art introduced in the shape of turrets and door jambs and surmounted by Dravidian pierced-stone-jali work. This combination renders the work more attractive and appreciable. The pilasters in the walls of the *mukhamaṇḍapa* have each a subsidiary pillar and the pilasters between the niches have yalis and warriors. All the doorways are exquisitely carved, especially the inner doorway of the *mukhamaṇḍapa.*

Above the turreted columns on the outer walls runs a band of 6″ carved mostly with figures of birds. There are 3 niches on the three sides of the outer wall of the *garbhagṛiha* and a platform of five feet wide runs all round the *garbhagṛiha* and the outer wall. On the east side beyond the platform, a beautifully carved drain projects at a height of about four feet and below the drain there is an elephant with a seated female figure holding *pāśa* and *aṅkuśa* in the two upper hands and lotus and fruit in the two lower hands. From an inscription on the basement of the temple which reads: "*Yī maṇḍapada kelasaya geyida achāri Hombuchada Venkaṭaiyaṇu*", it is clear that one Venkaṭaiya of Humcha was the principal architect responsible for the design and construction of the *mukhamaṇḍapa.* Except the western wall which is a bit out of plumb, the rest of the structure is in a very good state of preservation. To the left of the main temple stands the shrine of the goddess. It consists of a *garbhagṛiha,* a *sukhanasi* with two small shrines on either side, a *navaranga* and a porch.

The *navaranga* has an arched doorway with a window of jali work on either side. The front *maṇḍapa* has four pillars with figures of elephants supporting yalis and riders. There is a stone railing consisting of turrets and lions alternating with each other above the basement on either side of the central bay. The original image in the *garbhagṛiha* is stated to have been destroyed and another one is now placed. The name of the goddess is Akhilāṇḍēśvarī.

There is a pavilion in front of the main entrance of the Aghōrēśvara temple in which, a well carved Nandi is kept. The pavilion is in the Vijayanagar style of architecture with arched openings and is very elegantly carved.[111]

The temple of Aghōrēśvara now consists of three buildings enclosed within a compound wall of jambattige or laterite blocks. The wall appears to have had gateways on the north and south leading into the courtyard. In the yard are the Nandi Pavillion, a small Pārvatī temple and the temple of Aghōrēśvara. These structures are mostly of slightly greenish trap stone, hard to carve out but fine grained and exceedingly well suited for the construction of a large and enduring structures.

The main temple has a *garbhagriha* with a narrow *pradakshiṇa* branching from the inner *Sukhanasi,* two *Sukhanasis,* and a very large hall or maṇḍapa with closed sides, which is also its *Navaraṅga.* The building is well placed upon a high basement which develops into a *pradakshina* platform around the *garbhagṛiha.* Above the latter rises a stone tower of mixed Hoysala and Dravidian type. The building is lofty and airy and is remarkable for its roominess and strength.

History: No inscription recording the date of construction of this temple has been found. A slab which looks like an inscription stone standing in the courtyard on the east of the *garbhagṛiha* has its surface chiselled off and shows no characters now. On the second cornice outside the north-east corner of the *navaraṅga,* as said earlier, there is a single line inscription stating that Āchari Venkaṭaiya

111. *MAR.,* 1928, pp. 5-6.

of Humcha constructed the *maṇḍapa.* In the *navaraṅga* hall near the *Sukhanasi* doorway on the floor are two images in low relief of bhaktas whose names are mentioned in Kannaḍa as "'*Sadāśiva nāyaka*" and "*Bhadra Nāyakam.*" Near them is a half engraved figure pointed out as of Huchcha. On the sill of the *Śukhanasi* is a *bhakta* figure whose name has been lost. It might be, probably that of Śadāśiva Nāyaka. It is most likely that the temple was constructed during the time of Sadāśiva or Śaṅkaṇṇa Nāyaka.

The temple is a remarkable piece of work specially because it is the largest and finest example of the Ikkēri school of architecture which flourished in Malnad during the Vijayanagar period. It combines Hoysala with Dravidian features and suggests that the architecture of the Malnad was not overwhelmed by the Southern or Dravidian style but retained numerous features of the old Hoysala style. The Hoysala features in the Ikkēri temple are:

1. The high platform around the *garbhagṛiha* and its deeply cut tower.
2. The Stone tower.
3. The rounded and sixteen sided fluted pillars of the *navaraṅga;* and
4. The ornamentation and sculpture of the outside walls.

The Dravidian features of the temple are:

1. The storey with doorways in the tower.
2. The square shape of the *navaraṅga.*
3. The numerous Dravidian pillars and pilasters of the composite lion bracket type in the *navaraṅga.*
4. The Pradakshiṇa around the *garbhagṛiha;* and
5. Two *Sukhanasis.*

An Indo-Saracenic feature is also seen in the arches of the windows and of the Nandi *maṇḍapa.*[112]

112. For a detailed description of the basement, garbhagṛiha, navaraṅga, Sukhanasis and the tower of the Aghōrēśvara temple see *MAR.*, 1932, p. 40 ff.

Directly to the west of the main temple of Aghōrēśvara stands the temple of Pārvatī built in a similar style but with smaller dimensions and fewer sculptures. It has a *garbhagṛiha*, a *Sukhanasi*, a small *navaraṅga* without pillars, and a *mukhamaṇḍapa* closed on three sides and open in front. Outside the *garbhagṛiha* the walls bear turretted pilasters, padmas and swans in imitation of the main temple. The pillars and pilasters of the *navaraṅga* are Dravidian in form with brackets formed of heroes riding on lions which rear up on the backs of elephants. The door frame and perforated windows of the *navaraṅga,* however, are shaped like pointed arches showing Indo-Moslem influence. Around the *mukhamaṇḍapa* is the usual stone bench as also around the *navaraṅga.*

The image of Pārvatī has an unworked *tōraṇa* and a broken nose and is evidently not the original image. The original liṅga of the main temple, two images of its *navaraṅga* niches and the original Pārvatī image have all disappeared and been substituted by later images. On the sill of the *navaraṅga* is *bhakta* vigraha with the Kannaḍa inscription '*Bhadrappa Nāyakaru*'.

The Nandi Maṇḍapa: There is a square Bull pavilion facing the Aghōrēśvara Liṅga which is unique in its design and execution. On a platform about four feet high are seven pointed arches of stone, the walls between which are ornamented with indented square shaped Dravidian pillars borne on the heads of groups of lions. On the walls are sculptured images of drummers, dancers, attendants, Kāliṅgamardana etc., and above the walls project straight-shaped eaves. Further up there is a parapet of trefoil discs.

Five steps supported by Yalis lead up to the *maṇḍapa* in which is kept a magnificient stone wall, about 11 feet long and 10 feet high.

Ramēśvara temple at Keladi: At the northern end of Keladi is a large courtyard enclosed in a tiled verandah. In the middle of the courtyard, stand three temples consisting of a Ramēśvara temple in the centre with Vīrabhadra to the right and the Dēvi temple to the left. The latter is a separate building apart. But the other two touch each other and have a common railing between them.

The Ramēśvara temple is a medium sized structure built completely of greenish grey stone in the mixed Hoysala Dravidian style which was prevalent under the Nāyaks. It consists of a small *garbhagṛiha* with *pradakshina,* a small *navaraṅga* with two pillars only and a *mukhamaṇḍapa.*

History: No definite inscriptional evidence about the construction of this temple is available. A number of *bhakta* relievos appear in the eastern and western parts of the *navaraṅga,* a few of which only are named. Traditionally this temple is said to have been built by Chauḍappa Nāyaka, the founder of Ikkēri Nayakship.

Outer view of the Garbhagṛiha: The western part of the temple enclosing the *garbhagṛiha* is square in plan and raised on a platform about 2¾ feet high. The platform is adorned with four cornices one of which is ornamented with ḷow relief sculptures of drummers, dancers etc. The wall above it has square pilasters in the corner and is practically plain except for the following sculpture. In the east wall is a very low relief are carved Kaṇṇappanāyanar, Garuḍa and Hanumān fighting for a fruit, camel, elephant, yali, obscene figures, elephant killing a man, Rāhu attacking the disc of the moon in which is a stag. West Wall: A drummer with ḍavaṇe. North wall: Ramēśvara seated in Yōgāsana, between Hanumān and Garuḍa. The eaves are straight and above them a row of small sculptures consisting of a Vīrabhadra, Tāṇḍavēśvara, Pārvatī, Mōhini, Vēṇugōpala, Kālingamardana, Bhairava etc. None of these sculptures are of any beauty or importance. Above the *garbhagṛiha* is a stone tower, square in plan, with bulls in the corners and a metal *Kalaśa* on top.[113]

Vīrabhadra temple: The Vīrabhadra temple is more ornate and interesting and is nearly similar in form to the

113. For detailed description of maṇḍapa, ceilings, etc., see *MAR.*, 1932, pp. 45-47; 1928; p. 7.

Rāmēśvara temple. The main difference however is that the *navaraṅga* has in its centre a depressed *pātālāṅkaṇa.*

It looks very probable that the Vīrabhadra temple was built by one of the Bhadrappa Nāyakas of the Keladi dynasty. On the assumption that the Rāmēśvara temple was built by Chauḍappa Nāyaka, we may reasonably infer that his brother Bhadrappa Nāyaka might have put up the Vīrabhadra temple. Since one of the ceilings of the temple contains a gaṇḍabhēruṇḍa[114] bird very prominently, the crest particularly of Achyutarāya, this temple might have been built between A.C. 1530 and 1540 when Bhadrappa and Achutarāya were both living.

Outer view, Garbhagriha: The *garbhagṛiha* of the Vīrabhadra temple is very similar to that of the Rāmēśvara temple except that the basement has a large number of small relief sculptures and the wall has a few more pilasters. The most interesting of the sculptures of the outer wall is the relief image on the west wall. It is popularly pointed out as *Vāstupurusha.* He is a flat figure with two elephantine legs and tail and his hands are shaped like elephant trunks. His face is that of a lion with a longish beard and his belly is covered with seals. To the right is a boy with lifted hands seated between a man playing on a Vīṇa and a woman offering him a toy. On his left stands Mōhinī with a mirror dressing her hair while Bhasmāsura dances near her. To the right of the panel is shown in relief a measuring rod, 36 inches long, divided into lengths of 8 inches 4 inches etc., Outside the *Vāstupurusha* group are eight small panels containiṇg obscene and other figures. The tower is a little short.

Outer view of the Maṇḍapa: Here also there is a successful imitation of the basement and the railings of the Rāmēśvara temple. The chief difference consists in the large num-

114. For the origin and growth of *Ghaṇḍabhēruṇḍa* emblem see *IHQ.*, Vol. XX, p. 341, *n* 2. For the evolution of *Gaṇḍabhēruṇḍa,* see *QJMS.*, XXXI, p. 357 ff.

ber of small sculptures and the eastern poch which is the only one of its kind in the temple. The porch has sixteen sided fluted pillars with cubical mouldings, rounded imitation Hoysala railings and a padma railing.

The Navaraṅga: The larger part of the *navaraṅga* is a low *pātālāṅkaṇa* around which is a stone platform corresponding in level to the floor of the neighbouring *navaraṅga*. The wide span of the nave which is about 14 feet and its greater height give it a better appearance. On its north, is the outer face of the railing of the Rāmēśvara temple bearing turretted pilasters and niches. The opposite railing on the east is similarly sculptured on the inside and the north-west corner is pierced by a narrow passage leading to the space between the two *garbhagṛihas*. Against the west wall of the *navaraṅga* are found two large images of *Dakshabrahma*—human body with goat head, a *kamaṇḍalu* on the right and a mace on the left—and Narasiṁha (5 feet) both standing with folded hands.

Pillars: There are eight pillars in the *maṇḍapa*, six of which are square in plan with lion brackets, the other two being fluted sixteen sided ones with subsidiary pilasters. Some of the faces of the pillars contain interesting sculptures among these may be noticed:

1. Swan with elephant face.
2. A *yōgi* on whom a tree is growing, the group being surrounded by six monkeys in worshipful attitudes;
3. A towered canopy under which is seated on a bench a bearded chief, holding up a flower and wearing a low ribbed conical cap, *uttarīya* and dhoti, and supported by a long coated attendant on either side. It is possible that this is the representation of the builder of the temple, perhaps Bhadrappa Nāyaka.

Ceiling: The ceilings of the *maṇḍapa* which are twelve in number are tastefully designed and skilfully executed. They consist of padmas or ornamentally twisted bands, set in circles in the outer ring. The central ceiling consists of a large slab with ten panels containing Sūrya, surrounded by other grahas. Among these are deities rising on:

1. Deer (chandra).
2. Elephant.
3. Lion.
4. A flower.
5. Vyala.
6. A hill.
7. A man.
8. Bull.

The sun is surrounded by radiant rays and is driving in a chariot drawn by horses; on either side of the navagraha panel is another with five or seven hooded cobras whose coils form highly ornate designs.

The ceilings to the east of the central one has a large relief representation of *Gaṇḍabhēruṇḍa* or the two-headed eagle which is represented as flying, bearing a tusker elephant in each of its two talons, with each of its two beaks holding by the snout a lion which in turn is trampling on a trumpeting elephant; the group is exactly like that appearing on some of the varahas of Achyutaraya and is much grander than the simple double-headed eagle adopted for the Mysore crest after 1881 A.C.

Navaraṅga and Pradakshina: The doorway whose jambs are supported by five Dravidian pilasters borne on bases ornamented with elephants and lions, has Gaṇēśa on the lintel and a canopy surmounted by five towers above. The *navaraṅga* is narrow and small and has a continuation in the pradakshina. The ceiling of the *navaraṅga* has however, a beautiful lotus with more than 250 petals.

Garbagriha: The *garbhagṛiha* is a plain commonplace room containing a small image of Vīrabhadra.

Dvajastambha: Opposite to the eastern porch of the Vīrabhadra temple stands a large pillar of about 25 feet which according to an inscription in it was constructed in Śaka 1603 or 1681 A.C. As usual, from bottom to top it progresses from a square through an octagon and a sixteen sided shaft to a circular wheel above which is the abacus bearing under a small stone canopy, a bull. On the four lower panels of the pillar are the following figures:

West: Gaṇēśa with a royal party of five persons below the pedestal (a lady with her son and two female and male attendants, evidently, the person who set up the pillar.)

South: Śiva and Nandi.

East: Pārvatī.

North: Bhairava.[115]

Pārvatī temple: This is the shrine of the goddess standing by the side of the main temple. The shrine consists of a *garbhagṛiha* with a passage surrounding it for circumambulation and a small verandah in front. In front of this there is a hall about 15′ × 20′ which has got a tiled roof and a wooden ceiling of good workmanship. This is a small building with the old back portion of stone and the front portion of brick. On the west wall is carved an Umāmahēśvara group. The *garbhagṛiha* contains a two-handed image of Pārvatī. On the east stone wall, there are a number of well carved panels consisting of Bhairava, Shaṇmukha, Ganēśa, Śiva dancing on Andhakāsura with Nandikēśa beating time on mṛdaṅga. Above this row are carved smaller sculptures among which are *Purushamṛga* worshipping a liṅga, Saint Kaṇṇappa, Gajalakshmī and a warrior and lady conversing.

The front maṇḍapa is, on the inside, a finely carved woodwork with a large number of wood carvings among which are the eight *Dikpālakas* and other deities.

In the compound are now found a Hanumān, two sets of *Saptamatṛikas*, two *Viragals*, one of which has an inscription, and a number of stray sculptures.[116]

115. *MAR.*, 1928; pp. 6-7; 1932, pp. 45-9.
116. *MAR.*, 1932, p. 49; see also 1928, p. 7.

There are also three small shrines to the west of Keladi. Two of these are small stone structures of one *ankāṇa* each. The third is also of one *ankaṇa* but with a tiled roof. The first two are dedicated to Āñjanēya and Durgā and third is a Viṣṇu temple. The image of Viṣṇu is two feet high with four hands holding *chakra* and *śaṅkha* in the two upper hands and bow and arrow in the two lower hands. Garuḍa is carved on the pedestal of this image.

There is also a Jain Basti in the village. It appears that the ground where the basti stands was covered with thick jungle and that it was cleared and a small structure built over it by a Jaina residing in the village. The image is that of Pārśvanātha with a serpent hood. It is very small, nearly a foot in height. There is also a brass image of Anantanātha.[117]

Other temples: There are four temples in Nagar which belong to the Nāyaka period. The Nīlakaṇṭhēśvara temple is one among them. It is typical of Mālnad architecture in that it has two high jagalis in front and has a *garbhagṛiha*, a wide *Sukhanasi*, and a wide *navaraṅga*. The *garbhagṛiha* only is of stone and the tower is quite like a Moslem dome, the only difference being that in the place of the minarets at the four corners, are *kalaśas*. The ceiling of the *garbhagṛiha* is square with a padma medallion.

There is a black stone (*Tiruvehere kallu*) bull in the *navaraṅga*, well carved though out of proportions.

The goddess' shrine has an image of Pārvatī rudely executed.

Āñjanēya temple: The Āñjanēya temple is almost similar but for the existence of the high platform and the two stone elephants which flank either side of the flight of steps, which are of good workmanship.

Gudde Venkaṭaramaṇa temple: The Gudde Venkaṭaramaṇa temple is typically a structure of the Keladi type and

117. *MAR.*, 1928, p. 7.

consists of a *garbhagṛiha* and *mukhamaṇḍapa* only. The outer walls and basement cornices have, here and there, figured sculptures while the *garbhagṛiha* outer wall has a horizontal band. The *garbhagṛiha* doorway however, is old and of the Hoysala type. Very likely it has been brought from elsewhere. There are two big metallic bells one of which is from Amsterdam (1713 A.C.) and which originally belonged to a Roman Catholic Church of the place.

A study of these temples shows that the Keladi style of architecture was influenced by Moslem designs.[118]

Raṅganāthasvami temple at Hampanūr: Hampanūr is a small village in the Chitaldrug taluk and situated about two miles from Yemmehaṭṭi, a village by the side of the road between Devanagere and Chitaldrug. To the east of the village there is a hillock on which a granite temple is built for Raṅganātha.

The temple seems to belong to the Nāyak period. The outer walls have in the middle a horizontal plain cornice as in the structures at Ikkēri. The temple consists of a *garbhagṛiha*, a *vestibule,* a *mukhamaṇḍapa* and a front verandah. The pillars in the *mukhamaṇḍapa* are square with cubical sixteen and eight sided mouldings. The jambs of the vestibule doorway have *kalaśas* from out of which lotus buds issue. The main god Ranganātha inside the *garbhagṛiha* is really Janārdana (*abhaya, Chakra, Śaṅkha,* and *gadā*). To the north east of the temple is a small shrine containing a relivo figure of Hanumān. In front of the temple there is a tall *garuḍasthambha,* about 28 feet high. It has the carvings of the Śrī Vaishṇava *teṅgalai* caste mark and a bhakta couple, the latter representing perhaps the builders of the temple. To the southwest corner of the *Navaraṅga,* on the outside of the temple is kept a Sala group of granite which is said to have been brought from Kodehindi near Humsikaṭṭi.[119]

118. *MAR.*, 1936, p. 43.
119. *MAR.*, 1939, p. 94.

Pietro Della Valle gives us a graphic description about a temple in Honnali, dedicated to Vikramadēva. He observes:

"In the body of the temple were many other wooden statues of idols, plac'd about in several places, as't were for ornament, some of which were figures of their Gods, others not of Gods, but for ornament of several shapes. Many of these figures represented dishonest actions. One was of a woman kissing, the Man holding his hands on the Woman's breasts, and sundry such representations fit indeed for such a temple. But these were not figures of gods. Of Gods there was a *Brahma* with five heads and three arms on a side, sitting astride a peacock, which in their language they call *Nau Brahma.* That is the Peacock of Brahma. Another god was call'd *Naraina,* with four arms on a side; another with an elephant's head and two hands to an arm, whom they call *Ganesa* and others *Bacra-Tundo,* that is *Round Mouth;* for one and the same God hath diverse names. Another call'd *Fuena* had the shape of a man, holding a naked sword in his right hand and a Buckler in his left. Another had a man under his feet upon whose head he trampled and so many others of various sorts.

In the middle of the temple between the chief entrance and inner shrine, was another dark enclosure, separated from the chief entrance, but not to the same extent as was the inner shrine, that is to say about half way between the two, wherein stood fastened to the ground, certain slender slaves with others across them in two rows, making a little stockade or Palisade, of a long form, and there were to hang lamps and tapers upon at more solemn dayes and hours.

Within the circuit of this temple, but on one side of the Court as you go in, were three other little cells, separate from the body of the great Temple, two of which were empty, perhaps not yet well prepared, but in the other was an idol of an ox; it was half lying or rather sitting upon the floor with the head erect, like which ox, or *Basauna* stood another in the upper part of the temple, before the Tribunal of the Idol Virena as it stood there for his guard."[120]

Among the other interesting temples may be mentioned the Sadāśiva temple at Varadamūla which appears to have been constructed perhaps by Sadāśiva Nāyaka. The temple has a *garbhagṛiha* which is round backed with a masonry *vimāna*, a *Sukhanasi*, with a fine Chalukyan doorway and *mukhamaṇḍapa* with four pillars on the steps leading to which is an outline carving of Sadāśiva Nāyaka wearing turban, uttarīya, long coat, kammar band and necklace with his hands joined over his head in reverence. There is a one line Kannaḍa inscription above his head.

The pillars and doorway are ornamented and fine. The former are bell shaped with varied rope ornamentation below the bells and garland and other hangings on the bells with floral devices above.

The *Sukhanasi* doorway has two bands of variedly headed gryphons and the lintel bears a fine panel of Gajalakshmī which is indeed most beautiful. Lakshmī is seated in Padmāsana with five rearing elephants on each side, each pouring water on her from a jug like vessel held in the trunk. The goddess has only two hands and holds a padma in each. Her *kīrīṭa* is very ornate.

Near the Lakshmītīrtha there is a stone vessel 6 feet long which has two compartments each with the double lead out. It is evidently the sacrificial vessel used at sacrifices performed during the Nāyak days.[121]

Jaina Monuments: The prevalence of religious toleration in the Ikkēri kingdom is amply borne out by the existence of Jain bastis also within the empire of the Nāyaks. In Mēlige, six miles to the south east of Tīrthahaḷḷi there is a Jaina basti dedicated to Ananthanāthasvāmi. There is also

120. Pietro Della Valle, II, pp. 235 ff. He also gives a sketch of the ground plan of an Indian temple, see *Ibid.*, p. 241-42.

121. *MAR.*, 1945, p. 42.

a temple of Venkaṭaramaṇa there. According to an inscription in its *mukhamaṇḍapa,* it was rebuilt of stone about 1608 A.C. Hence we may be definite of the date of its architectural features. This fact helps us to assign it to the style prevalent in Malnad and Keladi period.

The Jaina basti is entered by the side of a *mānastambha* through an uppanage or *dvāramaṇḍapa* and the main structure consists of a straight sided oblong structure with a wide *garbhagṛiha,* a wide *Sukhanasi,* a *navaranga* of nine squares, and an open *mukhamaṇḍapa* also of nine squares. To this has been added a porch of four pillars, which is reached by a flight of steps flanked by spiral designs.[122]

Civil Architecture: The palaces and other civil buildings constructed by the Nāyakas are now in various stages of dilapidation. In Nagar stand the ruins of the palace of Sivappa Nāyaka. It appears to have been in good enough condition at the commencement of the 19th century but due to occupation and use by an English garrison as Catholic church, it was completely desolated.[123] Other noteworthy monuments of the Keladi rulers is the *Champaka sarasi maṭha* at Ānandapura and the tank in it called *Champakasaras,* both stated to have been built by Venkaṭappa Nāyaka.[124] About these Rice says that this maṭha "must also probably have been a superior building. There still remain some fine stone elephants and a splendid tank built with steps of laterite belong to it.[125] About two miles to the north of Ānandapura is a large pond which is said to belong to the Mahanti *Māṭha.* A story is narrated that this pond was built by Śivappa Nāyaka for purposes of his recreation and that his concubine lived there. But the situation of the pond in front of a gadige and the existence of a Basava shrine on an island in the middle of the pond suggest

122. For a detailed description of the pillars, Mahādvāra, Maṇḍapa and Mānastambha see *MAR.*, 1936, p. 38 ff.

123. *Ibid.*, p. 44.

124. *STR.*, VI. XIII.

125. *EC.*, VIII. Intro., p. 16.

that Vīraśaiva saint lived here during the 17th century. The pond is said to have been fed by a tank situated about a mile and a half to the north. The channel which is said to have conveyed the water from the tank is reported to have become silted up. To the north of the pond there is a bull carved out of stone with its mouth open and it is said that the water used to flow through the mouth of this bull into the pond. To the south of the pond is a sluice through which water is said to have been conveyed by means of a channel to irrigate the wet lands of Mallandūr.[126]

Dēvaganga ponds, Nagar: The Keladi chiefs appear to have lived in considerable comfort and luxury and they selected a little natural stream flowing down from the horse-shoe shaped valley about a mile north of Bednur and constructed tanks and wells in a large courtyard about 285′ × 98′ to which flights of steps lead down from the east and from the west. At the north end of the court is the largest of tanks which is about 83′ × 58′. It is only about 5′ deep, the water being about 10′ only, the sides being stone built and the bottom paved with stones. From the north end a narrow bridge leads to a low platform which offers a fine seat during the cool hours and perhaps a jumping platform when the sun is warm. The tank has plenty of fish of various kinds. A stone drain leads the water southward to a second tank which has a square bottom. This and the other tanks of the place are small ones. Between the first and the second tanks are stone pillars which were perhaps meant to receive covering of cloth or green leaves. Including the largest there are seven of these tanks, two of which have peculiarly shaped bottoms, one having the Padma shape and the other a star shape. At the south end is a bathing place paved with stone.

The Devaganga ponds are situated in a charming locality and were once the sporting ground of the royal families.[127]

126. *MAR.*, 1941, p. 72.
127. *MAR.*, 1936, p. 41.

Town planning had also reached a high level of excellence during this period. The city of Ikkēri which was visited by Pietro Della Valle is described by him as follows:

> "The city is seated in goodly plain, and as we enter'd we pass'd through three gates with small forts and ditches and consequently three enclosures; the two first of which were not walls, but made of very high Indian canes, very thick and close planted, instead of a wall, and are strong against foot and horse in any case, hard to cut and not in danger of fire. Besides that the herbs which creep upon them together with their own leaves make a fair and great verdure and much shadow. The other inclosure is a wall, but weak and inconsiderable. But having passed these three we pass'd all. Some say that there are others within, belonging to the citadel or Fort, where the palace is; for Ikkēri is of good largeness, but the houses stand thinly and are ill built, especially without the third inclosure; and most of the situation is taken up by great and long streets, some of them shadow'd with high and very goodly trees growing in lakes of water, of which there are many large ones, besides fields set full of trees, like groves, so that it seems to consist of a city, Lakes, fields and woods mingled together and makes a very delightful sight."[128]

Forts: There is a fort of Śivappa Nāyaka at Nagar. The fort is entered by a gateway supported by two round bastions and having a sally port on the left side. By the side of the sally port is the design of a Dravidian tower with seven *kalaśas.* Opposite to the tower is a niche. On the inside, one of the pillars of the high jagalis on either side contains in high relief, the figure of Hanuman sitting on his tail with his right forefinger lifted up as if in warning.

The courtyard inside shows signs of a former guard room with another short wall inside. The path passes through another wall just on the east taking a 'Z' shape.

128. Della Valle, Travels II, p. 245.

The outer wall is well supplied with a high parapet of laterite blocks having musket holes and canon mouths at the corners. A little further up is a very large well divided into compartments provided with flights of laterite steps. This appears to have been formerly a water lift perhaps for storing water and supplying it through a drain.

The inner wall is entered by a breach. At some distance lies a mutilated stone elephant, well caparisoned. Inside the third wall is a large open court, facing which is a terrace overlooking the west. The fort palace or citadel of Śivappa Nāyaka appears to have stood here with an octagonal well (three feet in width). There are two stone tablets set up here. The smaller one reads: "This tablet marks the site of the palace of Śivappa Naik, chief of Bednur 1648-1660." The larger one which evidently has been set up recently reads: "This is the site of Durbar Hall of Śivappa and his successors 1649-1763."

Between the first wall and the second on the south west side is a powder magazine with the roof and walls ruined. Some distance from it, is another round bastion.

Following up the line of this wall we ascend a flight of steps and reach another bastion to the north of which is the bateri which served the purpose also of an observatory. A broken cannon is lying on the top of the bateri.

On the north west are two more bastions provided with bay windows. On all the sides, some of them have pillars with lion brackets. The middle bay window of the first bastion on this side is directly opposite to the Nīlakaṇṭhēśvara temple so that it was possible for the inmates of the palace to obtain a good view of the procession of the image.

Further up on the extreme north-west of the fort wall is carved the relief figure of Hanumān with lifted tail. On the whole there are about nine bastions and a moat runs all round.[129]

Hill Fort at Channagiri: The hill of Channagiri which rises to a height of about 200 feet to the west of the town con-

129. *MAR.*, 1936, p. 43.

sists of a single soft dark rock covered with earth which commands a fine view of the wide plain which is now the taluk. It is said that the hill was fortified by Queen Cannammāji and was named after her. The fort consists of two rubble walls defended by moats, the chief gate being on the north where the gradient is lowest. To the north-west close to the top is a natural hallow, the rain water collecting in it being a source of water supply to the hill. On the north-east there is another rock-cut *hoṇḍa* with stone cut steps. This is a much better source of water supply.

On the top of the hill is an area about a hundred and fifty yards in diameter in which are found a number of rubble basements of old buildings. Of these a round cavalier exists on the south east. On the peak stands a temple dedicated to Śrī Raṅganātha. Architecturally the structure is quite an unimportant Hoysala temple. The structure is all of brick and mortar with stone pillars of Ikkēri type having square base, octagonal shaft, wheel moulding and a capital of dentil drops. The image is interesting iconographically. It is called Beṭe Raṅganātha and depicts Viṣṇu standing in Samabhaṅga holding *chakra* and *Śaṅkha* in his back hands and arrow and bow in his front hands with a low Garuḍa pedestal below him and a consort in relievo on the *prabhāvalī* on each side. The image though not handsome is peculiar. The temple has a wooden disc-like image of five-headed Hanumān sitting on a demon. The image is eight handed and the attributes are not easily distinguishable as the image is much coated over with muck. Just to the south of the temple is the old flag staff built of rubble stones. It is square in shape and its top commands a fine view of the country around.

To its south-west is a small shrine dedicated to Bhūtappa which contains the head of the god, whose tongue projects out of his mouth.[130] On the whole situated on an eminence, the hill commands a fine view of the surrounding parts, and along with the temple in it adds much beauty to the town.

130. *MAR.*, 1937, p. 56.

Appendix A. No. 1.

TREATY DOCUMENT BETWEEN VĪRAPPA NĀYAKA AND THE PORTUGUESE

(Pazes-e-Tratados, No. 2, Ano de 1715/1716, Fol. 69)

"In the name of God let all those who see this document of contract and friendship know that in the year 1631, on the 7th March on this bar of Barcelor and in the royal ship, before His Excellency the Conde de Linhares of the state Council of His Majesty Viceroy and Captain general of India and of Bishop of Athogia Dom Jao da Rocha, of His Majesty's Council and of Dom Francisco de Moura, Camp Master of His Majesty's Council, the admiral of this fleet and of Domingos da Conde de Noronha, and Dirgo de Souza de Menezes, both members of the Council, and of Ruy Dias da Cunha, Captain of Royal galley and of the captain General of the fleet Manuel da Canam Norinha, Dom Manuel de Menezes, Hope Gomez da brew, baspar Daquiar de Magathay, Domingos Ferreira Beliago, of Luis Mergathao Bonzes, Chief Justice and of the Finance Secretary of the Fleet Ambroisio de Freitas de Canara, Secretary of State, and Captain of His Excellency's staff; being likewise present Vitula Sinay and Trimalia (Tirumala), Ambassadors of the king Vira Naique, it has been declared that the said Vitula Sinay with the embassy of the aforesaid king Virapa Naique having been in Goa for many days to discuss the contract finally several doubts occurred to solve which, the said Vitula went to Ecquiry to consult his king about them. Finally by decision of the aforesaid king, he came back to aliterate this treaty with the following clauses as he (the said king) was indebted to His Excellency for having encouraged and helped him after taking possession of his kingdom, His Excellency being the first in congratulating him on the occasion since he knew the justice of his cause. Thus by virtue of the credentials shown by the aforesaid Vitula and Trimala — which are copied at the end of the document the following clauses and conditions were entered into:

1. First of all, the aforesaid king, on his own behalf and on behalf of his successors will always be loyal and faithful friend of this state of India (Portuguese) and friend of its friends and enemy of its enemies. Accordingly he will give all help and aid to the state of India for the wars undertaken by the State, whenever his help is required. Similarly the state of India will be bound to give the same help and aid to king Virapa Naique.

2. The aforesaid king grants and gives since today and for good the dominion and possession of the island of Cambolin to His Majesty. It is understood that by the word island, we mean the whole island from one end to the other down to the small temple of Mardamy so that he (the king of Portugal) might have, retain, possess and enjoy it together with all its privileges in the same way that the House of the Quelady and the kings of the said island possessed, and even with better right, if possible, for the income of the temple created in the island will not go to the state. The people that live in the aforesaid island will not be disturbed in the practices of their own religion and customs; finally the Viceroy and his successors may order fortresses with walls to be built in the aforesaid island, as a thing of their own property.

3. King Virapa Naique and his successors will allow to cut and take all trees of his kingdom, whenever the best wood needed by the Viceroy will be found and will be taken to the shores of His Majesty without paying any tax or interest and the foresaid king and his governors will watch over the wood and labourers working in it, as far as possible, and their watchmen will be paid by the aforesaid viceroy.

4. King Virapa Naique and his successors will not allow in their harbours any other ships of the Malavars which would not be furnished with a charter (or permit)

of the State (Portuguese) and he will not allow the aforesaid Malavars to take seamen or Victuals from his harbours and land.

5. The Taurim (?) of Onor will be free as he has always been so.

6. The five hundred sackfuls of rice of the tribute will be punctually paid, both the future ones and those which are actually due.

7. The dues enforced eight years since, on the things that will be sold to or bought from the Portuguese will be abolished; similarly the dues on ships coming from Muscat.

8. Since king Virapa Naique has instantly demanded through the aforesaid ambassadors, that the lands and palm groves which exist next to the fort of Barcelor, and within its limits, and possessed by the monied people and inhabitants of the said Barcelor, should be given to him, and that instead of them, and many other possessions and lands with great advantage will be given in the island of Cambolin the aforesaid Conde Viceroy consulted the whole affair with Mastum Supeao Dazevedo, Captain of the Barcelor fortress and with some of those who are mentioned, All determined that they agreed to this exchange if it was with evident advantage and accordingly the Conde the Viceroy agreed to this clause.

9. All the pepper of the kingdom of Gercoppa and other kingdoms possessed by the said king Virapa Naique and his successors, will be sold freely and without difficulties to the buyers, and the Viceroy of India will not be bound to buy pepper from the aforesaid king Virapa Naique nor his successors will be obliged to sell it. But supposing that the state of India would like to buy it, if the aforesaid king or his successors would sell it, the price will be that which both parties freely agree; yet in case it would not come to an agreement as regards the price, neither the aforesaid king nor his successors will on account of that alter the prices of other things or

victuals, but on the contrary they will allow that they would be sold at the same usual price and in the same way (without altering the price).

10. King Virapa Naique, on his own behalf and on behalf of his successors is satisfied in acknowledging the said Viceroy as the competent judge who might solve the doubtful cases and differences that king Virapa Naique, as king of Quelady, may have with other kings, who are allied with the state of India. And the decision of the viceroy will punctually be accepted by king Virapa Naique for he trusts that the viceroy will decide with justice, for the sake of his honour, credit and income, and according to customs and statutes drawn between the same kings and the House of Quelady. And for this, the said Viceroy will naturally take first of all the necessary and true information. And the aforesaid ambassadors bind themselves under obligation that their king will swear this clause, and the others that are included in the contract of peace and friendship. And the aforesaid Conde de Linhares, the Viceroy, on behalf of his Majesty and of the State of India and of all other Viceroys who would succeed him, was pleased in swearing the peace and he bound himself to the following causes:

(1) First of all the aforesaid Viceroy and the Viceroys and generals, his successors will be friends of the aforesaid king Virapa Naique, and of the kings or his successors, and of their vassals and friend of his friends and enemy of his enemies. And supposing the case in which the allied kings would not accept the decision of the aforesaid Viceroy as regards the doubts existing between them and the aforesaid Virapa Naique, Viceroy will declare himself as the enemy of those who would not accept his decision and the friend of those who would accept it.

(2) The aforesaid Viceroy in order to honour and favour the aforesaid king Virapa Naique and his successors permits on behalf of his majesty that every year,

while the peace would last, they might take from the city of Goa Iron, and besides ten riding horses without paying any tax, for which no other thing will be necessary but the permit of the viceroy to take them through any place they would wish.

(3) The Viceroy in the name of His Majesty gives two ships that may be taken away at once, and it has been determined that they will belong to him and the two ships are now anchored off the fortress of Sao Miguel of the island of Cambolin and belong to his Majesty at present for they were captured during the war waged with the state of India.

(4) Furthermore the aforesaid Viceroy and the aforesaid ambassadors declared that according to the text of this contract and to oath and word given to each other either of the parties that would break these clauses, either all or any of them will pay the sum of 10,000 pagodas that makes 35,000 xerafins in the currency of Goa. And in case that this contract is broken by either of the parties either by the State of India or by the king Virapa Naique, it will be impossible to renew it unless the aforesaid 10,000 pagodas are paid.

Thus the Conde Viceroy on behalf of His Majesty and the aforesaid ambassadors on behalf of King Virapa Naique and his successors, declare that this contract has finally been celebrated and solemnised for the good, and accordingly two copies of the same were made, one to remain with the Viceroy and the other with the Ambassadors and their king Virapa Naique.

Appendix A No. 2

TREATY DOCUMENT

(Pazes-e-Tratados, No. 1, Ano de 1671, Fols. 17-19)

The treaty document runs as follows: "In the name of god the Almighty, let all those who come to see the treaty of peace, and eternal friendship, know that in the year of our Lord Jesus Christ of 1633, on April 5th, in the city of Goa at the Royal Hall of the fortress where the Viceroys, grant their audience, being present His Excellency Dom Miguel de Noronha, Conde de Linhares of the Council of State of His Majesty and one of his gentilhomes Viceroy, Captain General of India and likewise Vitula Sinay, ambassador of Quelady Virabadar Naiqùe, king of Equeri, and Ambrosio de Freitas de Canara, Secretary of State and Appagi Sinay, the interpreter of the aforesaid ambassador and moreover the Right Rev. Bishop Dom Joao da Rocha of the Council of State of His Majesty and Captain of this city and Joseph Pinto Pereira Tinomes, Secretary, and Lourenzo de Melo deca, and all being together, the credentials brought by the aforesaid Vitula Sinay in order to settle this peace between the State and Virabadar Naique were examined and these credentials be copied at the end of this treaty. This letter being read, and there being a long discussion about the clauses of the aforesaid peace during several days, finally the treaty was settled with following capitulations:

That as regards the island of Cambolin and fortress of Barcelor, there will be no change, and everything will remain in the same state in which everything was when king Virabadar Naique wrote to His Excellency through the aforesaid ambassador Vitula Sinay about the settlement of this peace, order of the king has come, that king, Virabadar Naique was satisfied of this settlement and in the same way the Conde Viceroy.

That there will be a eternal friendship between both States, being friends of friends and enemies of those who are not friends of the State and to these he will give all help and possible favour and treat, King Virabadar Naique will not tolerate any private nor Malabar in any of the harbours under his jurisdiction.

That king Virabadar Naique and his successors will be bound to give up all the rice and other vituals of his country and harbours to this city and other fortresses and will order his Tanadar of upper Barcelor to give back the sackfuls of rice that were taken from the vassals of His Majesty on account of the rights over them. That the aforesaid king Virabadar Naique will be bound to pay the State 500 sackfuls of rice as tribute every year in the same way it will be paid by the chatris (kṣatriyas) of upper Barcelor.

That the State will be bound to take from king Virabadar Naique every year, in case, ships (from Portugal) would come, three hundred and fifty candies of pepper, for each ship that would sail from the kingdom, at the price of 22 pagodas each candil and in order to pay this sum the aforesaid Viceroy will take for granted that one hundred and two old Sao Tomes are equivalent to 100 pagodas of the aforesaid Ecquery and in case the State would take more pepper, its price will be as settled with the aforesaid Virabadar Naique, as between two merchants.

That the State will be bound to give him in perpetuity 12 horses every year and they will be passed free through any place of the island according to his will, without paying any tax whatsoever, and the aforesaid king will be bound to give place in the rivers of Garcopa and Sanyan near the shore as broad as 24 mastroes (?) for the ships of the fleet of His Majesty.

That the Viceroys and Governors of this State will give three charters (of Navigation) to king Virabadar Naique and his successors for three ships that would go to the straits of Mecca, to Muscat according to old custom.

That the aforesaid king Virabadar Naique will allow us to cut all the wood of his kingdom that would be required for the fleet of His Majesty, without asking for any price whatsoever, for which he will give all possible help.

That the aforesaid king Virabadar Naique will be bound to order his boatmen who live under his jurisdiction not to take more boats than those allowed according to old custom during the lifetime of his grandfather, when he began to reign.

That the Viceroy will order to give the aforesaid king Virabadar Naique two ships that are next to the island of Cambolin, in their present state.

And this treaty and clauses and things contained in it and the friendship that is now renewed, the aforesaid ambassador Vitula Sinay, on behalf of the aforesaid king Virabadar Naique and of his successors promised to fulfil and keep everything as it is herewith contained, and in case of not doing so, they will be obliged to pay all the losses and prejudices that would come on account of breaking of the treaty and the aforesaid king accepted it on behalf of the king Gur Loso, and promised to keep this friendship and to fulfil all the things contained in this treaty on his own behalf, and on behalf of the Viceroys and Governors his successors under the same punishment of paying the aforesaid king Virabadar Naique all the losses and prejudices caused by it not being kept.

The aforesaid ambassador Vitula Sinay, accepted everything in the name of the king Virabadar Naique, his Lord, and to strengthen everything they took on oath, the aforesaid Conde Viceroy upon a mission which he placed in his hands and similarly the aforesaid Vitula Sinay according to the custom of Brahmans took an oath that the aforesaid Virabadar Naique and his successors would keep this treaty as it is and thus this peace and friendship between the state and the aforesaid king Virabadar Naique was solemnised for good; and accordingly a copy of it was given to the aforesaid Vitula Sinay, signed by the aforesaid Viceroy, ambassador and other persons mentioned above; so that the aforesaid king should publish it at his own court as the Conde Viceroy will also do so in this city and at all fortresses which this document makes mention of. All signed Gaspar da Costa did it on the said day, month and year and I, Secretary Ambrosio de Freitas de Canara wrote it and signed as an eye witness of everything.

Conde de Linhares
Vithula Sinay
Appagi Sinay.

Francis de Moura deca
Ambrosio de Freitas de Canara

Appendix A. No. 3

Extracts from voyages of Weddel's Fleet

State Papers, Dom Chas I ccli, No. 3.

The extract runs as follows: Coming to Icary, in the afternoon, we were met and entertigned by anlient gentlemen, who is the master of the king's horse and whose sonne is Register (Secretary) at Baticola. He invited us to his house where we supped and lodged that night, the king being a mourner for the death of his nurse (buried that daie) and so not to be spoken with; but early in the morninge we had a house appointed for us, whether upon our entrance, were sent provisions of sheepe, hens, rice by the kinge, and after dinner we were called to the pallace for our entertynment with a tragicall representation of some ancient history of those parts as also sundrie dances of men and women.

After giving the letters of credit Robinson and Mundy kissed his hand and they were asked to sitt down upon a large carpet about 2 yeards distant from himself, who satt in very great state with most of his nobilitie about him in most and reverent manner far beyond the ordinary port of these heathen princes.

Then we brought in our present and laid it before him and delivered him the draught of the great gunne, wherewith hee expressed himselfe highlie contented, and with a royall promise of his absolute firmana to all our demands investing us after the countrie manner with certaine slight slothes, dismissed us for the present. The next daie he sent us word to have all our messages and demands drawn out into the Language of the countrie, promising us in audience the morrow followinge.

We supped with greate variete of cheese after the Bramenes manner (who eate nothing that has life) himself with a long wand in his hand reachinge from dishe to dishe and invitinge us to taste thereof. After supper he formed his grant to our demands and sent it to the Governor of Baticalla by ourselves, the contents whereof, together with somme of our whole message thus:

(1) We desired a plott of ground and materialls to build with and to be supplied for our money with workmen and Labourers.

(2) We certefied him what benefitt acrewed to the Mogull by our nation trading at Suratt and that the like or greater might be brought to this place, if clothe and other commodities may be here had at reasonable rates.

(3) We desired to be informed what quantities of pepper maie be had here yearlie and what cloth, lead and other commodities of our countrie he would take of for the same in exchange.

(4) Wee might be licensed to plant some force on shore for our defence against the Portugalls.

(5) We desired to know what he required either out of England or out of China.

(6) We craved his firmana for our accord. To each of these particulars he answered as follows:

(i) He granted us by pattent a large plott of ground lying very commodiously by the river side to build us a house, the ruyned parts whereof will afford us squarred stone enuffe for that purpose and moreover, in the same pattent he hath given us timber, of which there is no want, and all materials, we paying onlie for labourers hire, which in these parts is very cheape.

(ii) He seemed very sensible of the benefit which the port of Surat had gained by the trade of the English and promised to endeavour his best for the bringing in of weavers into his countrie of the effecting whereof in a short time he is very confident.

(iii) For pepper, he assured us that we might find yearlie between 1500 and 2000 candils in that port, each candil conteyninge about 4 kintalls Portuguez and that he would incourage his subjects in the manuringe of trees, which of late, in the dead times of trade, they have neglected, and would likewise publish an edict through all his countries that all the pepper should be for us and none to be exported either by sea or by land. For cloath, Lead, Corall, or any other rarities out of Earth he will take of them in barter of pepper and paie us the overplus in money.

(iv) From England and China he desireth all rarities, for which we shall receive satisfaction to our but chieflie horses from Persia and Arabia to which end a ship from that port may yearlie be sent thither in September or October to return again in March.

(v) He desired to see those merchants who were to live in his countrie, with whom he promised to contract both for the premises and for whatsoever else in season they desire, and to grant them his absolute firmana interchangeablie subscribed on both parties, which is also performed."

Appendix A. No. 4.

Extract from Courteen Papers (Ms. Rawl A. 299, Fol. 188-189 in Peter Mundy, Travels III, p.92)

The letter runs as follows: "By a lettre received from you I understand of your good health of which I am right glad. I have ordered Mange Naique that he presentlie out of hand weigh you out 300 candies of pepper and for the other 200, it shall be in due time in September next delivered to your agent that remains at Battecalla. I have likewise enordered the governor of Battecalla that hee appoint you a ware house to laie upp the 250 candies of lead which I understand you have landed.

And likewise that he see to the delivery of 300 candies of pepper in trucke of the lead which you are to deliver at the rate of 22½ pagodas the candee. And for the overplus arising from the price of pepper 7½ pagodas, upon the candee I have endordered Mange Naique to buy commodities of you for it, if you can agree on the price or else money.

Touching the procurement of weavers which you solicited they dwell not in my countrie, but I will invite them to come from whence they are and will cause you to be served with cloth of my countrie here, such as you desire to buy and will also delivere you all my pepper every yeare according to this price agreed.

If you bring good horses of Persia or Arabia I will buy them and paie you in pepper.

Likewise if you bring corall, silke, pearle, or anie other good commoditie of value, I will pae you for them in pepper and money.

Touching a house to dwell in and ware house for your goods and a wharf I have written to the governor of Battecalla to furnish you with materialls, you only paying the workmens charge. He is also enordered to appoint you a buriall place for your dead.

You write to me how some people have misinformed mee of your nation, but I knowe and believe that you are grave persons, and if anie man shall speak evill of you unto me I promise you for my part not to give credit to them.

All things else I have referred to Mange Naique and he shall inform you in particular." Icary, March 1637.

Appendix A. No. 5.

Instrucoes No. 3, 1641-47, Fols. 113-114.

In instructing Antonio Da Costa in the matter, the Portuguese Viceroy Dom Phillipe Mascarenhas wrote on December 4, 1646, as follows:

"As for the ships, the aforesaid king (Śivappa Nāyaka) demands as being at Cambolin, you will escape the question by saying that they are destroyed by time and that there is no memory of them and will make him notice that the past kings, seeing the unreasonableness of his demands, never mentioned it and they received benefits from the State (of Portuguese India) and we shall proceed in the same way with him.

"For he is to know how much we love our friends and if the aforesaid king besides, demands another ship, which was according to his statement, taken by Antonio Carueiro Salena, you will reply that this man was imprisoned and sentenced to forced labour and this sentence would have been carried out had he not died in jail. And coming to the main point about the pepper tell him that if he gives at the price of 21 *pagodas* that is a reasonable price according to the Council of Finance paying attention to the difference of prices from all days down to the present, as it becomes dearer than before at 28 *pagodas,* we shall take it and such is the loss that the kingdom is experiencing that we cannot in any way buy it, but at the aforesaid price of 21 *pagodas* and that this should be made clear to him that we would prefer to take his pepper that is so close than that of Cochin, that is so far though it is much better and its prices are more reasonable. As soon as the king agrees to selling us the pepper at the mentioned price, you will induce him to send the pepper at once towards Barcelor, whence it will be at once be sent.

"For as we do not know, for certain, whether he will agree to our price, it has not been sent through you, but then all will be punctually paid.

"In the note given to me by the ambassador of this king, he seems to complain that in our fortress of Barcelor, we have made provisions of victuals, which are in the prejudice of those they have at upper Barcelor. Tell him that this must be done by the people."

Appendix A. No. 6.

Instrucoes No. 4, 1647, Fol. 42.

In communicating the instructions the Portuguese Viceroy wrote as follows:

"As soon as your Reverence would reach Onor, your Reverence will make enquiries about the state of things and the disturbances of Cambolin whether they are over and settled and without doing this your Reverence will not leave Onor, saying to that king that your Reverence was going to treat with him as a friend.

"As regards the affair of the pepper that is the main one and about which he has spoken most, it has been determined by the Finance Council that in order to please the king we shall take only 200 *candies* of pepper at the price of 25 *pagodas* and no more pepper, for it is more, the price of this extra portion to be reduced according to instructions which will be given to you. As regards the help he expects from us against the Moors, that we are always ready for this unless the war would be against the king of Cannanor, who is brother of the king of Portugal and we cannot go against the peace promised to him though in case his ships would bring pirates I shall capture them. In case he would speak of Cambolin as is expected and that he will give us lands in Canhorto (Kasargod) or some of those he intends to conquer from the Naires, instead of Cambolin, your Reverence will not hear his demands, saying that we are not conquerors in Canara. We only have those fortresses because they are old and for the traffic of rice and pepper, which things are not made round Canhorto, so it would not incur expense on the garrisons and fortresses.

"As regards the things that occur, your Reverence will inform us about them. Your Reverence must during the journey, instruct the ambassador telling him how unwise it would be of his king not to procure the friendship of the Portuguese in everything, in order to have them as friends in a special case, for it is well known how many enemies he has, on one side the Naires, on the other Messur (Mysore) and on his head the Moors of Idalcao (Bījāpūr) who are the most numerous and worst enemies of all.

"Try to obtain from the king consent for the captain of Onor to cut some trees to make masts, and on coming back tell him to have these ships made out of the wood that would not be bought by the aforesaid king nor by that of Cannanor."

Appendix A No. 7.

Moncões do Reino, No. 23, Anno de 1653, Fol. 395.

The letter runs as follows:

"Sir,

The Conde de obidios informed your Majesty in last years of the war that Canara was waging against the fortress of the Coast, and since the fleet sailed till now the war continues there with greater violence. And since the fortresses are weak and not easily defendable, he attacked them one by one, with much superior strength, it was impossible to defend them though the Conde de Obidios had sent one hundred soldiers to Mangalore with ammunition and money. But the army of the enemy overpowered them by ways of mines in such a way that the walls of the towns were all ruined; and they entered it in last August, some of our people being killed in the mines, the rest retreating to the fortress the walls of which were more in a state of decay, and older than those of the town, and it was like a big square bastion without water nor victuals whatsoever. There our people remained till the Periches from Cannanor arrived, and then reaching the foot of the fortress that is built on the sea itself our people escaped leaving the pieces of ordinance to the enemy. The captain of the fortress Sebastio de Carvalho died at Cananor a few days after.

"The fortress of Onor is now in the same danger and is in need of greater help of God, for the other fortress were next to sea, and that of Onor is built on the top of a hill far from the river. It is now besieged all throughout with trenches and mines of the enemy and there is only one free entrance though one of the bastions defended by our people for the maintenance is already taken, and if the enemy would take this pass or would apply fire to the mines, as they inform me, that fort is in greatest danger in spite of great help rendered to it. One cannot believe the expenses incurred into on account of this Canara war. Nothing is enough, for the enemy wages war by means of mines; our people labour in order to counteract their effect, but he does not mind. For he is not in lack of soldiers as we are; we have no soldiers enough to fight with them a pitche battle and on account of this Conde thought of receiving an envoy representing the city of Bednūr, Court of the king to make a composition. This composition did not nevertheless take place and the sending of Fr. Gonzalo Martin had no other success; in spite of having been called by them to discuss this composition.

"In point of fact, the Canara (king of) has become very proud. Just now as the king of Sunda, his neighbour though not very powerful to lead soldiers of the Idalcao (Bījāpūr) and in order to carry out this project he sent another envoy to speak with me. I accepted his offer and promised to give him help by sea. But his reply is delayed so long that I am afraid that nothing will come out of it. A Tanadar of Ancola also offered himself to speak of a composition of peace. I replied that the state could not hear of this peace but in case the Canara (king) would be sensible to his demands. But nothing has been settled hitherto.

"I am now preparing other ships for Onor, besides those which are always at the coast, as I inform your Majesty through another of my letters by post. Let God keep the Catholic person of your Majesty as Christendom and your vassals require.

Goa, 20th Jan. 1654."

Appendix A No. 8.

Notions of the Reign, No. 22, Year 1652

Fol. 436

The letter runs as follows:

"In another letter of mine I have given an account to your Majesty as to how I found the fort at Canara at war and in the last days of August, the fort of Barcelor was given up and how with power and effect was the fort of Cambolin fighting which I helped with all my might the entrance to the barrier was effected with the help of the fleet and a boat the barrier was well fortified and as the enemy was attacking three forts at the same time it was necessary to divide and with the limited power we had, however, help was rendered in turns and at Cambolin all kinds of arms were doubled with the help of these vassals and the greatest attack of the batteries was made on a weak and tottering fortification and Manoel de Souza found himself in the river with some vessels and the chief captain outside the barrier at this juncture came Tristad de Silveira de Menzes from the Cape and ordered him to enter the river and the state, in which the fort of Cambolin was. It was resolved to give up returning with the artillery and all that was inside and practically kept it dismantled. This is in substance what had happened and more will be known from the assent of the judge if the happening which I have ordered to enquire that the time is short and I asked him to finish it as soon as possible in order to send it to your Majesty.

Goa, 26th January, 1653,

Conde de Obridos."

Appendix A No. 9.

Instrucoes, No. 4. 1647, Fols. 83-84.

The extract reads:

"It is well known to you how on the part of king Sivappa Naique, it has been proposed to make peace, which it seemed to us to accept, but not in the form drafted by Francisco de Souza (for according to that) the quantity of pepper he (Sivappa Naique) demands from us to take is too great.

"And thus after consultation in my council I ordered him to continue discussing this treaty of peace with the Ambassador for which purpose the necessary documents go now with you.

Goa. Luis Calderira wrote it on March 6, 1654.

Dom Bras de Castro."

Appendix A No. 10

Treaty between Sōmaśēkhara Nāyaka and the Portuguese

(1671)

(Pazes-e-Tratados-No. 1, 1671, Fols. 57-59)

The treaty runs as follows: "In the name of All powerful God, ye who see this contract of peace and friendship know that in the year of our Lord 1671, on the 20th day of April in the city of Goa, in the Royal Hall of its fort in which the viceroys give their assent, in the presence of Their Excellencies the Governors Antonio de Mello de Castro and Manoel Corte Real de Sampayo succeeded in the first place on the death of the Count of St. Vincient, Viceroy, as well as Vithula Mallo, ambassador of Quellady Somaxa Carnaik, king of Ikkeri, and Dr. Andre Friere de Anthonde, Secretary of State and Copana (Gopana) Sinay Lingoa of the said ambassador and also Manoel Mascaren has, Superintendent General of the Treasury, Diogo de Mello de Castro, Captain of the city Joao de Mello de Sampayo and Dom Francisco Luiz and all being together, was examined the letter of credency which the said ambassador Vithula Mallao has brought from the king for the governors to give their assent to peace contracted between the state and king Somaxacarnayak, after having examined the conditions of the peace on many occasions and having conferred on different days. This contract was assented to and the following capitulations there, in the following manner:—

That the said king shall give to the state factories at Onor, Barcelor and Mangalore with lands to build them with their fence round a unit of a shot of hand rifle, being the property of the same demarcation, and factories shall not be built of double walls but single, without bulwarks, fortifications, battlements, canals nor shall encroach on the land beyond the one that is marked.

That in the said places no oil mills shall be constructed nor balances and weights be used except those used by the king.

There shall be no forced conversion nor taking of orphans or killing cows or Brahmins.

If the prisoners of the Portuguese run away to the lands of the same king, they shall be extradicted in a good and willing manner. In fear of the enemy and dacoits there shall be kept in the factory gunpowder and balls.

The factory hands shall be styled according to their antiquity.

As soon as the fleets of the state arrive, there may be no delay in the loading. The factory hands shall take the rice before hand and shall load it with the help of the king's boat master.

The officers of the fleet wishing to talk to the factory hands, shall first of all ask permission and the factory agents shall not use force in the lands of the above king.

The Portuguese merchants shall lodge all their goods in the factories and shall pay the duties only of those they sell and shall be able without impediment to take those they have not sold and on the other hands the factory hands shall bring from the hill of the king all that is necessary for their service and the use of their household without paying the duty or tax which the said king shall give up if asked for.

The boats, vessels and the machuas of the Portuguese merchants entering the rivers and ports of the said king shall not levy any duty of those goods they have not sold and good passage and shelter shall be given to them.

The Patamarins (boats) of the Portuguese going or coming with letters shall be allowed to go free without any search. If any vessels of the thieves who do stay in the lands of the said king imprison any boats of the Portuguese or the merchants of their mills, they shall be ordered to be let off as of old.

The boats, machuas, and the vessels from Canara shall take bills as they did formerly and the boats of the said king that go with the cargo of chilleys shall receive bills from the secretariat in the old style, however they shall not be able to go to the ports of the enemies of the state.

The said king being at war with the enemies of the state, he shall be helped with fleet as of old nor shall this state unite with enemies of Canara.

The boats of the king of Canara coming to the ports of the state, shall be allowed good passage and on the occasion of a storm they shall be given shelter without being forced to land their goods, nor to pay duties except on those they sell willingly.

The boats, vessels and machuas of the king of Canara shall not pay toll and anchorage fees.

Finally they shall be bound to order to hand over at once if they have not done it still, 60 measures of chilleys as a reward to the risks undergone in one of the ports of Canara, for having entered with a cargo below the safety line.

Which contract and capitulations and this friendship which has been newly obtained, the said ambassador Vithula Maloe promised in the name of the said king Somaxacarnaick, who is his master and Lord and also in the name of his successors to obey and keep, hold and maintain, all that it contains, on the penalty of paying to the state all the losses and damages that are caused by its being disobeyed and the said governments shall accept in the name of the prince overlord, and shall promise on the other hand to obey and keep and maintain this friendship and all that is contained in this contract for themselves and for the viceroys and governors, who henceforward shall be of this state on the same penalty of paying to the said king Somaxacarnaick all the losses and expenses and damages that are thereby caused which the said ambassador Vithula Maloe has accepted in the name of his Master and Lord and for the firmness of the contract all the governors swore declaring that a person shall go to the king from the city so that he may swear to all that is capitulated as if all the successors were represented by his person and as the peace and friendship is celebrated and solemnised the said king Somaxacarnaik shall assent to the contents of this treaty whose copy is sent to him so that he might publish it in his court, which also shall be done in this city, and so that it may be obeyed. This assent is given with signatures of those present on the same day, month and year."

Subsequently the governors Antonio de Mello de Castro and Manoel Corte Real de Sampayo seem to have felt the need for including in the treaty the following clauses: "The king of Canara should force those Christians who live in his kingdom to obey our laws as also the Portuguese who live there shall be able to be priest in their misdemeneaours against the law.

We are also informed that some brahmans forced the Christians to go to their temples on feast days to fire salutes of musketry, and to do other things which our law forbids and thus the king of Canara ought to order that henceforward this should not be done and those who disobey shall be punished."

The letter of Sōmaśēkhara Nāyaka to the Portuguese runs as follows: "To the possessors of happiness, Governors of the State of India Antonio de Mello de Castro and Manoel Cortes Real de Sampayo to whom I Quelladi Somaxacarnaik with great love and courtesy between myself and the king of Portugal there shall be much friendship as has been formerly with whose contact and adjustment I celebrate on the 14th February 1671 in the following manner.

At Mangalore, Barcelor and Onor, in these three ports I shall give you places to build your factories and Bungalows and also surrounding places. In the same places you shall neither build double walls nor raise bulwarks and battlements and canals nor shall you encroach upon the ground besides the one I give you. In the same place you shall not use oil mills and the balances and weights shall be those that are used in our lands. You shall not convert by force nor shall take orphans nor mollest cows or brahmins. The Portuguese captains who enter my lands shall keep in the factories the necessary gunpowder for fear of dacoits and enemies. The factories should, however, pay anchorage in conformity with old custom. I have ordered the boatmen to be paid from the money of the parias. As soon as the vessels reach, they may not be delayed from the cargo; The Portuguese shall bring the rice and other things beforehand. When they load it, it shall be in the presence of my boatmen. The officers of the Aramane wishing to speak to the millhands shall ask first of all permission and the Tanadars shall not send their officer to exercise force and violence and in particular I shall order what is necessary and in the same manner the agents of the mill hands coming to my lands shall not exercise any force nor shall mine given any scandal and if this takes place to the contrary I shall order what is right and shall pass orders accordingly.

The Portuguese merchants, buying their goods by the river shall keep them in the factories and shall pay duties on those that are sold and shall not pay anything for those they take back and they shall not be harassed in any way in this matter and all that the factory hands bring in for the service and use, use of their house, though the duty belongs to me, I shall give it up if they ask for it.

The boats, the vessels and the Machuas of the merchants coming from the lands of the Portuguese to my lands with their goods shall pay duties of the goods sold and with this shall be given good passage. The post coming or going with the letters of the Portuguese shall not be searched and shall be let free for which I shall give orders.

The boats and the vessels from Canara shall take bills and shall pay in the accustomed manner and bills shall pass to the boats that take the cargo of the chilleys.

On any occasion the Portuguese shall send their fleet with powder and balls to help me against the moors, the naires and others, they shall not unite with my enemies nor shelter them.

They shall help me when I send my army against those I referred above. My boats and vessels that go to the Portuguese ports shall pay their duties and good passage shall be given to them. In case of any storm or contrary wind turning the ships and vessels to your ports, they shall be given permission and let off without forcing them to unload their goods. The Portuguese and the merchants bringing their goods loaded in the vessels and boats shall pay duties of those that are taken from our lands in the presence of our boatmen and the clerk shall not do it absolutely and by this there shall be commerce with our vessels, boats, and machuas supplying the necessaries going and coming without paying for shelter and anchorage and the Portuguese binding themselves to keep and concur with the clauses of this contract without failing on their part. In the same manner I shall not fail to obey and as a means to that effect I give this paper written by me."

Appendix A No. 11

Letter from Viceroy of Goa to Cannammājī

Riez Vizinhos No 2 Ano de 1681-93

The letter runs as follows:

"One of the Frigates of this state of which Joao Monteiro da Rocha is Captain General of sea and war captured in the port of Baticala, a vessel that was unloading Arabian horses from Muscat against the contents of the charter (or permit) given to it. On account of this, the vessel could be confiscated, yet paying attention to the good conduct of your Highness towards the State and because the vessel is the property of your Highness I present the same to your Highness and am giving orders to the Captain of the same frigates to take it to the aforesaid port. It is nevertheless expected that your Highness will show your gratefulness to his kindness by ordering to give soon the amount of Rice for the *kafila* without delay.

Moreover, we expect that your Highness will give the necessary orders so that the vessels will be faithfully observed. Let God enlighten the person of your Highness with his Divine Grace.

Goa, January 16, 1683.

Francisco de Tavore."

Appendix A No. 12

Letter from Portuguese King to Cannammājī

Notions of the Reign: No. 3, 1685-1698, Fols. 77-78.

The letter of the Portuguese king dated 6th February 1687 runs as follows:

"The license Gaspar de Manel whom you sent with chilleys wrote to me that in the river of Barcelor there is an island on the side of Goa which gives an income of 10,000 *pagodas* from palm trees to the Canaras. It is from this that leaving aside 30 paces of a point which comes to join with land, a fort could be ordered that could defend itself with a custom house with great income which could in the least yield 10,000 coins.

And as on this matter also the Superintendent of the Treasury of Cochin wrote to me I recommend to you that you should deal in this matter with persons who understand this and send the information which you obtain on this matter so that I may write to you what is good and best.

Lisbon, 6 February 1687.

The king."

Appendix A. No. 13

Extract from Archivo-Portuguese Oriental, III, pt. I, No. 95

The letter runs as follows: "To the king of Canara, I have received the letter of your Majesty in which you mentioned the friendship that you have towards the king of Portugal, my Lord. Your Majesty should allow the army of the State easy passage. I have ordered that the price of rice should be promptly paid. The previous dues are still uncleared because of our not receiving remittance. Do not receive the Arabs, who are enemies of the state, into the ports. Your Majesty had experience in their traditions and having done what was due to our state on my part I will not fail to give the necessary help against your enemies. I remit the letters which your Majesty asked for, very willingly and as a sign of affection, I send a return present that your Majesty will accept.

Goa, 15-2-1701

Antonio Luis."

Appendix A No. 14.

Extract from Archivo Portuguese Oriental, III, pt. I No. 275.

The letter is as follows:

"King of Canara and the Arabs,

Sir,

After the departure of the two ships that I have sent last year to that kingdom, I have news that Canara pursuaded by the Arabs and being afraid of their powerful army, with which they passed the coast, they resolved to deny access to the state, facilities of trade. Under the pretext of asking to return what they had seized, Governor Almo taza More, expected that the Arabs were victorious and went with an army to Carregar to fill in with rice as agreed before. This facilitated more the boldness of closing the ports to us knowing that one 'Galiot' and 2 manchuas had been caught with arecanut, the Canarese resolved to seize in their ports two captains of the ships and manchuas and 16 or 18 soldiers and sailors who were on board. After handcuffing them, they took Gold and silver, from the merchants and some parangis of the Cafila, who could not get out of the ports immediately. But having heard that the Canarese and our armies were fighting the rest of the parangies and a part of the soldiers and sailors began to cut the communication.

Goa, 4th December 1704."

Appendix A No. 15.

Archivo Portuguese Oriental, III, pt. II, No. 65.

Das Pazes; Fol. 274.

Basavappa's letter runs as follows: "written by me Quelady Basavappa Naique to the Gracious Vasco Fernandes Cesar de Menzes. Friendship was with Courtesy maintained between me and the king of Portugal and presently I hope that with the arrival of your Excellency it may increase day by day. I am sending an envoy Damarasa Prabhu with a present which your Excellency will accept. Let your Excellency hear whatever the envoy may say and let us strive to maintain the friendship of both the parties."

Appendix A No. 16

Archivo Portuguese Oriental, III, pt. II, No. 65

The document runs as follows:

"It was necessary to punish Canara both by remittance of rice to this city and by the exhorbitant selling price and the carelessness with which they used to treat the officials and soldiers of the army had departed in which there were 350 men, disembarked, the captain Joseph being qualified for such a post, so by the value of his endowment as for having a great desire of honour, integrity etc.,

On the 15 of January, the army started from this bank of Goa, which army contained 13 ships of war inclusive of small boats and on the 18th they arrived at the port of Commuta (Kumta) which was shallow as usually the ports of Canara are, could not enter except the small boats, in that were found 11 canaras who immediately set fire to the port, to prevent the Portuguese ships from entering. From here the captain ran to Onor with orders to harm the fort for it had no security during war. It was not exactly to put in danger our first success, for it would be a disgrace to contact our forces and the enemies. And the Captain examined what was necessary and in spite of difficulties because the fort was the best in Canara and having a moat around it and being well protected he wished to take it but as he saw 3 ships in the sea he went to recognise Barra de snor, he gave up the idea.

On 21st January he arrived at Barcelor and ordered the captain of two small ships to enter, even with risk, and he with the people also went into the small boats. From those boats, he dashed furiously against the fort and our soldiers disembarked with impetus and resolution that they went on destroying and setting fire to everything. The fire lasted from sunset to midnight and they burnt 10 ships of the Portuguese, one from Calcot. While this was going on the Captain got the news that that one part was well protected by men and arms (artillery). In the early morning of 22nd January he came with sword in hand, took the artillery and burnt the rich ship, also burnt 10 ships big and small. The greatest loss was one godown of provision and cargo for many ships, which were burnt. And the captain did not conduct our army but sent parts of the battery and those in the fort were also destroyed. On 23rd January our army reached the bank of Kalyanpur which was defended by a fort by 7 citadels from where they constantly fired. In spite of that our ships crossed over but the big ones could not go. Entering the port they went on burning all the ships and causing havoc to Canara, because it was thickly populated....and the fire lasted one day. At night they kept awake to attack the fort while the people slept. At dawn the captain set fire to everything and collected the artillery which was there. On the 25th they arrived at Catapalle where they burnt everything. On 27th, when they were at Moloquim, to avoid the havoc, the governor of the place ordered the men to defend, himself taking another route and at night and in the morning they went near the fort and joined the 500 Canarees and went on fighting. Among them 50 soldiers acted so powerfully that they drove away the rest and caused damage.

The last port was that of Mangalore, which was well protected by 4,000 men and 1,500 men with horses (cavalry) when the captain arrived on 30th January and gave orders to enter. They observed the order with resolution; for two days, they attacked the fort which was opposed equally. The governor of the place wanted to suspend hostilities and make peace. There was suspension. But even though they did not cause harm to the city the captain divided his army in the port from there in four autumns did not go a single ship out of the place.

It was already the middle of April when the army should have been gathered and though he pretended to adjust, could not make up his mind, asked the captain to recollect his army in Angedevia....and on the way to destroy Commuta (Kumta) Gecorna (Gokarna) and so it has been done. These ports did not expect such punishment in its being damaged by the many articles burnt and among them a big temple, of great veneration of the Hindus. This was a great success, which few have attained so that within 36 miles of Canara no ship was allowed to pass unhurt. Things burnt were 82 big and small ships, 4 forts, 30 persons injured and 12 dead. But the great shock was the death of the Captain, who died shortly.

The particular captain and other officers fulfilled their duties. The soldiers acted well. The enemys besides hostilities in the population and forts destroyed were a large number who died. The reason being, their soldiers were warned to continue to fight until death. As the Canarese published afterwards that in no war, the state lost so much life lost 600 and articles worth five millions of pagodas. But as the principal motive this king had to give occasion to this excess is to be supposed in the total dependence that we had of their ports so much so that no provision was cheap in Goa and with this experience they proposed a peace through an ambassador who is at Goa to transact business and it is certain that he will adjust to the convenience of the state."

BIBLIOGRAPHY

I. CONTEMPORARY SOURCES.

A. Archaeological

Annual Reports of the Archaeological Survey of India.
Annual Reports of the Mysore Archaeological Department.
Annual Reports on South Indian Epigraphy (1887-1945).
Annual Reports on Indian Epigraphy (1946-1956).
South Indian Inscriptions.
List of Antiquarian Remains in Madras Presidency by R. Sewell, 2 Volumes, Madras 1882-84.
List of inscriptions and Dynasties of Southern India (Madras, 1932).
Topographical Lists of the Inscriptions of the Madras Presidency (with notes and references by V. Rangacharya 3 Vols. Madras, 1919).
Epigraphia Indica Volumes I to XXX.
Epigraphia Carnatica Volumes I to XIII.
Revised List of Antiquarian Remains in the Bombay Presidency by Burgess and Cousens. (Bombay, 1885).

B. Chronicles and Traveller's accounts

Albuquerque: *Commentarios do Grande Afonso de Albuquerque*, Translated by Walter de Gray Birch, 4 Volumes, (Hakluyt Society, 1875-84).
Buchanan: *Journey Thro' Madras, Mysore and Canara*, 3 Volumes, (London, 1807).
Bulhao Pato: *Documentos.*
Ceaser Frederick: *Purchas, Samuel, His Pilgrims*, (Glasgow, 1905).
Correa: *Lendas da India*, (Lisboa, 1864).
Ferishta: *History of the Rise of the Mahomedan power in India*—Translation from the original Persian of Mohamed Kasim Ferishta by John Briggs, 4 Volumes, (Calcutta, 1908).
Edward Grey: *Travels of Pietro Della Valle*, 2 Volumes, Haklyut Society's Edition, (London, 1892).
Faria-Y-Souza: *Asia Portuguesa*, 3 Volumes, Lisboa, 1674-1675.
Dr. Fryer: *Travels.*
Ditto: *East India and Persia.*
Gracia de Orta: *Tratado delas drogas.*
Gubernatis, Angelo de.: *Storia dei Viaggiatori* (Livomo, 1775).
Hamilton: *A New Account of the East Indies.*
Lima felner: *Subsidos* (Lisboa, 1868).
Peter Mundy: *Travels.*
Peter Mundy: *Travels in Europe and Asia.*

Pinkerton: *Voyages.*

Pyard-de-Leval: *Travels.* (Haklyut Society's Edition).

Taylor: *A Catalogue Raisonne of Oriental Manuscripts,* in the Government Library, (3 Volumes, Madras 1857-1862).

Wassaf and Elliot and Dowson: *History of India as told by its own Historians.*

Wilson: *Mackenzie Collections,* (Madras, 1882).

C. *Traditional and Literary*

Achyutarāyābhyudayam: By Rājanātha Diṇḍima. Ed. by R. V. Krishnamāchariar (Śrīraṅgam, 1907).

Apratima Vīracaritram: Edited by M. A. Rāmānuja Ayyangar. (Karnāṭaka Kāvya Mañjari Series, Mysore, 1931).

Cikkadēvarājavamśāvali: Karnāṭaka Kāvya Mañjari Series No. 13, (Mysore, 1932).

Cikkadēvarāja Vijayam: Karnāṭaka Kāvya Mañjari Series No. 17, (Mysore, 1897).

Keladinṛpavijayam: Edited by R. Shama Sastry. (University of Mysore: Oriental Library Publication, Kannada Series, No. 9, 1921).

Śivatattvaratnākara: Edited by B. Rama Rao and Sundara Sastriar (1927).

Vishṇu Purāṇa: Venkaṭēśvara Press, Bombay.

II. MODERN WORKS.

Aiyangar, Dr. S. K.: *Historical Inscriptions of Southern India,* (Madras, 1924).

Aiyangar, Dr. S. K.: *Sources of Vijayanagar History,* (Madras, 1924).

Aiyangar, Dr. S. K.: *Ancient India.*

Aygal: *History of South Kanara.*

Brown: *The Coins of India* (Calcutta, 1922).

Colebrook, H. T.: *Miscellaneous Essays.*

Danvers: *The Portuguese in India,* 2 Volumes, (London, 1894).

Danvers: *Portuguese Records.*

De La Tour: *New Memoirs concerning the East Indies,* (London, 1784).

Elliot, Sir Walter: *Coins of Southern India* (The International Numismatia Orientalia), (London, 1885).

Fawcett, Sir Charles: *English Factories in India.*

Foster: *English Factories in India.*

Fleet, J. F.: *Bombay Gazetteer,* Vol. I, Part II, (Bombay, 1896).

——: *Gazetteer of North Kanara.*

Gode, P. K.: *Studies in Indian Literary History* (Singhji Jain Series, No. 38).

Grant Duff: *History of the Marathas,* (Calcutta, 1912).

Hayavadanarao, C.: *History of Mysore,* 2 Volumes, (Mysore, 1953).

Hayavadanarao, C.: *Mysore Gazetteer,* (Mysore, 1930).

Hegde: *History of South Kanara.*

Heras, Rev. Fr. H.: *The Aravīḍu Dynasty of Vijayanagar,* (Madras, 1927).

Hopkins: *Religions of India,* (Boston, 1895).
Indica: *Indian Historical Research Institute Silver Jubilee Commemoration Volume,* (Bombay, 1954).
Keay: *Ancient Indian Education.*
Kirmani Mir Hussain Ali Khan: *The History of Hyder Naik; Col. W. Mule's Translation,* (London, 1842).
Kittel: *Kannada Dictionary.*
Logan, William: *Malabar* (Madras, 1887).
Macleod: *De Oost Indische Compagnie.*
Mahalingam, T. V.: *Administration and Social Life under Vijayanagar,* (Madras, 1940).
Michaud, J.: *Histoire des progre's et de la chute del'Empire de Mysore sous les regnes d'Hyder Aly et Tippoo Sahib,* (Paris).
Moraes, G. M.: *Mangalore.*
Nagam Aiya: *Travancore State Manual* (Trivandrum, 1906).
Nainar, Muhammad Hussain: *Tuzuk-i-Walājahi* (English Translation, Madras, 1934).
Narasimhachar, R.: *Karnāṭaka Kavi Charite,* 3 Volumes, (1927-1929).
Narasinga Rao, Ullal: *A Kisamwar Glossary of Kanarese Words,* (Mangalore, 1891).
Nilakanta Sastri, K. A. and Venkataramanayya, N.: *Further Sources of Vijayanagar History,* 3 Volumes, (Madras, 1946).
Orme: *Historical Fragments,* (London, 1805).
Rice, Lewis: *Mysore Gazetteer.* (Revised Edition, 2 Volumes, 1897).
Robson, Francis, Capt.: *Life of Hyder Ally,* (London, 1786).
Saletore, B.A.: *Social and Political Life in the Vijayanagara Empire,* 2 Volumes (Madras, 1934).
Sarkar, Jadunath: *Sivaji* (Calcutta, 1929).
Satyanatha Ayyar: *History of the Nāyaks of Madura,* (Madras, 1924).
Sewell Robert: *A Forgotten Empire.* (Reprinted, London, 1924).
Souza: *Oriente Conquistade.*
Srinivasachari, C. S.: *History of Gingee and its Rulers,* (Annamalainagar, 1943).
Sturrock, J.: *South Canara Manual* (Madras, 1894).
Vijayanagara Sexcentenary Commemoration Volume, (1936).
Vriddhagirisan: *The Nayakas of Tanjore,* (Annamalainagar, 1942).
Wilks: *Mysore* (2 Volumes, Madras, 1869, Revised Edn., Mysore 1930).
Wilson: *Glossary of Judicial and Revenue Terms.*
Yule, Sir Henry: *Cathay and the Way Thither* (4 Volumes, Haklyut Society, London, 1913-16).

III. JOURNALS

Annals of the Bhandarkar Oriental Research Institute.
Annals of Śr Veṅkaṭēśvara Oriental Institute.
Archivo Portuguese Oriental (4 Volumes, Nova Goa, 1860-61).
Asiatic Researches (Calcutta from 1888).

Bulletin of the Deccan College Research Institute.
Indian Antiquary.
Indian Culture.
Indian Historical Quarterly.
Journal Asiatique.
Journal of the Bombay Branch of the Royal Asiatic Society.
Journal of the Royal Asiatic Society of Great Britain and Ireland.
Journal of the Bombay Historical Society.
Journal of Indian History.
Journal of the Oriental Institute, M. S. University of Baroda.
Journal of Oriental Research.
Journal of the Asiatic Society of Bengal.
Karnataka Historical Review.
Poona Orientalist.
Proceedings of the Indian Historical Records Commission.
Quarterly Journal of the Mythic Society.

INDEX

[The figures refer to pages; *n* after a figure to foot-notes and *add* to additions. The following other abbreviations are also used:— *au* = author; *ca* = capital; *ch* = chief; *chron* = chronicle; *ci* = city; *co* = country; *com* = composer, *di* = district or division; *do* = ditto; *dy* = dynasty; *E* = eastern, *engr* = *engraver; ep*= epithet; *fe* = female; *fo* = fort or fortress; *fued* = feudatory; *g* = god; *gen* = general; *Hist* = historical; *k* = king; *l* = locality; *l.m.* = linear measure; *m* = male; *min* = minister; *mo* = mountain; *myth* = mythological; *n* = name; *N* = Northern; *off* = Officer; *pr* = prince; *q* = queen; *rel* = religious; *ri* = river; *S* = Southern; *s.a.* = same as; *sur* = surname; *te* = temple; *t.d.* = territorial division; *tit* = title; *tn* = town; *tk* = taluk; *vi* = village; *W* = Western; *wk* = work.]

Fig. 1. Aghōrēśvara temple, Ikkēri, Shimoga District.

Fig. 2. Doorway, Aghōrēśvara temple, Ikkēri.

Fig. 3. Interior view, Aghōrēśvara temple, Ikkēri.

Fig. 4. Bull Mandapa, Aghōrēśvara temple, Ikkēri.

Fig. 5. Pillar, Aghōrēśvara temple, Ikkēri.

Fig. 6. Pillar, Aghōrēśvara temple, Ikkēri.

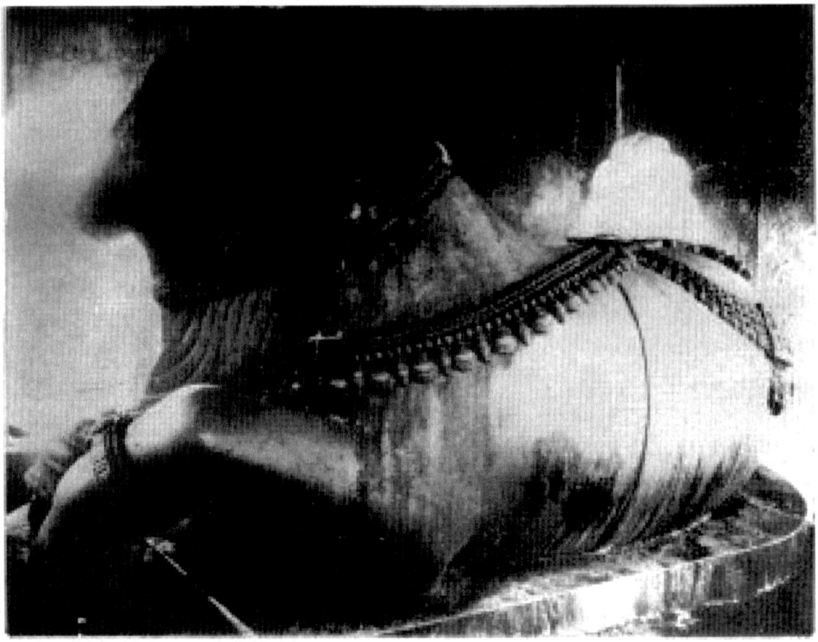

Fig. 7. Bull, Aghōrēśvara temple, Ikkēri.

Fig. 8. Votive bas reliefs of Sadāśiva Nāyaka and Bhadrappa Nāyaka in the Aghōrēśvara temple, Ikkēri.

Fig. 9. View of Virabhadra temple, Keladi.

Fig. 10. Gaṇḍabhēruṇḍa ceiling, Virabhadra temple, Keladi.

Fig. 11. Relievo Portrait of a Chief, Virabhadra temple, Keladi.

Fig. 12. Gaṇapathi image on the Dīpasthambha, Virabhadra temple, Keladi.

Fig. 13. Daksha figure, Virabhadra temple, Keladi.

Fig. 14. Narasimha figure, Virabhadra temple, Keladi.

Fig. 15. Vāstupurusha, Virabhadra temple, Keladi.

Fig. 16. Interior view, Rāmēśvara temple, Keladi.

Fig. 17. Fort gate of Śivappa Nāyaka's palace, view from south, Nagar, Shimoga District.

Fig. 18. View of Mūkāmbika temple, Kollūru, South Kanara.

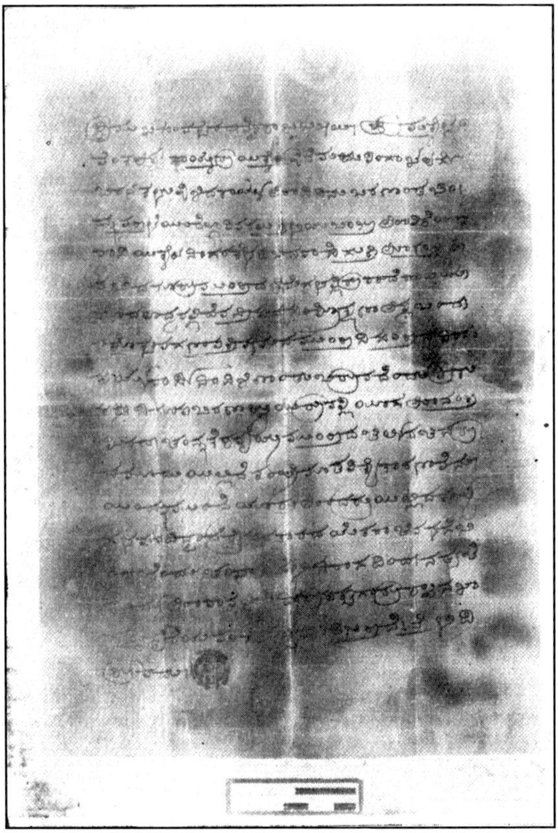

Fig. 19. Manauscript Sannad issued by Venkatappa Nāyaka, now in the possession of Śrī Rāma Bhat of Ikkēri.